Decidability of
Parameterized Verification

Synthesis Lectures on Distributed Computing Theory

Editor
Jennifer Welch, *Texas A&M University*
Nancy Lynch, *Massachusetts Institute of Technology*

Synthesis Lectures on Distributed Computing Theory is edited by Jennifer Welch of Texas A&M University and Nancy Lynch of the Massachusetts Institute of Technology. The series publishes 50- to 150-page publications on topics pertaining to distributed computing theory. The scope largely follows the purview of premier information and computer science conferences, such as ACM PODC, DISC, SPAA, OPODIS, CONCUR, DialM-POMC, ICDCS, SODA, Sirocco, SSS, and related conferences. Potential topics include, but not are limited to: distributed algorithms and lower bounds, algorithm design methods, formal modeling and verification of distributed algorithms, and concurrent data structures.

Cooperative Task-Oriented Computing: Algorithms and Complexity
Chryssis Georgiou and Alexander A. Shvartsman
2011

New Models for Population Protocols
Othon Michail, Ioannis Chatzigiannakis, and Paul G. Spirakis
2011

The Theory of Timed I/O Automata, Second Edition
Dilsun K. Kaynar, Nancy Lynch, Roberto Segala, and Frits Vaandrager
2010

Principles of Transactional Memory
Rachid Guerraoui and Michal Kapalka
2010

Fault-tolerant Agreement in Synchronous Message-passing Systems
Michel Raynal
2010

Communication and Agreement Abstractions for Fault-Tolerant Asynchronous
Distributed Systems
Michel Raynal
2010

The Mobile Agent Rendezvous Problem in the Ring
Evangelos Kranakis, Danny Krizanc, and Euripides Markou
2010

Decidability of Parameterized Verification

Roderick Bloem, Swen Jacobs, Ayrat Khalimov, Igor Konnov, Sasha Rubin, Helmut Veith, and Josef Widder

ISBN: 978-3-031-00883-2   paperback
ISBN: 978-3-031-02011-7   ebook

DOI 10.1007/978-3-031-02011-7

A Publication in the Springer series
SYNTHESIS LECTURES ON DISTRIBUTED COMPUTING THEORY

Lecture #13
Series Editors: Jennifer Welch, *Texas A&M University*
                Nancy Lynch, *Massachusetts Institute of Technology*
Series ISSN
Print 2155-1626   Electronic 2155-1634

Decidability of Parameterized Verification

Roderick Bloem and Ayrat Khalimov
Graz University of Technology, Austria

Swen Jacobs
Graz University of Technology, Austria
Saarland University, Saarbrücken, Germany

Igor Konnov, Helmut Veith, and Josef Widder
Vienna University of Technology, Austria

Sasha Rubin
University of Naples "Federico II", Italy

SYNTHESIS LECTURES ON DISTRIBUTED COMPUTING THEORY #13

ABSTRACT

While the classic model checking problem is to decide whether a finite system satisfies a specification, the goal of parameterized model checking is to decide, given finite systems $\mathbf{M}(n)$ parameterized by $n \in \mathbb{N}$, whether, for all $n \in \mathbb{N}$, the system $\mathbf{M}(n)$ satisfies a specification. In this book we consider the important case of $\mathbf{M}(n)$ being a concurrent system, where the number of replicated processes depends on the parameter n but each process is independent of n. Examples are cache coherence protocols, networks of finite-state agents, and systems that solve mutual exclusion or scheduling problems. Further examples are abstractions of systems, where the processes of the original systems actually depend on the parameter.

The literature in this area has studied a wealth of computational models based on a variety of synchronization and communication primitives, including token passing, broadcast, and guarded transitions. Often, different terminology is used in the literature, and results are based on implicit assumptions. In this book, we introduce a computational model that unites the central synchronization and communication primitives of many models, and unveils hidden assumptions from the literature. We survey existing decidability and undecidability results, and give a systematic view of the basic problems in this exciting research area.

KEYWORDS

parametrized model checking, concurrent systems, distributed systems, formal verification, model checking, decidability, cutoffs

Contents

Acknowledgments

We are grateful to Paul Attie, Giorgio Delzanno, Sayan Mitra, and Kedar Namjoshi for carefully reading an earlier draft of this manuscript, and providing detailed and constructive comments.

Supported by the Austrian National Research Network RiSE (S11403, S11405, S11406) and project PRAVDA (P27722) of the Austrian Science Fund (FWF), by the Vienna Science and Technology Fund (WWTF) through grant PROSEED, by the German Research Foundation (DFG) through SFB/TR 14 AVACS and project ASDPS (JA 2357/2-1), and by the Istituto Nazionale di Alta Matematica through INdAM-COFUND-2012, FP7-PEOPLE-2012-COFUND (Proj. ID 600198).

Roderick Bloem, Swen Jacobs, Ayrat Khalimov, Igor Konnov, Sasha Rubin, Helmut Veith, and Josef Widder
August 2015

CHAPTER 1

Introduction

Reasoning about the correctness of concurrent and distributed systems is an inherently difficult task. A main challenge comes from the fact that many processes run concurrently and interact with each other, which results in non-determinism and large execution and state spaces. Thus, it is easy for a system designer to miss a bug related to concurrency, e.g., an unforeseen race condition, deadlock, livelock, etc. Finding these kinds of bugs motivated research in model checking for many years [Baier and Katoen, 2008, Clarke et al., 1999, Emerson and Clarke, 1980, Grumberg and Veith, 2008, Queille and Sifakis, 1982]. The central problem for model checking (and of many other techniques) is state explosion. Research in model checking made several breakthroughs and developed methods to deal with this problem. Over the years, these methods have been implemented in industrial tools, which are used to verify hardware designs (e.g., microprocessors and cache coherence protocols), predominantly sequential software (e.g., device drivers), and network protocols [Grumberg and Veith, 2008]. The main line of research in model checking of concurrent systems considers systems with a fixed and a priori known number of processes.

Some designs, however, need to be proven to work independently of the system size (e.g., hardware protocols, network protocols, distributed algorithms). The engineering intuition says that if a system has been carefully debugged on a small number of processes, then it should also work with a large number of processes. This intuition is sometimes wrong. For instance, Clarke et al. [1992] applied model checking on the Futurebus+ cache coherence protocol for small sizes. After discovering several bugs, Clarke et al. proposed an improved version of the protocol, and verified that the new version of the protocol is correct on various instances of small size. Later, Kesten et al. [1997] performed model checking on the new protocol for larger system sizes and discovered new bugs.

This book focuses on the verification of systems where the number of processes is not known a priori. Because the number of processes is not known, the challenge is to verify a system for all system sizes. This motivates the study of *parameterized model checking*. In this book we survey results regarding the decidability of this problem for concurrent systems, and we thus make explicit the limits and strengths of automated verification methods. For instance, we will see cases where one can prove that it is sufficient to verify only system instances of small size, that is, special cases where the intuition mentioned above is actually justified. However, we will also see that parameterized model checking is undecidable for many interesting classes.

These decidability results, and the border between decidability and undecidability of the parameterized model checking problem, are the topics of this book. In the decidable cases we, in general, do not cover complexity results. Many existing formalizms (e.g., Petri-nets, process algebra) are related to concurrent systems, and complexity results regarding these formalizms may carry over to the parameterized model checking problem. As there is a wealth of complexity results related to such formalizms we cannot cover them in this book. Also, we do not cover infinite-state systems such as automata with unbounded channels or external storage, or concurrent systems in all generality. We focus on concurrent systems that are composed of a parameterized number of identical finite-state processes, where the local state space is independent of the parameter. Consequently, each system instance we consider has a finite state space.

The rationale of this book is to give an overview of the positive and negative results, and to ease the understanding by expressing system models and proofs in a unified model. Thereby, we hope to shed some light on the border between decidability and undecidability of the parameterized model checking problem.

1.1   MOTIVATION

If the number of components in a concurrent system is known a priori and every component has finitely many states, then the verification problem corresponds to finite-state *model checking* [Baier and Katoen, 2008, Clarke et al., 1999]: given the specification as a temporal logic formula ϕ, and given the system with n components as a finite-state transition system M, check whether M satisfies ϕ. In practice, reasoning about properties of concurrent systems is complicated because the interleaving of steps leads to combinatorial explosion.

Many protocols like cache coherency or bus protocols are defined as *parameterized* systems. Intuitively, a parameterized system is a sequence $(\mathbf{M}(n))_{n \in \mathbb{N}}$ of systems, where $\mathbf{M}(n)$ consists of n copies of similar or identical processes. The *parameterized model-checking problem* (PMCP) is then to decide whether $\mathbf{M}(n)$ satisfies the specification for every n. We survey the work in this area, focusing on decidability and undecidability results, and putting less emphasis on pragmatic solutions for real-life systems.

A tempting approach to the PMCP is to check the system for small values of n and *assume* that if there is a bug in a system with a large number of components, then it already appears in a small system. This assumption is widely used; for instance, Lamport [2006, p. 13] writes "Almost every error manifests itself on a very small instance — one that may or may not be too large to model check." For specific classes of systems, this approach can be formalized as a *cutoff* or *decomposition* statement [Clarke et al., 2004, Emerson and Namjoshi, 1995] that reduces the PMCP to a finite collection of classic model checking problems.

Unfortunately, not all bugs of large systems can be found in small ones, and the PMCP is undecidable in general. Indeed, Apt and Kozen [1986] formalized the PMCP and were the first to address the question of its decidability. However, they considered systems where the implementation of a single process S depends on the parameter n, and treated concurrency only superficially. To prove undecidability of the PMCP, Apt and Kozen considered the following program: Given a deterministic Turing Machine T, let $S(n)$ be the finite-state system represented by the following code:

```
flag := false
for i := 1 to n do
  simulate one step of T
if T has not halted then flag := true
```

Hence, the system $S(n)$ simulates the first n steps of the Turing machine T. Let ϕ be the formula stating that eventually the flag is set to true—in linear temporal logic this is written as F*flag*. Then T does not halt *if and only if* $\forall n \in \mathbb{N}.\, S(n) \models \phi$. As the non-halting problem is undecidable, one immediately finds the PMCP to be undecidable. Furthermore, as $S(n)$ is a degenerate case of a concurrent system (concisting of only one process), one may conclude that the PMCP for concurrent systems is undecidable in general.

However, the undecidability result by Apt and Kozen [1986] does not directly apply to a particularly interesting class of concurrent systems, namely those that are composed of n copies of a finite-state process P, where P is independent of n. We call these *uniform concurrent systems*. Examples of such systems solve classic problems such as mutual exclusion [Pnueli et al., 2002, Wolper and Lovinfosse, 1989], or scheduling [Milner, 1989]. For specific fault-tolerant distributed broadcasting algorithms [Srikanth and Toueg, 1987], John et al. [2013] obtained a uniform concurrent system after a data abstraction of the parameterized process code of the broadcasting algorithm. Hence, PMCP of specific uniform concurrent systems can also be used as part of a tool chain in the verification of concurrent systems where P actually depends on n.

Whether the PMCP for a uniform concurrent system is decidable depends on several factors, the most important being the underlying communication graph (e.g., rings, stars, cliques), and the means of synchronization (e.g., token passing with/without information-carrying tokens, handshake). For instance, Suzuki [1988] proved that Apt and Kozen's idea of reducing the PMCP to the non-halting problem can be extended to token rings in which tokens carry information. The basic idea is to use each of the n replicated finite-state processes to store the content of one cell of the tape of a Turing machine, and implement the movement of the head by shifting information around the ring using tokens. As n cells can be stored in a system with n processes, such a system can be used to simulate n steps of a Turing machine, and undecidability follows as in Apt and Kozen [1986]. Suzuki's construction is prototypical of the undecidability results surveyed in this book.

However, the parameterized model checking results in the literature are not limited to token rings. Rather, there are many different computational models that differ in the underlying graph, and the means of communication. These computational models are scattered over the literature, use different terminology, with slightly different assumptions.

Hence, if one is faced with a PMCP in a given system, it is difficult to tell whether there is a published computational model that naturally captures the system's semantics. The main goal of this work is to provide a *one-stop source* for existing models for asynchronous *uniform concurrent systems*, along with known (un)decidability results. To this end, we provide a single definition that incorporates many of the foundational computational models that have appeared in the parameterized model checking literature on undecidability and decidability. The later chapters then specialize specific features of the general model to systems that can be found in the literature, and discuss the applicable (un)decidability results.

1.2   WHO SHOULD READ THIS BOOK?

This book was written for people who are interested in the principles of concurrent systems and parameterized model checking. This includes graduate students and senior undergraduate students in computer science who are interested in the basic principles of parameterized model checking for concurrent systems. For researchers this book surveys the principles that have been used to obtain decidability and undecidability results in the context of parameterized model checking. We are convinced that many of the techniques surveyed in this book can be used to derive new results in the field.

1.3   ORGANIZATION OF THE BOOK

In Chapter 2 we introduce definitions of a computational model and parameterized specifications that cover most of the existing decidability results in parameterized model checking. In Chapter 3 we explain foundational ideas from the literature for proving decidability or undecidability of different subclasses of the PMCP.

   Subsequently, we consider four classes of systems where decidability results have been obtained.

1. The well-studied class of *token-passing systems*, where communication is restricted to passing a single token among all processes. This includes the important special case of *token rings* (Chapter 4).

2. Systems where communication is based on synchronized steps between two processes, called *pairwise rendezvous*, or one-to-many synchronization, called *broadcast* (Chapter 5).

3. *Guarded protocols*, where local transitions of one process can be restricted with respect to the global state of the system (Chapter 6). This includes combinations with other forms of synchronization, like broadcast and rendezvous.

4. *Ad-hoc networks*, where broadcast communcation between processes may be lossy, or equivalently, communication networks can change during runtime (Chapter 7).

   For all classes, we survey decidability and undecidability results from the literature. After briefly discussing related work that is not surveyed in this book in Chapter 8 and giving an overview of existing parameterized model checking tools in Chapter 9, we conclude in Chapter 10.

CHAPTER 2

System Model and Specification Languages

In this chapter we present definitions of parameterized systems, parameterized specifications and the parameterized model-checking problem. The rationale behind our definitions is to make explicit many of the commonalities of the different system models and results found in the literature.

A concurrent system $\overline{P}^G$ (called a *system instance*) is composed of a vector of *process templates* $\overline{P} = (P^1, \dots, P^d)$, with copies of the templates arranged on a graph G (called the *connectivity graph*). We consider discrete time, and at each time step either one process acts alone, or some process v initiates an action and some set of processes that are connected to v in G simultaneously synchronize with v.

Synchronization primitives result from restricting the number of processes that can simultaneously synchronize with the initiating process. We capture a given synchronization primitive (e.g., pairwise rendezvous, broadcast) by a *synchronization constraint* card $\subseteq \mathbb{N}_0$. Roughly, the number of synchronizing processes should be a number in card. For instance, pairwise rendezvous is captured by defining card $= \{1\}$: every synchronous transition must be taken by the initiating process and exactly one other process.

We define $\overline{P}^G$ as a labeled transition system, and thus need to specify its labeling function. If p is an atomic proposition of the process template and v is a vertex in G, then p_v is an atomic proposition of the composed system—an *indexed atomic proposition*—meaning that p holds in the current state of the process at vertex v.

Then, a *parameterized system* is a sequence of system instances formed from a fixed vector of process templates and a sequence of graphs $\mathbf{G}$. Typical sequences of graphs are rings of size n, cliques of size n, or stars of size n, where n is the parameter. The nth instance of a parameterized system is the system instance $\overline{P}^{\mathbf{G}(n)}$. *Parameterized specifications* make statements about parameterized systems by quantifying over process indices (i.e., vertices of $\mathbf{G}(n)$), e.g., "every process v of $\mathbf{G}(n)$ eventually satisfies p." The *parameterized model checking problem* is to decide whether for all $n \in \mathbb{N}$ the instance $\overline{P}^{\mathbf{G}(n)}$ satisfies the specification.

2.1 PRELIMINARY TERMINOLOGY AND DEFINITIONS

A *labeled transition system (LTS)* over AP is a tuple $(Q, Q_0, \Sigma, \delta, \lambda)$, where AP is a set of *atomic propositions* or *atoms*, Q is the set of *states*, $Q_0 \subseteq Q$ are the *initial states*, Σ is the set of *transition labels* (also-called *action labels*), $\delta \subseteq Q \times \Sigma \times Q$ is the *transition relation*, and $\lambda : Q \to 2^{AP}$ is the *state-labeling* and satisfies that $\lambda(q)$ is finite (for every $q \in Q$). A *finite LTS* is an LTS in which AP and Q are finite. Transitions $(q, a, q') \in \delta$ may be written $q \xrightarrow{a} q'$. A *transition system* is an LTS without the state-labeling λ, and sometimes without initial states.

A *path of an LTS* $(Q, Q_0, \Sigma, \delta, \lambda)$ is a finite sequence of the form $q_0 a_0 q_1 a_1 \ldots q_n \in (Q\,\Sigma)^* Q$ or an infinite sequence of the form $q_0 a_0 q_1 a_1 \cdots \in (Q\,\Sigma)^\omega$ such that $(q_i, a_i, q_{i+1}) \in \delta$ for all i. A *run of an LTS* is a path that starts in an initial state, i.e., $q_0 \in Q_0$. A *state-labeled path* of an LTS is the projection $q_0 q_1 \ldots$ of a path onto states Q. An *action-labeled path* of an LTS is the projection $a_0 a_1 \ldots$ of a path onto transition labels Σ.

When it is clear from the context, a path may omit either actions or states (e.g., LTL formulas are interpreted over infinite state-labeled paths $q_0 q_1 \cdots$).

2.2   SYSTEM MODEL

Given a finite set of atomic propositions AP_{pr} (for individual processes), and process identifiers from the set $\mathbb{N}$, define the set of *indexed atomic propositions* $AP_{sys} := AP_{pr} \times \mathbb{N}$. The set of atomic propositions for a system instance with k processes is $AP_{pr} \times [k] \subseteq AP_{sys}$. For $(p, i) \in AP_{sys}$ we may also write p_i.

INGREDIENTS OF SYSTEM INSTANCE

Transition labels.   Write Σ_{int} for a finite non-empty set of *internal transition labels* and Σ_{sync} for a finite non-empty set of *synchronous transition labels*. Throughout this book, when we use τ, we assume that is an action with $\tau \in \Sigma_{int}$. Define Σ_{pr} as the disjoint union $\Sigma_{int} \cup \{out_a : a \in \Sigma_{sync}\} \cup \{in_a : a \in \Sigma_{sync}\}$, where out_a and in_a are new symbols. An action out_a will be called an *initiate action* and an action in_a a *receive action*. Formally, in_a may be defined as $(a, 0)$ and out_a as $(a, 1)$.

System-arity d.   Let d be a positive integer called the *system-arity* or just *arity*.

d-ary system template $\overline{P}$.   A d-*ary system template* is a d-tuple $\overline{P} = (P^1, \ldots, P^d)$ where each P^ℓ, called a *process template*, is a finite LTS $(Q^\ell, Q_0^\ell, \Sigma_{pr}, \delta^\ell, \lambda^\ell)$ over atomic propositions AP_{pr}. The elements of Q^ℓ are called *local states* — the Q's are assumed to be pairwise disjoint — and the transitions in δ^ℓ are called *local transitions of P^ℓ*. Furthermore, we require the modest restriction that every δ^ℓ is total in the first coordinate: for every $q \in Q^\ell$ there exists $\sigma \in \Sigma_{pr}, q' \in Q^\ell$ such that $(q, \sigma, q') \in \delta^\ell$. In case d $= 1$ we write P instead of $\overline{P}$.

d-ary connectivity graph **G**.   A d-*ary connectivity graph* is a d-colored directed graph $G = (V, E, \text{type})$ where $V = [k]$ for some $k \in \mathbb{N}$, $E \subseteq V^2$ and $\text{type} : V \to [\text{d}]$. Vertices are called *process indices*. For $i \leq$ d let n_i denote the cardinality of $\{v \in V : \text{type}(v) = i\}$. If $(v, w) \in E$ then we say that *w is a recipient of v*, and also write $w \in E(v)$. In case d $= 1$ we may write $G = (V, E)$ instead of $G = (V, E, \text{type})$. To distinguish vertices and edges of different graphs, we introduce the notation $V(G)$ and $E(G)$ to refer to the set of vertices and the set of edges of graph G, respectively. A connectivity graph is sometimes also-called a *topology*.

Example 2.1   Simple Client/Server System.   As an example, consider a simple client/server system consisting of a server and three clients. In our model, this is captured by a 2-ary connectivity graph with $V = \{1, 2, 3, 4\}$: vertex 1 is the server and thus type(1) = 2, and vertices $2, 3$, and 4 are clients so that type(i) = 1 for $i \in \{2, 3, 4\}$. To model that only the clients can initiate synchronization, we set $E = \{(2, 1), (3, 1), (4, 1)\}$. The connectivity graph is depicted in Figure 2.1(a).

Now, suppose the implementations of server and client (as LTSs) are based on internal transition labels $\Sigma_{int} = \{\tau\}$ and synchronous transition labels $\Sigma_{sync} = \{\text{enter, leave}\}$. Very simple implementations S and C for the server and client, respectively, are depicted in Figure 2.1(b) and Figure 2.1(c) (omitting state labels).

In the composed system, client processes can take internal transitions (labeled with a) independently of the others, while for the other transitions they need to synchronize with the server. The details of synchronization are defined in the following.

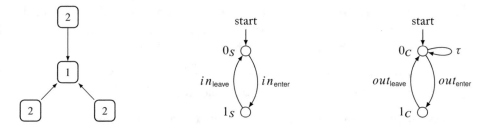

(a) Star-shaped communication graph for the client/server system.

(b) Process template S for the server.

(c) Process template C for the clients.

Figure 2.1: Communication graph and process templates for simple client/server system. Circles represent local states of a process, labeled with state names.

Synchronization constraint card.   A *synchronization constraint* is a set card $\subseteq \mathbb{N}_0$ of natural numbers. This set is used to define the number of processes that participate in a synchronized action: The idea is that if a process with index v takes an out_a action then simultaneously some subset of v's recipients take in_a actions. The cardinality of this subset must be in card. See Section 2.2.1 for synchronization cardinalities that correspond to standard synchronization primitives such as pairwise rendezvous, asynchronous rendezvous, and broadcast, in which card are very simple sets such as $\{1\}$, $\{0, 1\}$ and $\mathbb{N}_0$.

Example 2.2   Synchronization in Client/Server System.   In our client/server system in Figure 2.1, consider the synchronization constraint $\{1\}$. Intuitively, this means that whenever a client wants to take a synchronous transition, labeled out_{enter} or out_{leave}, it can only do so when there is at least one other process which synchronizes with the client by taking a transition labeled with in_{enter} or in_{leave}, respectively. In the given communication graph, this other process can only be the server.

In the following definition of a system instance, we formalize the notion of synchronization.

SYSTEM INSTANCE $\overline{P}^G$

Given a system arity d, a d-ary system template $\overline{P}$, a d-ary connectivity graph $G = (V, E, \text{type})$ with $|V| = k$, and a synchronization constraint card, define the *system instance* $\text{sys}(\overline{P}, G, \text{card})$, also written $\overline{P}^G$ if card is clear, as the *finite* LTS $(S, S_0, \Sigma_{int} \cup \Sigma_{sync}, \Delta, \Lambda)$ over indexed atomic propositions $\text{AP}_{pr} \times [k]$, where the following holds true.

- The state set S consists of all $|V|$-tuples $s = (q_1, \ldots, q_{|V|}) \in Q^{\text{type}(1)} \times \cdots \times Q^{\text{type}(|V|)}$. For $v \in V$, let $s(v)$ denote q_v, the local state of the process at v. Each s is called a *global state*.

- The set of *global initial states* is defined as $S_0 := Q_0^{\text{type}(1)} \times \cdots \times Q_0^{\text{type}(|V|)}$.

- The *global transition relation* $\Delta \subseteq S \times (\Sigma_{int} \cup \Sigma_{sync}) \times S$ is defined as the set of all internal transitions (in which a single process acts) and synchronous transitions (in which some set of processes act simultaneously, where we have the following.

  - An *internal transition* is an element (s, a, s') of $S \times \Sigma_{int} \times S$ for which there exists a process index $v \in V$ satisfying the following two conditions:

    (int-step) $s(v) \xrightarrow{a} s'(v)$ is a local transition of process template $P^{\text{type}(v)}$.
    (int-frame) For all $w \in V \setminus \{v\}$, $s(w) = s'(w)$.

  - A *synchronous transition* is an element (s, a, s') of $S \times \Sigma_{sync} \times S$ for which there exists a process index $v \in V$, called the *initiator*, and a set $\mathcal{I} \subseteq \{w \in V : E(v, w)\}$ of recipients of v in G such that:

    (card) $|\mathcal{I}| \in \text{card}$.

    (step) $s(v) \xrightarrow{out_a} s'(v)$ is a local transition of process template $P^{\text{type}(v)}$.

    ($\mathcal{I}$-step) For every $w \in \mathcal{I}$, $s(w) \xrightarrow{in_a} s'(w)$ is a local transition of process template $P^{\text{type}(w)}$.

    (frame) For every $w \in V \setminus (\mathcal{I} \cup \{v\})$, $s'(w) = s(w)$.

    (max) There does not exist a strict superset $\mathcal{I}' \supset \mathcal{I}$ of recipients of v in G such that

      (i) $|\mathcal{I}'| \in \text{card}$, and (ii) for all $w \in \mathcal{I}'$ there exists $r \in Q^{\text{type}(w)}$ such that $s(w) \xrightarrow{in_a} r$ is a local transition of process template $P^{\text{type}(w)}$.

- The labeling $\Lambda(s) \subseteq \text{AP}_{pr} \times [k]$ for $s \in S$ is defined as follows: for $v \in V$, $p_v \in \Lambda(s)$ if and only if $p \in \lambda^{\text{type}(v)}(s(v))$, and for $v \notin V$, $p_v \notin \Lambda(s)$ for all $s \in S$.

2.2.1   SOME STANDARD SYNCHRONIZATION PRIMITIVES

We give various synchronization constraints card that model standard forms of communication, namely pairwise rendezvous, asynchronous rendezvous, and broadcast (Chapter 5). Variations of the primitives, along with extensions of our basic system model, are used to define the Token-Passing Systems (Chapter 4), Guarded Protocols (Chapter 6), and Ad-Hoc Networks (Chapter 7); see Figure 2.2.

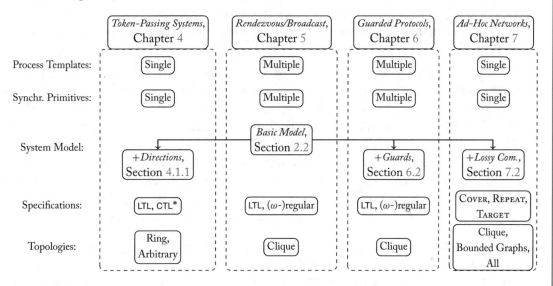

Figure 2.2: Basic system model and extensions in this survey. For topologies, "All" refers to the parameterized topology with all possible topologies in it, while "Arbitrary" refers to an arbitrary parameterized topology.

Pairwise Rendezvous. The synchronization constraint card = $\{1\}$ captures pairwise rendezvous — i.e., synchronization between pairs of processes. In this case it is customary to write $a!$ instead of out_a and $a?$ instead of in_a.

To illustrate, we instantiate the definition of synchronous transition for card = $\{1\}$. *Pairwise-rendezvous transitions* are of the form (s, a, s') for which there exists $(v, w) \in E$ such that:

(STEP) $(s(v), a!, s'(v))$ is a local transition of process template $P^{type(v)}$;

($\mathcal{I}$-STEP) $(s(w), a?, s'(w))$ is a local transition of process template $P^{type(w)}$; and

(FRAME) for all $z \notin \{v, w\}$, $s(z) = s'(z)$.

Note that this incorporates the (CARD) condition with $\mathcal{I} = \{w\}$, and the (MAX) condition is trivially satisfied since $\mathcal{I}' \supset \{w\}$ implies $|\mathcal{I}'| \notin$ card.

Figure 2.3(a) illustrates some possible configurations for a pairwise-rendezvous step.

Asynchronous Rendezvous.   The synchronization constraint card $= \{0, 1\}$ captures asynchronous rendezvous. The idea is that a process can synchronize with zero or one other process. The maximality condition (MAX) ensures that asynchronous rendezvous is like pairwise rendezvous except that a process taking a transition labeled out_a is not blocked when there are no corresponding processes that are able to take a transition labeled in_a.

Figure 2.3(b) illustrates some possible configurations for an asynchronous-rendezvous step.

Broadcast.   The synchronization constraint card $= \mathbb{N}_0$ captures broadcast. The idea is that if vertex v wants to broadcast message a then every recipient of v that is ready to receive the broadcast message a does so. If no process is ready to receive the broadcast then since $0 \in$ card, the initiating process makes its local transition anyway. For broadcast, out_a is written $a!!$ and in_a is written $a??$.

Again, we instantiate the definition of synchronous transition to illustrate. *Broadcast transitions* are of the form (s, a, s') where there exists $v \in V$ and a subset $\mathcal{I} \subseteq V$ of recipients of v, such that (STEP) $s(v) \xrightarrow{a!!} s'(v)$ is a local transition of $P^{\text{type}(v)}$, ($\mathcal{I}$-STEP) for all $w \in \mathcal{I}$, $s(w) \xrightarrow{a??} s'(w)$ is a local transition of $P^{\text{type}(w)}$, (FRAME) for all other z, $s'(z) = s(z)$, and (MAX) there is no recipient w of v not already in $\mathcal{I}$ such that $s(w) \xrightarrow{a??} r$ is a local transition of $P^{\text{type}(w)}$ for some state r.

Thus, the (MAX) condition ensures that when a process v takes a transition labeled $a!!$ then every recipient w of v that can take a local transition labeled $a??$ does so. As a special case we get the broadcast protocols of Esparza et al. [1999, Section 2.1] in which "a process is always willing to receive a broadcast message."

Figure 2.3(c) illustrates some possible configurations for a broadcast step.

Variations on standard primitives.   To model token passing systems, in Chapter 4 we introduce a variation of pairwise-rendezvous synchronization which keeps track of who has the token, and only allows this process to initiate a synchronization. To model synchronization failures in ad hoc networks, in Chapter 7 we introduce a *lossy* variant of broadcast synchronization by removing condition (MAX) from the definition of synchronous transition. Informally, lossy broadcast is to broadcast what asynchronous rendezvous is to pairwise rendezvous.

Figure 2.3(d) illustrates some possible configurations for a lossy broadcast step.

Notation.   Note that, in general, the definition of a process template, including its transition labels, does not determine a synchronization primitive. This is highlighted in Examples 2.1 and 2.2, where the transition systems for server and client use the generic notation for actions $in_{\text{enter}}, in_{\text{leave}}, out_{\text{enter}}, out_{\text{leave}}$, and one can consider systems that use these process templates, but differ in the synchronization primitive.

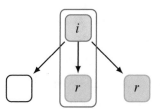

(a) **Pairwise rendezvous**: synchronization with exactly one recipient. If more than one process is ready to synchronize, only one of them can take the synchronous transition.

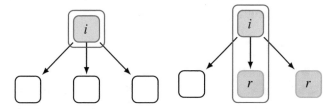

(b) **Asynchronous rendezvous**: synchronization with at most one recipient. If no process is ready, the initiator can take the transition on its own. Otherwise, exactly one of the recipients synchronizes.

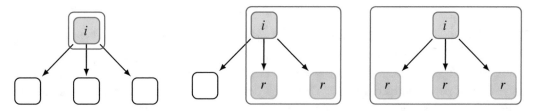

(c) **Broadcast**: synchronization with all recipients that are ready. If no process is ready, the initiator can take the transition on its own. Otherwise, all recipients that are ready synchronize.

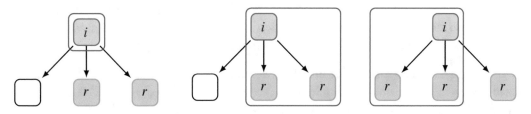

(d) **Lossy broadcast**: synchronization with some of the recipients that are ready. Even if other processes are ready, the initiator can also take the transition on its own.

Figure 2.3: **Synchronization primitives**: pictures show initiator of a synchronous transition, marked with i, with all its recipients. Processes that are ready to take the receive action are marked with r. The processes in the box take the synchronous transition.

In the following, when we use the special notation of the form $a!, a?$ for pairwise-rendezvous actions, or $a!!, a??$ for broadcast actions in a process template, then we implicitly fix the synchronization primitive to correspond to these action labels.

Systems with multiple primitives $\text{sys}(\overline{P}, G, \overline{\text{card}})$. By introducing a little more notation into Definition 2.2 we may define a parameterized system that allows more than one synchronization primitive. In this case, we have a tuple of synchronization constraints $\overline{\text{card}} = (\text{card}_1, \ldots, \text{card}_k)$ and an equal number of sets of synchronizing-action labels $\Sigma_{\text{card}_i} \subset \Sigma_{sync}$. Then define card_i-*synchronous transition* as in the definition of synchronous transition but replace Σ_{sync} with Σ_{card_i}. Now define Δ to be the union of the internal transitions and all the card_i-synchronous transitions. Write $\text{sys}(\overline{P}, G, \overline{\text{card}})$ for the resulting system instance.

2.2.2 RUNS AND DEADLOCKS

A state s of an LTS M is *deadlocked* if there is no transition with source s. Given that the synchronization primitives discussed above are non-trivial, deadlocks may occur in a system instance. The existence of deadlocks leads to two problems. First, a deadlock is usually considered as an error that we would like to detect. Second, a deadlocked run is *finite*, and the specifications we consider are usually interpreted over *infinite* runs (see Section 2.4). Therefore, we need special ways to interpret runs that end in a deadlock.

Deadlock detection. Deadlock detection, i.e., checking whether deadlocked states are reachable, is a problem on its own, and solutions depend heavily on the underlying synchronization primitives. We are interested in *parameterized deadlock detection*, i.e., checking if there exists an instance of a parameterized system in which a deadlocked state is reachable. For some of the systems that we consider, certain assumptions guarantee that there can never be deadlocks. This is the case for token-passing systems without direction-awareness (cf. Section 4). In a few cases, deadlocks are possible and there exist decidability results for parameterized deadlock detection. For example, some of the cutoffs for parameterized model checking of guarded protocols in Section 6 are also cutoffs for the parameterized deadlock detection problem. In most of the cases, however, there are no known results for parameterized deadlock detection.

Interpreting deadlocked runs. The literature we survey here has three ways to deal with deadlocked runs, i.e., finite paths (starting in initial states) which end in deadlocked states.

1. Define a run to be an infinite path starting in the initial state. Thus, we evaluate specifications over infinite paths only and ignore maximal finite paths. This is the approach taken by German and Sistla [1992].

2. Define a run to be a maximal (finite or infinite) path that starts in the initial state. This requires one to use a specification language that can also be interpreted over finite paths. This is the approach taken by Emerson and Namjoshi [1995, 2003], Baier and Katoen [2008], and Delzanno et al. [2010].

3. Change the LTS M to get an LTS M' that does not contain deadlocked states by (i) introducing a new symbol τ into the set of action labels and (ii) for every deadlocked global state s add the transition (s, τ, s). Evaluate specifications over infinite paths of M' that start in an initial state. This is the approach taken by Clarke et al. [1999].

Throughout this book we will explain in every chapter how deadlocked runs are interpreted, and mention known results for the parameterized deadlock detection problem.

2.3   PARAMETERIZED FAMILY OF UNIFORM CONCURRENT SYSTEMS

A *parameterized* d-*ary connectivity graph* is a sequence $\mathbf{G}$ of d-ary connectivity graphs. Observe that as a special case, $\mathbf{G}(n)$ may contain n vertices and $\mathsf{d} = 1$, e.g., $\mathbf{G}(n)$ may be the ring of size n. In general $\mathbf{G}(n)$ need not have n vertices.

Fix a d-ary system template $\overline{P}$, a parameterized d-ary connectivity graph $\mathbf{G}$, and a synchronization constraint card. These determine a *parameterized family of uniform concurrent systems* or simply a *parameterized system*, defined as the sequence

$$n \mapsto \mathsf{sys}(\overline{P}, \mathbf{G}(n), \mathsf{card}).$$

Notation $\overline{P}^{\mathbf{G}(n)}$.   As a shorthand we may write $\overline{P}^{\mathbf{G}(n)}$ instead of $\mathsf{sys}(\overline{P}, \mathbf{G}(n), \mathsf{card})$ if card is clear from the context.

2.4   PARAMETERIZED SPECIFICATIONS

Specifications express the required behavior of systems. Typical specifications for concurrent systems are that no bad *global* state is ever reached (safety specifications), and that individual processes make progress (liveness specifications). Both kinds of specifications are naturally expressed by quantifying over the processes of the system: the canonical approach is to index processes as well as atomic propositions, so that one can express, e.g., that process i is in the critical section by "critical$_i$," and further one can express that some process is in the critical section by $\bigvee_{i \in [n]}$ critical$_i$. Observe that this Boolean formula is actually parameterized by n, and further that the formula—and the set of atomic propositions—grows with n. Using indexed propositions and parameterized Boolean operations in temporal logic, we obtain *indexed temporal logics*. In this book, instead of parameterized Boolean operations we will use the more intuitive notation of quantification over indices. That is, $\bigvee_{i \in [n]}$ critical$_i$ will be expressed as $\exists i.$ critical$_i$.

Apart from being a natural formalizm, the question arises whether it is *necessary* to resort to a logic that induces an unbounded number of atomic propositions to express properties of parameterized systems. To answer this question, first consider the mutual exclusion property, stating that two distinct processes are never in the critical section at the same time, i.e., $\mathsf{G}\left(\forall i, j, i \neq j. (\neg\text{critical}_i \vee \neg\text{critical}_j)\right)$. This formula belongs to the interesting fragment of indexed temporal logic in which temporal operators do not appear inside the scope of index quantifiers. If a given specification is in this fragment, we can also express it in (non-indexed) temporal logic, for a modified system that can be obtained from the original one by introducing additional atomic propositions. For this example, introduce a proposition p and define a labeling function that maps a global state s to p if at most one process is in the critical section in s. (Browne et al. [1989] made this observation for the property that *exactly* one process is in the critical section.) Then, mutual exclusion is expressed as $\mathsf{G}p$, which is a formula in (non-indexed) temporal logic. Other specifications in this fragment can be found in distributed algorithms. Examples are the consensus problem [Lynch, 1996], where several processes need to agree on a common output after limited communication, or the reliable broadcast specification [Srikanth and Toueg, 1987], which ensures that all processes deliver the same set of messages.

However, one can show that even if we allow to redefine systems in such a way, non-indexed temporal logic is not sufficiently expressive for other specifications: for instance, consider the property that any process that tries to enter the critical section will eventually enter it, i.e., $\forall i.\, \mathsf{G}(\mathrm{trying}_i \to (\mathsf{F}\mathrm{critical}_i))$. Note that in this case, quantified subformulas contain temporal operators. To express this specification, we need to distinguish global states according to the processes that are in specific local states (e.g., trying or critical) in order to evaluate that some process actually makes progress along a path of a computation. As the number of processes is a priori not fixed in parameterized model checking, a fixed finite set of atomic propositions is not sufficient for this purpose. We are hence forced to use a logic where the number of propositions grows with the system size, and indexed temporal logic is a very natural choice for the formalization of such specifications.

2.4.1 INDEXED TEMPORAL LOGICS

Indexed temporal logics were introduced by Browne et al. [1989] to model specifications of certain concurrent systems. They are obtained by adding *index quantifiers* to a given temporal logic over indexed atomic propositions.

For example, we can specify a mutual exclusion property as $\mathsf{G}\left(\forall i, j : i \neq j.\, (\neg\mathrm{critical}_i \vee \neg\mathrm{critical}_j)\right)$. Furthermore, in a uni-directional ring, we can express that if a property p holds for some process, then p' should hold for its successor in the ring by writing $\forall i, j : j \in E(i).\, p_i \to p'_j$.[1]

In the following, we first recall the syntax and semantics of CTL*. Then we extend CTL* to *indexed* CTL*. By restricting the temporal logic one gets fragments such as *indexed* LTL\X. All variations of indexed temporal logics from the PMC literature are fragments of indexed CTL*.

CTL*

We briefly describe syntax and semantics of CTL* (see, for instance, Clarke et al. [1999], and Baier and Katoen [2008]).

---

[1]Emerson and Namjoshi [1995, 2003] write such formulas as $\forall i.\, p_i \to p'_{i+1}$ where addition is modulo the size of the ring.

Syntax.   The syntax of CTL* over a set AP of atomic propositions is defined as follows.

State formulas are formed according to the grammar

$$\Phi ::= \top \,\Big|\, p \,\Big|\, \Phi_1 \wedge \Phi_2 \,\Big|\, \neg \Phi \,\Big|\, \mathsf{E}\varphi,$$

where $p \in \mathrm{AP}$, Φ_1 and Φ_2 are state formulas and φ is a path formula.

Path formulas are formed according to the grammar

$$\varphi ::= \Phi \,\Big|\, \varphi_1 \wedge \varphi_2 \,\Big|\, \neg \varphi \,\Big|\, \mathsf{X}\varphi \,\Big|\, \varphi_1 \mathsf{U}\varphi_2,$$

where Φ is a state formula and $\varphi, \varphi_1, \varphi_2$ are path formulas. From these we derive, as usual, Boolean operators (like $\vee$), temporal operators F (eventually) and G (always), and the universal path quantifier A.

Semantics.   Formulas are interpreted in labeled transition systems $M = (Q, Q_0, \Sigma, \delta, \lambda)$ over atomic propositions AP. For a state s of M, define

- $M, s \models p$ iff $p \in \lambda(s)$,

- $M, s \models \Phi_1 \wedge \Phi_2$ iff $M, s \models \Phi_1$ and $M, s \models \Phi_2$,

- $M, s \models \neg \Phi$ iff not $M, s \models \Phi$, and

- $M, s \models \mathsf{E}\varphi$ iff $M, \pi \models \varphi$ for some infinite path π of M starting in s.

For an infinite path π of M starting in s, write π^j for suffix of π starting at position $j \geq 0$, and define

- $M, \pi \models \Phi$ iff $M, s \models \Phi$,

- $M, \pi \models \varphi_1 \wedge \varphi_2$ iff $M, \pi \models \varphi_1$ and $M, \pi \models \varphi_2$,

- $M, \pi \models \neg \varphi$ iff not $M, \pi \models \varphi$,

- $M, \pi \models \mathsf{X}\varphi$ iff $M, \pi^1 \models \varphi$, and

- $M, \pi \models \varphi_1 \mathsf{U}\varphi_2$ iff $\exists j \geq 0\ \forall k < j.\ \big(M, \pi^j \models \varphi_2 \text{ and } M, \pi^k \models \varphi_1\big)$.

Finally, define $M \models \Phi$ if for all initial states s of M, it holds that $M, s \models \Phi$.

Note that action labels Σ are not used in the semantics.

Fragments.   An important fragment of CTL* is LTL, which consists of all CTL* formulas that start with a universal path quantifier A, followed by a CTL* formula without path quantifiers E or A. If it is clear that a formula is in LTL, then the leading path quantifier A may be omitted. From CTL* and LTL, we obtain fragments CTL*\X and LTL\X, respectively, by only considering formulas that do not contain the next-state operator X.

Indexed CTL*

Fix an infinite set $I = \{i, j, \ldots\}$ of index variables.

Syntax.   The syntax of indexed CTL* over a set AP of atomic propositions and set I of index variables is defined as follows.

State formulas are formed according to the grammar

$$\Phi ::= \top \ \Big|\ p_i \ \Big|\ \forall i : r.\, \Phi \ \Big|\ \exists i : r.\, \Phi \ \Big|\ \Phi_1 \wedge \Phi_2 \ \Big|\ \neg \Phi \ \Big|\ \mathrm{E}\varphi,$$

where $p \in AP$, $i \in I$, Φ, Φ_1, Φ_2 are state formulas, φ is a path formula, and r is a list of *range expressions* from

$$\mathrm{type}(i) = t \ \Big|\ neq(i_1, \ldots, i_n) \ \Big|\ i \in E(j),$$

where $t \in \mathbb{N}$ and $i, i_1, \ldots, i_n, j \in I$.

Path formulas are formed according to the grammar

$$\varphi ::= \Phi \ \Big|\ \forall i : r.\, \varphi \ \Big|\ \exists i : r.\, \varphi \ \Big|\ \varphi_1 \wedge \varphi_2 \ \Big|\ \neg \varphi \ \Big|\ \mathrm{X}\varphi \ \Big|\ \varphi_1 \mathrm{U}\varphi_2$$

where Φ is a state formula and $\varphi, \varphi_1, \varphi_2$ are path formulas.

Our notation is inspired by that of Emerson and Namjoshi [1995, 2003]. The symbols $\forall$ and $\exists$ are called *index quantifiers*. If r is empty, we just write $\forall i.\, \phi$ or $\exists i.\, \phi$. The expression $neq(i, j)$ may also be written $i \neq j$. Variable i and atoms p_i in an indexed CTL* formula are *bound* if they are in the scope of a quantifier $\forall i : r$ or $\exists i : r$. An indexed CTL* formula Φ is a *sentence* if every atom in it is bound. An indexed CTL* formula ϕ in which index variables $i_1, \ldots, i_k$ are not bound by index quantifiers may be written $\phi(i_1, \ldots, i_k)$. We say that $i_1, \ldots, i_k$ are *free* in ϕ.

Semantics.   An indexed CTL* formula ϕ is interpreted over a system instance $\overline{P}^G$ (with $\overline{P}$ a system template and $G = (V, E, \mathrm{type})$ a connectivity graph) and a *valuation of the index variables* $e : I \to V$.

A *valuation e satisfies* the range expression $\mathrm{type}(i) = t$ if $\mathrm{type}(e(i)) = t$. Similarly, it satisfies $neq(i_1, \ldots, i_n)$ if $e(i_1), \ldots, e(i_n)$ are pairwise distinct, and it satisfies $i \in E(j)$ if $(e(i), e(j)) \in E$. Finally, it satisfies a list of range expressions if it satisfies every element of the list. A valuation $e : I \to V$ is an *i-variant* of a valuation e' if $e'(j) = e(j)$ for all $j \in I \setminus \{i\}$.

Define $\overline{P}^G, e, s \models \Phi$ inductively:

- $\overline{P}^G, e, s \models p_i$ iff $p_{e(i)} \in \Lambda(s)$,

- $\overline{P}^G, e, s \models \forall i : r.\, \Phi$ iff for all i-variants e' of e that satisfy r it holds that $\overline{P}^G, e', s \models \Phi$,

- $\overline{P}^G, e, s \models \exists i : r. \Phi$ iff there exists an i-variant e' of e that satisfies r and it holds that $\overline{P}^G, e', s \models \Phi$,

- $\overline{P}^G, e, s \models \Phi_1 \wedge \Phi_2$ iff $\overline{P}^G, e, s \models \Phi_1$ and $\overline{P}^G, e, s \models \Phi_2$,

- $\overline{P}^G, e, s \models \neg \Phi$ iff not $\overline{P}^G, e, s \models \Phi$, and

- $\overline{P}^G, e, s \models \mathsf{E}\varphi$ iff $\overline{P}^G, e, \pi \models \varphi$ for some infinite path π of $\overline{P}^G$ starting in s.

For an infinite path π of $\overline{P}^G$ starting in s, define

- $\overline{P}^G, e, \pi \models \Phi$ iff $\overline{P}^G, e, s \models \Phi$,

- $\overline{P}^G, e, \pi \models \forall i : r. \varphi$ iff for all i-variants e' of e that satisfy r it holds that $\overline{P}^G, e', \pi \models \varphi$,

- $\overline{P}^G, e, \pi \models \exists i : r. \varphi$ iff there exists an i-variant e' of e that satisfies r and it holds that $\overline{P}^G, e', \pi \models \varphi$,

- $\overline{P}^G, e, \pi \models \varphi_1 \wedge \varphi_2$ iff $\overline{P}^G, e, \pi \models \varphi_1$ and $\overline{P}^G, e, \pi \models \varphi_2$,

- $\overline{P}^G, e, \pi \models \neg \varphi$ iff not $\overline{P}^G, e, \pi \models \varphi$,

- $\overline{P}^G, e, \pi \models \mathsf{X}\varphi$ iff $\overline{P}^G, e, \pi^1 \models \varphi$, and

- $\overline{P}^G, e, \pi \models \varphi_1 \mathsf{U} \varphi_2$ iff $\exists j \geq 0 \; \forall k < j. \left(\overline{P}^G, e, \pi^j \models \varphi_2 \text{ and } \overline{P}^G, e, \pi^k \models \varphi_1 \right)$.

If Φ is a sentence, define $\overline{P}^G, s \models \Phi$ if for all evaluations (equivalently, for some evaluation) $e : I \to V$ it holds that $\overline{P}^G, e, s \models \Phi$. Finally we define:

$$\overline{P}^G \models \Phi$$

if for every initial state s of $\overline{P}^G$ it holds that $\overline{P}^G, s \models \Phi$.

Notation.   We write $P^G, s \models \Phi(c_1, \ldots, c_k)$ if for all evaluations e in which i_j maps to c_j (for $j \leq k$) it holds that $P^G, e, s \models \Phi(i_1, \ldots, i_k)$.

Fragments.   A *prenex* formula is of the form $Q_1 i_1, \ldots, Q_k i_k : r. \phi(i_1, \ldots, i_k)$, where the Q_j are index quantifiers and $\phi(i_1, \ldots, i_k)$ has no index quantifiers. Formulas of the form $Q_1 i_1, \ldots, Q_k i_k : r. \phi(i_1, \ldots, i_k)$, for some range expression r, will be referred to as *k-indexed*.[2]

---

[2]Note that in these formulas only the last quantifier has a range expression. This is not an additional restriction, however, since semantically $Q_1 i_1 : r_1 \ldots Q_k i_k : r_k. \phi(i_1, \ldots, i_k)$ with separate range expressions $r_1, \ldots, r_k$ is equivalent to $Q_1 i_1, \ldots, Q_k i_k : r_1 \wedge \ldots \wedge r_k. \phi(i_1, \ldots, i_k)$ with the conjunction of all range expressions.

Since the results in the literature concentrate on the prenex fragment of indexed-temporal logic, we introduce some shorthands for important fragments. Write ICTL* for the set of all prenex indexed CTL* sentences, and k-CTL* for the set of all k-indexed formulas in ICTL*.

Prenex indexed LTL, written ILTL, is defined as the linear-time fragment of ICTL*, i.e., formulas of the form $Q_1 i_1, \ldots, Q_k i_k : r. A\phi(i_1, \ldots, i_k)$, where the Q_j are index quantifiers and $\phi(i_1, \ldots, i_k)$ has no index quantifiers and no path quantifiers.[3] Write k-LTL for the set of all k-indexed formulas in ILTL.

Fragments of ICTL* without the next operator, such as ICTL*\X and ILTL\X, are obtained by disallowing formulas that contain the X operator. Specifications without the next-time operator X are common in the literature, since they are stuttering-insensitive, and thus are a natural specification language for asynchronous concurrent systems. Moreover, the presence of X, even with weak communication primitives, leads to undecidability of the PMCP [Emerson and Kahlon, 2003b].

2.4.2   ACTION-BASED SPECIFICATIONS

In contrast to specifications in index temporal logic, which are formulas over indexed state labels, an action-based specification evaluates the sequences of action labels of $\overline{P}^{\mathbf{G}}$. An ω-*regular action-based specification* is an ω-regular language $\mathcal{L}$ over actions $\Sigma_{int} \cup \Sigma_{sync}$.

It is interpreted as follows: write $\overline{P}^{\mathbf{G}} \models \mathcal{L}$ if the projection onto $\Sigma_{int} \cup \Sigma_{sync}$ of every infinite path of $\overline{P}^{\mathbf{G}}$ starting in an initial state is in the language $\mathcal{L}$.

We also find *regular action-based specifications* which are (ordinary finite-word) regular languages $\mathcal{L}$ over actions $\Sigma_{int} \cup \Sigma_{sync}$. These are interepreted as follows: $\overline{P}^{\mathbf{G}} \models \mathcal{L}$ if every finite prefix of every projection onto $\Sigma_{int} \cup \Sigma_{sync}$ of every path of $\overline{P}^{\mathbf{G}}$ starting in an initial state is in the language $\mathcal{L}$.

We write Reg(A) and ωReg(A) for regular and ω-regular action-based specifications, respectively.

2.4.3   SPECIFICATIONS IN THE LITERATURE

Most of the decidability results in the literature are based on one of the following forms of specifications.

- Plain temporal logics (or ω-regular properties) over state labels of a specific process template [Emerson and Kahlon, 2003b, Emerson and Namjoshi, 1996, 1998, German and Sistla, 1992]. These are used for systems with a special *control* process and an unbounded number of *user* processes, and specify only the behavior of the controller.

---

[3]Note that the index variables are bound *outside* of the temporal path quantifier. In particular, for an existentially quantified formula to be satisfied there must exist a valuation of the variables such that ϕ holds for all paths (and not one valuation for each path).

- Indexed temporal logics over the state labels of all processes [Clarke et al., 2004, Emerson and Kahlon, 2000, 2003a,c, 2004, Emerson and Namjoshi, 1995, 2003, German and Sistla, 1992]. These are used for systems with or without a unique control process.

- Action-based specifications on global transitions [Emerson and Kahlon, 2003b, Emerson and Namjoshi, 1998, Esparza et al., 1999]. Specifications on the actions of the system do not directly talk about the state of local processes. However, as argued by Esparza et al. [1999], in many cases one can construct a modified system that satisfies an adapted specification over state labels if and only if the original system satisfies the original action-based specification.

In addition, we consider special parameterized model checking problems COVER (reachability of a local state in one of the components), REPEAT (repeated reachability of a local state in the same component), and TARGET (reachability of a certain state in all components simultaneously, not definable in prenex ICTL*) [Abdulla et al., 2013a, Delzanno et al., 2010, 2011, 2012b]. These are used when reasoning about ad-hoc networks with an arbitrary (and possibly changing) graph structure, and constitute small and important fragments that may be decidable even for systems where more general languages are undecidable (see Chapter 7).

2.5   MODEL CHECKING PROBLEMS FOR CONCURRENT SYSTEMS

Typical questions from the PMC literature are of the form: Is the PMCP decidable for a given class of systems (defined by system template, connectivity graph, and synchronization constraint) and a given class of specifications? We formalize such questions in the following. Fix:

- a set of system templates $\mathcal{P}$ (such as the d-tuples of finite process templates),

- a parameterized connectivity graph $\mathbf{G}$ (such as the sequence of rings),

- a tuple of synchronization constraints $\overline{\mathsf{card}}$ (which is often a singleton card), and

- a set of indexed-temporal logic or action-based specifications $\mathcal{F}$ (such as k-CTL*).

First, we define the (non-parameterized) model checking problem for our class of systems:

The model-checking problem $\mathrm{MCP}(\mathcal{P}, \mathbf{G}, \mathcal{F}, \overline{\mathsf{card}})$ is as follows:

Input. $\overline{P} \in \mathcal{P}, \phi \in \mathcal{F}$ and $n \in \mathbb{N}$.

Output. "Yes" if $\mathrm{sys}(\overline{P}, \mathbf{G}(n), \overline{\mathsf{card}}) \models \phi$; and "No" otherwise.

Unless explicitly stated otherwise, in this book we assume that all system instances $\text{sys}(\overline{P}, \mathbf{G}(n), \text{card})$ are finite-state, and thus that the (non-parameterized) model checking problem is decidable.

In contrast to this, in the parameterized model checking problem we do not give n as an input, but ask whether the specification holds for *all* n:

The parameterized model-checking problem $\text{PMCP}(\mathcal{P}, \mathbf{G}, \mathcal{F}, \overline{\text{card}})$ is as follows:

Input. $\overline{P} \in \mathcal{P}$, and $\phi \in \mathcal{F}$.

Output. "Yes" if $\text{sys}(\overline{P}, \mathbf{G}(n), \overline{\text{card}}) \models \phi$ for all $n \in \mathbb{N}$; and "No" otherwise.

When $\overline{\text{card}}$ is clear from the context, we write $\text{PMCP}(\mathcal{P}, \mathbf{G}, \mathcal{F})$.

Example 2.3   Consider the question: Is the PMCP decidable for token-passing systems on unidirectional rings, with specifications in $\text{ILTL}\backslash\mathsf{X}$? This problem is considered in Section 4.2.1 and written $\text{PMCP}(\mathcal{P}_{\text{simptok}}, \mathbf{R}, \text{ILTL}\backslash\mathsf{X}, \{1\})$ where $\mathcal{P}_{\text{simptok}}$ is a set of processes that are designed to simulate token-passing using pairwise rendezvous, i.e., $\text{card} = \{1\}$, and $\mathbf{R}(n)$ is the uni-directional ring of size n.

2.5.1   COMPUTABILITY ASSUMPTIONS

In parameterized model checking one usually makes the following very general assumptions. In the literature they are typically not made explicit.

- Each process template P is computable, meaning there is an algorithm that computes exactly the states and transitions of P.

- Each set $\text{card} \subseteq \mathbb{N}_0$ is computable.

- The parameterized connectivity graph is computable, meaning that there is an algorithm that on input $n \in \mathbb{N}$ outputs a list of the vertices and edges in $\mathbf{G}(n)$.

Note that for the systems under consideration in this book, the first two are satisfied by definition, since P is finite-state, and card is finite or co-finite for the standard communication primitives. Furthermore, note that the first assumption is also satisfied by various classes of infinite-state processes that are considered in the parameterized verification literature, such as pushdown machines or processes with variables that range over the natural numbers. From these assumptions we can conclude that:

(i) the inputs to the PMCP are finite objects, e.g., $\overline{P}$ may be finite state, or (the configuration space of) a counter machine; and

(ii) the parameterized system is computable, meaning that there is an algorithm that given n returns a finitary representation of the system instance $\mathsf{sys}(\overline{P}, \mathbf{G}(n), \mathsf{card})$, e.g., a list of the states and transitions, or in case the system instance is infinite it may be an algorithm that computes the states and transitions.

The first item is needed for the PMCP to be an algorithmic problem, and the second item is needed if there is to be any hope of deciding the PMCP (for particular cases).

CHAPTER 3

Standard Proof Machinery

The purpose of this section is to briefly summarize the typical principles and ingredients in proofs of (un)decidability for the PMC problem.

3.1 TECHNIQUES TO PROVE UNDECIDABILITY OF PMCP

To prove that $\mathrm{PMCP}(\mathcal{P}, \mathbf{G}, \mathcal{F})$ is undecidable it is sufficient to computably transform a given Turing Machine T into a tuple $(\overline{P}, \mathbf{G}, \phi) \in \mathcal{P} \times \mathcal{G} \times \mathcal{F}$ such that T does not halt on empty input if and only if for all $n \in \mathbb{N}$, $\overline{P}^{\mathbf{G}(n)} \models \phi$.

The first undecidability proof that applies to uniform parameterized systems is by Suzuki [1988], for systems consisting of identical processes arranged in a uni-directional ring with a single multi-valued token. The proof reduces non-halting of Turing machines to this problem. A neater exposition by Emerson and Namjoshi [1995] goes via two-counter machines. Informally, a two-counter machine [Minsky, 1967] has a read-only tape, finite control, and two counters, with operations to increment a counter, decrement a counter, test a counter for zero, and change its internal state. It accepts the word on its input tape if there is a run starting with zero in both of its counters that leads to a halting state. Two-counter machines are Turing-complete. Obviously, k-counter machines for $k > 2$ are also Turing-complete.

We use a formal definition of counter machine close to the one given by Emerson and Kahlon [2003b]. Although it may look more complicated than the usual Minsky machines, we picked their definition for the purpose of presentation, as it typically makes PMCP undecidability proofs easier.

Counter Machines.　An *input-free k-counter machine* (kCM) $\mathcal{M}$ consists of a set of locations $[m]$ (for some $m \in \mathbb{N}$), and action set $\mathcal{A} = \{inc(c_q), dec(c_q), zero(c_q) : q \in [k]\}$, and a set $\Delta \subseteq [m] \times \mathcal{A} \times [m]$ of *commands*. A *configuration* of $\mathcal{M}$ is a tuple $(i, \bar{v}) \in [m] \times \mathbb{N}_0^k$; so i is a location and v_j indicates the value of the j-th counter. The *initial configuration* is $(1, 0, \ldots, 0)$; so the machine starts in location 1 with empty counters). The *halting configurations* are $\{m\} \times \mathbb{N}_0^k$; so the machine halts whenever it reaches location m). The *configuration graph of* $\mathcal{M}$ is the directed graph whose vertices are all the configurations, and edges are defined as follows. There is an edge from configuration $(i, \bar{v})$ to configuration $(j, \bar{w})$ if (a) $i \neq m$ and (b) there exists a command $(i, \sigma, j) \in \Delta$ such that:

- if σ is $inc(c_q)$ then $w_q = v_q + 1$ and $w_p = v_p$ for $p \neq q$;

- if σ is $dec(c_q)$ then $w_q = v_q - 1$ and $w_p = v_p$ for $p \neq q$; and

- if σ is $zero(c_q)$ then $w_q = v_q = 0$ and $w_p = v_p$ for $p \neq q$.

Note that if σ is $dec(c_q)$ then the described edge exists only if $v_q > 0$ (i.e., there is an implicit test for non-zero).

This definition differs from Minsky's original definition of multi-counter machine in two ways: (i) a Minsky machine is deterministic while this definition is non-deterministic and (ii) a Minsky machine has no deadlocked configurations while this definition allows non-halting configurations with no outgoing edge. The translation of a Minsky machine into our definition results in a machine such that for every location $l \in [m]$ either there is exactly one outgoing transition, and it is labeled $inc(c_q)$ for some q, or there are exactly two outgoing transitions and they are labeled $dec(c_q)$ and $zero(c_q)$ for some q. From this translation and undecidability of the halting problem for Minsky machines [Minsky, 1967], the following theorem is immediate.

Theorem 3.1   *The following problem is undecidable: given an input-free k-counter machine $\mathcal{M}$ (for $k \geq 2$), where the counters are initialized with zeroes, does there exist a path in the configuration space of $\mathcal{M}$ from the initial configuration to a halting configuration?*

Undecidability of PMCP.   Thus, typical undecidability proofs in this area show how to simulate a 2CM by the composition of (uniform) finite-state processes. Typically one process, the *controller* process, simulates the internal state of the 2CM, while the remaining n *storage* processes collectively encode the counter values (the simulation either covers n steps of the 2CM, or a prefix of the computation as long as the counter values are bounded by n). The work in the proof is typically showing how the controller can issue commands to increment/decrement counters and test counters for zero. The prototypical such proof, following Emerson and Namjoshi [1995, 2003], is sketched in Section 4.2.3.

3.2   HOW TO PROVE DECIDABILITY OF THE PMCP

In this section we describe techniques that help one prove that the PMCP is decidable, i.e., symmetry arguments, reductions to well-structured transition systems or vector addition systems, and cutoff techniques.

A natural first step of a decidability proof is to use symmetry of the systems $\overline{P}^G$ as well as the specifications to simplify the problem. For instance:

- if the connectivity graph G is a clique, and all processes are instances of the same process template P, then $P^G \models \forall i.\phi(i)$ is equivalent to $P^G \models \phi(1)$, or

- as noted by Emerson and Namjoshi [1995, 2003], if the connectivity graph G is a ring, and all processes are instances of the same process template P, then $P^G \models \forall i, j : i \neq j.\phi(i, j)$ is equivalent to $P^G \models \forall j.\phi(1, j)$.

Such intuitions can be formalized following the approach by Emerson and Sistla [1996]. Formal treatment of symmetry is tedious and thus often only addressed implicitly in the literature (and this survey). Note that Emerson and Namjoshi [1995, 2003] treated symmetry explicitly.

We can reduce the PMCP to model checking a single infinite-state LTSs by combining $\overline{P}^G$ for $G \in \mathbf{G}$. Model checking is decidable for certain classes of infinite-state systems and certain specifications. Notably, the coverability problem (defined below) is decidable for well-structured transition systems (WSTS); see Finkel and Schnoebelen [2001] or Abdulla et al. [1996]. Vector addition systems with states (or equivalently Petri Nets) are special kinds of WSTSs for which repeated coverability and reachability problems are decidable. For classical results in Petri nets, see Esparza [1998] and Yen [1992]. Thus, for example, if the combined system is a WSTS or a VASS, then we can decide the PMCP. We review the definitions and decidability results for WSTS and VASS in Section 3.2.1.

Another approach is to reduce PMCP to model checking finitely many system instances, see e.g., Emerson and Namjoshi [1995, 2003] and Clarke et al. [2004]. Such results are often described as cutoffs and are typically proved by exhibiting suitable simulation relations between almost all system instances of the parameterized system and a fixed system instance. We formalize this in Section 3.2.3.

3.2.1 WELL-STRUCTURED TRANSITION SYSTEMS

Following the work by Abdulla et al. [1996] and Finkel and Schnoebelen [2001], well-structured transition systems became a popular framework for reasoning about infinite-state systems and parameterized systems. We begin by recalling some required notions.

A binary relation $\leq$ on a set X is a *quasi-order* if it is reflexive and transitive. For $T \subseteq X$ write $\uparrow T := \{x \in X \mid \exists t \in T, t \leq x\}$, called the *upward closure of* T. The *downward closure* of T is the set $\{x \in X \mid \exists t \in T, x \leq t\}$. A set T is *upward closed* if $T = \uparrow T$.

A quasi-order is a *well quasi-order* if for every infinite sequence $x_1, x_2, \cdots$ there exist indices $i < j$ with $x_i \leq x_j$. In particular, there are no infinite decreasing chains and no infinite anti-chains.

A typical example of a well quasi-order on $\mathbb{N}^n$ (for $n \in \mathbb{N}$) is defined by $(x_1, \cdots, x_n) \leq (y_1, \cdots, y_n)$ if for every $i \leq n$ it holds that $x_i \leq y_i$.

The following properties follow from the definition of well quasi-order $\leq$. If C is upward closed then there is a finite set $B \subseteq C$, called a *basis of* C, such that C is the upward closure of B: $C = \uparrow B$ (the word *basis* is used to mean that B generates C, and not that B is unique with this property). If $C_1 \subseteq C_2 \subseteq C_3 \subseteq \cdots$ is an infinite chain of upward closed sets then there exists k such that $C_k = \cup_{n \in \mathbb{N}} C_n$.

Let $\leq$ be a quasi-order on the set of states of a transition system M. For states s, t of M, write $s \xrightarrow{a} t$ if there is an edge in M from s to t labeled a, write $s \rightarrow t$ if $s \xrightarrow{a} t$ for some a, and write $s \xrightarrow{*} t$ if there is a path in M from s to t. For a set C of states of M, define the set $Pred(C)$ of states M as follows: $s \in Pred(C)$ iff either $s \in C$ or there exists $t \in C$ such that

$s \to t$. Say that $\leq$ is *monotonic* with respect to M if for all states s, s', t of M and all action labels a, if $s \leq s'$ and $s \xrightarrow{a} t$, then there exists $t' \geq t$ such that $s' \xrightarrow{a} t'$.[1] The following property holds if $\leq$ is monotonic: if C is an upward-closed set of states of M, then $Pred(C)$ is upward closed.

Definition 3.2   Let M be a transition system and let $\leq$ be an ordering on the state set of M. Then M is a *well-structured transition system* (WSTS) with respect to $\leq$ if the following conditions hold:

1. $\leq$ is a well-quasi ordering,

2. $\leq$ is monotonic with respect to M, and

3. one can compute, from a basis for an upward closed set C, a basis for $Pred(C)$.

Finkel and Schnoebelen [2001] gave a detailed discussion of fundamental computation models that are well-structured transition systems. Examples are variants of, e.g., communication finite state machines, basic process algebra, and Petri nets.

The following problem is parameterized by an infinite-state LTS M with initial states I and a quasi-ordering $\leq$ on the states S of M.

- The *coverability* problem:
  input: finite set of states $T \subset S$.
  output: 'Yes' if and only if there exist $\iota \in I$ and $t \in \uparrow T$ such that $\iota \xrightarrow{*} t$.

The following theorem can be easily obtained from the work by Abdulla et al. [1996] and Finkel and Schnoebelen [2001].

Theorem 3.3   *The coverability problem is decidable for WSTSs, if the initial state set I satisfies one of the following conditions.*

1. *I is finite.*

2. *I is downward closed, and has a computable set membership.*

Proof. The proof idea is similar in both cases. From a basis for C and n, one can compute a basis for $Pred^n(C)$. Thus, one can compute, given n, whether $Pred^n(C) = Pred^{n+1}(C)$: they are equal iff for every s' in a basis of $Pred^{n+1}(C)$ there is s in a basis of $Pred^n(C)$ such that $s \leq s'$. Thus, one can compute a number k such that $Pred^k(C) = \cup_{n \in \mathbb{N}} Pred^n(C)$, and hence a basis for $\cup_{n \in \mathbb{N}} Pred^n(C)$.

Now consider the coverability problem for state set T and initial state set I. Let B be a basis for $\cup_{n \in \mathbb{N}} Pred^n(\uparrow T)$. There exists $\iota \in I$ and $t \in \uparrow T$ such that $\iota \xrightarrow{*} t$ if and only if $I \cap \uparrow B \neq \emptyset$.

---

[1]Monotonicity is called "strong compatibility" by Finkel and Schnoebelen [2001].

In other words, we have reduced the coverability problem to checking if there is some $i \in I$ and some $b \in B$ such that $b \leq i$. If I is finite then there are only finitely many pairs to check. If I is downward closed then $I \cap \uparrow B \neq \emptyset$ is equivalent to $I \cap B \neq \emptyset$. If I also has decidable membership then one simply needs to check if one of the finitely many elements of B is in I. $\square$

This theorem is used to prove decidability of PMCP for safety properties in Theorem 5.7, Theorem 6.31, and Theorem 7.19.

3.2.2   VECTOR ADDITION SYSTEMS WITH STATES (AND PETRI NETS)

We define a *vector addition system with states* (VASS) M to consist of a finite set Q of states, an initial state $\iota \in Q$, a finite action set $A \subset \mathbb{Z}^d$, and finite transition relation $T \subseteq Q \times A \times Q$. The *configuration space* of a VASS M is the transition system with state set $Q \times \mathbb{N}_0^d$, initial state $(\iota, 0, \cdots, 0)$, and transitions defined by $(q, \bar{x}) \xrightarrow{a} (r, \bar{y})$ if $\bar{y} = \bar{x} + a$ where $(q, a, r) \in T$. Write $s \xrightarrow{*} t$ if there is a path in the configuration space (ignoring actions) from s to t.

The VASS with ordering $\leq$ defined as follows is a WSTS: $(q, \bar{x}) \leq (r, \bar{y})$ if $q = r$ and $x_i \leq y_i$ for $1 \leq i \leq d$. Besides the coverability problem, we also consider the following.

- The *reachability* problem:
  input: configuration $t = (q, \bar{v}) \in Q \times \mathbb{N}_0^d$.
  output: 'Yes' if and only if $\iota \xrightarrow{*} t$ for some $\iota \in I$.

- The *control-state repeated coverability* problem:
  input: $q \in Q$.
  output: 'Yes' if and only if there exist infinitely many configurations $t_1, t_2, \cdots$ each of whose first coordinate is q and such that $(\iota, 0, \cdots, 0) \xrightarrow{*} t_1$ and $t_i \xrightarrow{*} t_{i+1}$ for all $i \in \mathbb{N}$.

The following theorem summarizes results on Petri nets and VASS important for the exposition in this book, cf. [Esparza, 1998] for a detailed survey of this area.

Theorem 3.4   *The control state repeated coverability problem for VASS is EXPSPACE-complete. Moreover, the problem can be solved in space which is polynomial in the number of states of the VASS and exponential in the dimension of the VASS. The reachability problem is decidable (and EXPSPACE-hard).*

This theorem is used to prove decidability of special PMCPs of broadcast and pairwise systems for liveness properties in Theorem 5.8, Theorem 5.10, and Theorem 7.21.

A VASS in which $|Q| = 1$ is called a vector-addition system (VAS), which is a notational variant of Petri nets. Conversely, every VASS can be represented as a VAS (since the state component can be coded in $|Q|$ many additional coordinates).

3.2.3   DECOMPOSITIONS AND CUTOFFS

Some proofs that $\mathsf{PMCP}(\mathcal{P}, \mathbf{G}, \mathcal{F})$ is decidable also yield a computable reduction to a finite set of finite-state model checking problems. This is formalized as follows.

A *decomposition* for $(\mathcal{P}, \mathbf{G}, \mathcal{F})$ is a function mapping every pair $(\overline{P}, \phi) \in \mathcal{P} \times \mathcal{F}$ (where $\overline{P}$ and $\mathbf{G}$ have the same arity d) to a pair $(\mathrm{MC}_{fin}, \Phi_{\mathbb{B}})$, where

1. MC_{fin} is a set $\{(K_1, \phi_1), \ldots, (K_m, \phi_m)\}$, where each K_i is a d-ary connectivity-graph, each ϕ_i is a formula, m is a positive integer, and

2. $\Phi_{\mathbb{B}}$ is a Boolean formula $\Phi_{\mathbb{B}}(x_1, \ldots, x_m)$ (with m variables)

   such that the following are equivalent:

- $\forall n \in \mathbb{N}, \overline{P}^{\mathbf{G}(n)} \models \phi$,

- $\Phi_{\mathbb{B}}(c_1, \ldots, c_m)$ evaluates to $\top$ under the assignment $c_i = \top$ iff $\overline{P}^{K_i} \models \phi_i$.

Thus, a decomposition reduces the problem $\mathsf{PMCP}(\mathcal{P}, \mathbf{G}, \mathcal{F})$ to a Boolean combination of the finitely many model checking problems from the set MC_{fin}. Note that if the decomposition is a computable function, then $\mathsf{PMCP}(\mathcal{P}, \mathbf{G}, \mathcal{F})$ is decidable.

We identify a special case of this definition that appears in the literature: we say *m is a cutoff* (for $(\mathcal{P}, \mathbf{G}, \mathcal{F})$) if for all $(\overline{P}, \phi) \in \mathcal{P} \times \mathcal{F}$, the image of the decomposition function is the pair $(\mathrm{MC}_{fin}, \Phi_{\mathbb{B}})$ where $\mathrm{MC}_{fin} = \{(\mathbf{G}(1), \phi), \ldots, (\mathbf{G}(m), \phi)\}$ and $\Phi_{\mathbb{B}} = x_1 \wedge \ldots \wedge x_m$. In other words, m is a cutoff means that for all $(\overline{P}, \phi) \in \mathcal{P} \times \mathcal{F}$: $\forall n, \overline{P}^{\mathbf{G}(n)} \models \phi$ if and only if $\forall n \leq m, \overline{P}^{\mathbf{G}(n)} \models \phi$. Cutoff results appear in Section 4 and Section 6.

Proposition 3.5   *If $(\mathcal{P}, \mathbf{G}, \mathcal{F})$ has a cutoff, then $\mathsf{PMCP}(\mathcal{P}, \mathbf{G}, \mathcal{F})$ is decidable.*

Proof. Suppose m is a cutoff. This means that for all $(\overline{P}, \phi) \in \mathcal{P} \times \mathcal{F}$: $\forall n, \overline{P}^{\mathbf{G}(n)} \models \phi$ if and only if $\forall n \leq m, \overline{P}^{\mathbf{G}(n)} \models \phi$. Thus, an algorithm solving the PMCP is: given $\overline{P} \in \mathcal{P}, \phi \in \mathcal{F}$, output "Yes" if for every $n \leq m$, it holds that $\overline{P}^{\mathbf{G}(n)} \models \phi$, and "No" otherwise.   □

Remark 3.6   To solve PMCP, it is not enough to know that there exists a cutoff, one also needs to know the value of the cutoff in order to know when to stop enumerating the system instances.

For instance, suppose that for every $k \in \mathbb{N}$ the data $(\mathcal{P}, \mathbf{G}, k\text{-CTL}^*)$ has a cutoff. This means that for every k there is an algorithm deciding $\mathsf{PMCP}(\mathcal{P}, \mathbf{G}, k\text{-CTL}^*)$. However, it does not imply that there is an algorithm that can decide $\mathsf{PMCP}(\mathcal{P}, \mathbf{G}, \mathsf{ICTL}^*)$. However, if the cutoffs are computable (i.e., there is an algorithm that given $k \in \mathbb{N}$ outputs a cutoff for $(\mathcal{P}, \mathbf{G}, k\text{-CTL}^*)$), then $\mathsf{PMCP}(\mathcal{P}, \mathbf{G}, \mathsf{ICTL}^*)$ is decidable. Such a situation occurs in Section 4.

Cutoff results for $(\mathcal{P}, \mathbf{G}, \mathcal{F})$ are often obtained by showing that for any $\overline{P} \in \mathcal{P}$, the set of runs of all system instances of $\overline{P}^{\mathbf{G}}$ cannot be distinguished by any specification in $\mathcal{F}$ from the set of runs of the system instance $\overline{P}^{\mathbf{G}(m)}$, for some $m \in \mathbb{N}$. This is the case if one can show, for instance, that (i) for sufficiently many components, adding an extra component to the system only adds runs that can already be simulated in the smaller system, and (ii) a run in a system instance with many components can be simulated by a run in a system with a smaller number of components. This is often possible when the connectivity-graph is "homogeneous" (like a star or a clique), see Emerson and Kahlon [2000] and German and Sistla [1992]. For the case of uni-directional rings and specifications in indexed CTL*\X, Emerson and Namjoshi [1995, 2003] use stuttering bisimulations (see, e.g., Browne et al. [1988]) between tuples of processes in system instances of different size. To prove that two system instances are bisimilar, one has to find one or several maps (depending on the number of indexed variables) from components of the big system to components of the small system, such that any projection of a path of the big system with respect to these maps is stuttering equivalent to a path of the small system, and vice versa.

CHAPTER 4

Token-passing Systems

In a token-passing system (TPS), processes communicate by passing a token to their neighbors in the connectivity graph. We will define the passing of a token (with or without a value) as a special case of pairwise-rendezvous synchronization. In contrast to most of the other classes of systems in this survey, TPSs have been analyzed on complex connectivity graphs, where connections may or may not be labeled with directions. Thus, in order to define TPSs we extend our basic system model to *direction-aware parameterized systems*.

One special case has received attention in the literature, in particular in the work by Emerson and Namjoshi [1995, 2003] and Clarke et al. [2004] and recently by Aminof et al. [2014a]: connections in the graphs are not labeled with directions and the token does not hold a value. In this case, the only purpose of the token is to distinguish the process that currently holds it from all the other processes. This allows us to realize systems with mutual exclusion properties as TPSs, where the process with the token is the only one to access the shared resource. Connectivity graphs can then be used to model certain schedulings, e.g., token rings model a round-robin scheduling scheme.

Environment assumptions can be added to the specification in order to further restrict token passing, e.g., to only consider runs with fair token passing. Emerson and Namjoshi [1995, 2003] show that in this case the PMCP is decidable when the considered graphs are rings and specifications are in a fragment of ICTL*\X with purely universal index quantification, and Clarke et al. [2004] show decidability for arbitrary graphs and specifications in k-LTL\X (for any fixed k). Recently, these two decidability results have been unified and extended by Aminof et al. [2014a].

We also consider systems where the token can hold different values, and, in later sections, look at systems where processes are aware of direction labels in the connectivity graph. While it is known that multi-valued tokens lead to an undecidable PMCP in general [Suzuki, 1988], there are decidability results for systems with multi-valued tokens and direction-awareness, subject to additional restrictions on the process and the specifications.

Running Example.   As the running example of this chapter, we use a version of Milner's scheduler [Milner, 1989]. The scheduler is composed of an arbitrary number of components, each of which is responsible for activating one (unspecified) task and receives confirmation when its task has been executed. Scheduling should ensure that the tasks are activated in a round-robin scheme, and that every task has terminated before being activated again. This can naturally be modeled in token-passing systems, as noted by Emerson and Namjoshi [1995, 2003].

4.1   SYSTEM MODEL

To model TPSs, we first extend our general system model to *direction-aware parameterized systems*. Then we define TPSs as a special case, where token passing is modeled by restricted pairwise-rendezvous synchronization. Not all results of this chapter require this extension of the system model: results in Section 4.2 consider direction-unaware systems, while results in Section 4.3 consider direction-aware systems.

4.1.1   DIRECTION-AWARE PARAMETERIZED SYSTEMS

We extend the definition of parameterized systems to include additional labels on edges, called *directions*. The idea is that processes are allowed to restrict, depending on their local state, which edges of the connectivity graph can be used to synchronize with other processes.

A *direction-aware parameterized system* consists of the same ingredients as a (direction-unaware) parameterized system (see Section 2.2), except for the following modifications.

Directions.   Fix finite sets Dir_{out}, Dir_{in} of *outgoing* and *incoming directions*.

Directed connectivity graph.   A d-ary *directed connectivity graph* is a tuple $G = (V, E, \text{type}, dir_{out}, dir_{in})$, where (V, E, type) is a d-ary connectivity graph, and $dir_{out} : E \to Dir_{out}$ and $dir_{in} : E \to Dir_{in}$ are additional labeling functions. A *parameterized* d-*ary directed connectivity graph* is a sequence **G** of d-ary directed connectivity graphs.

Example 4.1   Bi-directional Ring.   Let $Dir_{out} = Dir_{in} = \{\text{cw}, \text{ccw}\}$, standing for clockwise and counterclockwise directions in a ring. A *bi-directional ring* is a directional connectivity graph $B = (V, E, \text{type}, dir_{out}, dir_{in})$ with

- $V = [k]$ for some $k \geq 2$,

- $E = \{(i, i +_k 1), (i, i -_k 1) \mid i \in V\}$, and

- $dir_{out}(i, i +_k 1) = dir_{in}(i, i +_k 1) = \text{cw}$, and $dir_{out}(i, i -_k 1) = dir_{in}(i, i -_k 1) = \text{ccw}$ for $i \in V$.

In general, type is arbitrary, but usually we consider bi-directional rings with a single process template.

A *parameterized bi-directional ring* **B** is a sequence of $B_1, B_2, \ldots$ of bi-directional rings, usually with $V(B_n) = [n]$. A bi-directional ring with $V = [4]$ is depicted in Figure 4.1.

Direction-aware Transition Labels.   In a direction-aware parameterized system, process templates use transition labels from

$$\Sigma_{pr} := \Sigma_{int} \cup \{(out_a, d) : a \in \Sigma_{sync}, d \in Dir_{out}\} \cup \{(in_a, d) : a \in \Sigma_{sync}, d \in Dir_{in}\}.$$

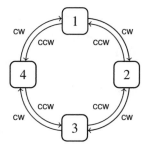

Figure 4.1: A bi-directional ring with 4 nodes. Since $dir_{out}(e) = dir_{in}(e)$ for all edges e, the direction is only displayed once.

Direction-aware Synchronous Transitions.   Internal transitions remain as before, but synchronous transitions are now direction-aware. That is, a synchronous transition must satisfy the same properties as before, and additionally the direction d in the local transition label of the sender must match the labeling of the used edge by dir_{out}, and similarly with dir_{in} for the receiver(s).

Formally, *direction-aware synchronous transitions* are elements (s, t, s') of $S \times \Sigma_{sync} \times S$ for which there exists a process index $v \in V$ and a set $\mathcal{I} \subseteq \{w \in V : E(v, w)\}$ of recipients of v in G such that:[1]

(CARD) $|\mathcal{I}| \in$ card.

(STEP) $s(v) \xrightarrow{out_a,d} s'(v)$ is a local transition of $P^{\text{type}(v)}$.

(DIR) For every $w \in \mathcal{I}$, $dir_{out}(v, w) = d$.

$(\mathcal{I}\text{-STEP-DIR})$ For every $w \in \mathcal{I}$, $s(w) \xrightarrow{in_a,d_w} s'(w)$ is a local transition of $P^{\text{type}(w)}$, with $d_w = dir_{in}(v, w)$.

(FRAME) For every $w' \in V \setminus \{v, w\}$, $s'(w') = s(w')$.

(MAX) There does not exist a strict superset $\mathcal{I}' \supset \mathcal{I}$ of recipients of v in G such that the conditions above are satisfied, with $\mathcal{I}'$ replacing $\mathcal{I}$, and s'' replacing s'.

Example 4.2   Directional Pairwise Rendezvous.   In a bi-directional ring, pairwise rendezvous as defined in Section 2.2.1 allows any process to synchronize with either of its two neighbors. We can define *directional pairwise rendezvous*, that may restrict which of its neighbors a process is allowed to synchronize with.

---

[1]Note that (CARD), (FRAME), and (MAX) are as before.

To obtain directional rendezvous, we instantiate the definition of directional synchronous transition for card $= \{1\}$. *Directional pairwise-rendezvous transitions* are of the form (s, a, s') for which there exists $(v, w) \in E$ such that

(STEP) $s(v) \xrightarrow{a!,d} s'(v)$ is a local transition of $P^{\text{type}(v)}$.

(DIR) $dir_{out}(v, w) = d$.

$(\mathcal{I}\text{-STEP-DIR})$ $s(w) \xrightarrow{a?,d_w} s'(w)$ is a local transition of $P^{\text{type}(w)}$, with $d_w = dir_{in}(v, w)$.

(FRAME) For every $w' \in V \setminus \{v, w\}$, $s'(w') = s(w')$.

As with non-directional pairwise rendezvous, this incorporates the (CARD) condition with $\mathcal{I} = \{w\}$, and the (MAX) condition is trivially satisfied since $\mathcal{I}' \supset \{w\}$ implies $|\mathcal{I}'| \not\subseteq$ card.

Remark.   Note that a direction-aware parameterized system degenerates to a parameterized system if $|Dir_{out}| = |Dir_{in}| = 1$. Also, by having either $|Dir_{out}| = 1$ or $|Dir_{in}| = 1$, we can define parameterized systems where processes can choose which edges to use for synchronization only for incoming or only for outgoing edges.

4.1.2   TOKEN-PASSING SYSTEMS

Fix a finite set T of token values. If $|T| = 1$, we call the token a *simple token*, otherwise a *multi-valued token*.

Token-passing system template.   For token-passing systems, we consider only 1-ary system templates, and therefore do not distinguish between process templates and system templates. A *token-passing process template* with token values T is a finite[2] LTS $P = (Q, Q_0, \Sigma_{pr}, \delta, \lambda)$ with the following restrictions.

1. The state set Q is partitioned into two non-empty sets: $Q = T \cup N$. States in T are said to *have the token*.

2. The initial state set is $Q_0 = \{\iota_T, \iota_N\}$ for some $\iota_T \in T, \iota_N \in N$.

3. The synchronous transition labels are given by the token values, i.e., $\Sigma_{sync} = T$.

4. Every transition $q \xrightarrow{out_t,d} q'$ with $t \in T$ satisfies that q has the token and q' does not. We say that P *sends the token* with value t in direction d.

5. Every transition $q \xrightarrow{in_t,d} q'$ with $t \in T$ satisfies that q' has the token and q does not. We say that P *receives the token* with value t from direction d.

---

[2]Note that all results of this chapter that state existence of a cutoff hold even for infinite-state process templates.

6. Every transition $q \xrightarrow{a} q'$ with $a \in \Sigma_{int}$ satisfies that q has the token if and only if q' has the token.

7. Every infinite action-labeled run $a_0 a_1 \ldots$ of P is in the set $(\Sigma_{int}^* Dir_{out} \Sigma_{int}^* Dir_{in})^\omega \cup (\Sigma_{int}^* Dir_{in} \Sigma_{int}^* Dir_{out})^\omega$. That is, the token is sent and received infinitely often in every run.

A More Liberal Token-passing Restriction.   Restriction 6 above was introduced for direction-unaware systems by Emerson and Namjoshi [1995, 2003]. Aminof et al. [2014a] extended it to direction-aware systems, and showed that all the results in this chapter that state existence of cutoffs for TPSs also hold for the following, more liberal restriction:

(†) From every state q that has the token there must be a path $q \ldots q'$ such that q' does not have the token, and from every state q that does not have the token there must be a path $q \ldots q'$ such that q' has the token.

Notation.   Let $\mathcal{P}_T$ be the set of all token-passing process templates with token values T. If $|T| = 1$ then we write $\mathcal{P}_{simp}$ instead of $\mathcal{P}_T$. Moreover, let $\mathcal{P}_T^u$ denote the set of all process templates for which $|Dir_{out}| = |Dir_{in}| = 1$, i.e., direction-unaware processes.[3] If we require $|Dir_{in}| = 1$, then processes cannot choose from which directions to receive the token, but possibly in which direction to send it. Denote the set of all such process templates by $\mathcal{P}_T^{snd}$. Similarly, define $\mathcal{P}_T^{rcv}$ to be all process templates where $|Dir_{out}| = 1$ — processes cannot choose where to send the token, but possibly from which direction to receive it.

Example 4.3   Processes in Milner's Scheduler.   Milner's scheduler is composed of a variable number of processes, each responsible for scheduling one of the tasks. An implementation of such a process is depicted in Figure 4.2, where label A stands for activation of the task, and label C for completion of the task. Transitions to a state labeled with C are assumed to synchronize with actual completion of the task by an external device.

After activating the task, the process sends the token in direction cw, and afterwards waits for the return of the token, which may happen before or after completion of the task. Only after both of these events, the process will activate its task again.

Token-passing System Instance.   To define token-passing systems, we instantiate the definition of a direction-aware parameterized system with

- $\Sigma_{sync} = T$,

- $d = 1$,

---

[3]For notational simplicity, we assume that Dir_{out} of the directed connectivity graph and the direction-aware process template are always identical, and similarly for Dir_{in}. One can easily define process templates to run on connectivity graphs with differing sets of directions, at the cost of notational overhead.

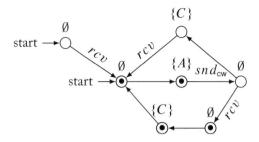

Figure 4.2: Process template for Milner's scheduler. States with token are depicted with a dot inside the circle. State labels are depicted above states. Label A stands for activation of the task, C for completion of the task.

- card $= \{1\}$ (i.e., directional pairwise rendezvous), and

- process templates from $\mathcal{P}_T$.

Additionally, the global initial states S_0 are restricted to those states s for which there exists a unique $v \in V$ such that local state $s(v)$ has the token.[4]

Example 4.4   Milner's Scheduler for 4 Tasks.   We obtain an implementation of Milner's scheduler for four tasks by constructing a system instance with four process templates as given in Figure 4.2, arranged in a bi-directional ring as given in Figure 4.1.

   Note that since the processes always send the token in direction cw, their behavior would be the same in a uni-directional ring. Our system model allows us to define variants of this example where, e.g., the token is non-deterministically sent in one of the directions cw, ccw, and where the receiving process may accept the token from both directions, or only from one.

Deadlocks.   Restrictions 6 and (†) for token-passing process templates both guarantee the absence of deadlocks for direction-unaware systems. Note that the same is not true for direction-aware systems: the processes which are ready to receive might accept the token only from certain directions, which may be different from the directions into which the process that has the token can send it. This can lead to a deadlock if all process run into states from which the only possible transition is a token-passing transition. There are no known decidability results for parameterized deadlock detection in direction-aware TPSs.[5]

---

[4]Note that there is a slight difference between our model and that of Emerson and Namjoshi [1995, 2003]: in our model, one of the processes starts with the token, while in the original model nobody has the token, and the first transition of the system is a receive action of one process. There is, however, no difference in decidability of the two models, and the only difference in satisfaction of properties is in properties that mention the initial position of the token.

[5]Absence of deadlocks is guaranteed if we require that either (a) the process must always be able to reach a state such that it can receive the token from any direction, or (b) the process must always be able to reach a state such that it can send the token into any direction. Both (a) and (b) are more restrictive than (†), and incomparable to 6. The undecidability results in

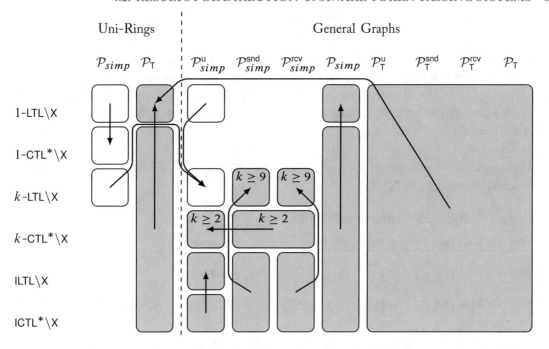

Figure 4.3: Decidability results and reductions for token-passing systems, distinguished into connectivity graphs and classes of process templates on top, and fragments of ICTL* on the left. White boxes are decidability results, dark boxes are undecidability results. An arrow from box A to box B means that the result of A follows from the result, or a variation of the proof, of B. Blank items are not covered in the literature.

Specifications. For token-passing systems, we use indexed temporal logic specifications in fragments of ICTL*\X. Unless a different fragment is specified, in the following $\varphi(i_1, \ldots, i_n)$ stands for a formula in ICTL*\X with free index variables $i_1, \ldots, i_n$.

4.2 RESULTS FOR DIRECTION-UNAWARE TOKEN-PASSING SYSTEMS

Figure 4.3 and Table 4.1 (on page 47) give an overview of the decidability results for TPSs. We consider results for direction-unaware systems (with process templates from $\mathcal{P}^u_{simp}$ or $\mathcal{P}^u_T$) in this section, and for direction-aware systems (with process templates from $\mathcal{P}^{snd}_T$, $\mathcal{P}^{rcv}_T$, or $\mathcal{P}_T$) in Section 4.3.

Theorem 4.17 and the first part of Theorem 4.18 also hold for templates that satisfy restriction (a), while the second part of Theorem 4.18 also holds for templates that satisfy (b).

4.2.1   DECIDABILITY FOR SIMPLE TOKEN-PASSING IN UNI-DIRECTIONAL RINGS

Consider the parameterized connectivity graph $\mathbf{R}$ of uni-directional rings of size n, i.e., $\mathbf{R}(n) = (V, E)$ with $V = [n]$ and $E = \{(i, j): j = i + 1 \mod n\}$. In a cornerstone paper, Emerson and Namjoshi [1995, 2003] prove that in uni-directional rings with a simple token it is enough to check a given property for all rings up to a given size, where the size depends on the quantification in the formula.

Theorem 4.5   [Emerson and Namjoshi, 2003].   *PMCP$(\mathcal{P}^{\mathsf{u}}_{simp}, \mathbf{R}, \mathcal{F})$ has a cutoff if $\mathcal{F}$ is one of the following fragments of* ICTL$^*\backslash$X:[6]

  (i) for $\mathcal{F} = \{\forall i . \varphi(i)\}_{\varphi(i) \in \mathsf{CTL}^*\backslash \mathsf{X}}$, the cutoff is 2.

  (ii) for $\mathcal{F} = \{\forall i, j : j \in E(i). \varphi(i, j)\}_{\varphi(i,j) \in \mathsf{CTL}^*\backslash \mathsf{X}}$, the cutoff is 3.

  (iii) for $\mathcal{F} = \{\forall i, j : i \neq j. \varphi(i, j)\}_{\varphi(i,j) \in \mathsf{CTL}^*\backslash \mathsf{X}}$, the cutoff is 4.

  (iv) for $\mathcal{F} = \{\forall i, j, l : neq(i, j, l), j \in E(i). \varphi(i, j, l)\}_{\varphi(i,j,l) \in \mathsf{CTL}^*\backslash \mathsf{X}}$, the cutoff is 5.

Proof idea. We first sketch the proof that 2 is a cutoff for formulas of the form $\forall i . \varphi(i)$, and then consider the case of multiple quantified index variables.

Consider formulas of the form $\forall i . \varphi(i)$. First, by symmetry of rings, a system instance $P^{\mathbf{R}(n)}$ in satisfies $\forall i . \varphi(i)$ if and only if it satisfies $\varphi(0)$. Second, consider system instances $P_0^{\mathbf{R}(n)}$, which are the same as $P^{\mathbf{R}(n)}$, except that the labeling function is restricted to atoms of the form p_0 for $p \in \mathrm{AP_{pr}}$. Then there is a stuttering bisimulation between $P_0^{\mathbf{R}(n)}$ and $P_0^{\mathbf{R}(2)}$ for all $n \in \mathbb{N}$. A stuttering bisimulation implies that both system instances agree on all CTL$^*\backslash$X formulas. The required bisimulation is defined as follows: two global states s, s', in $P_0^{\mathbf{R}(n)}, P_0^{\mathbf{R}(n')}$ are equivalent iff $s(0) = s'(0)$, i.e., the processes with index 0 are in the same state, and thus either both have the token or both do not have the token. The key reasons why this is a stuttering bisimulation is that

- the processes with index 0 can mimick each other,

- the behavior of other processes can be ignored, except that they must allow the token to arrive at process 0 again, and

- a process $j \neq 0$ with the token can, by (†), send the token to its successor.

---

[6]In fact, the results of Emerson and Namjoshi [1995, 2003] hold for a logic that can also talk about local actions a_i of components. In the same vein, Khalimov et al. [2013a] proposed a local X operator over state labels as an extension of the logic that preserves the existence of cutoffs. None of the other results in this survey support such local properties, and therefore we have not included them in our definition in Section 2.4.1. We conjecture that most of the results in this chapter could be extended to such a logic.

Moreover, the labels of process 0 do not change during steps of the other processes, i.e., the system "stutters."

For the case of multiple quantifiers, like $\forall i, j : i \neq j . \varphi(i, j)$, only the first quantifier can be instantiated with the fixed value 0, and for the second we need to consider all possible values for j in $[n] \setminus \{0\}$. In fact, we only need to consider the following cases:

  (i) j is recipient of i,

  (ii) i is recipient of j, and

  (iii) there is no edge between i and j.

We define a monotone function $h : [n] \to [m]$, where m is the cutoff, such that each of (i), (ii), and (iii) holds for $(0, j)$ in $P^{\mathbf{R}(n)}$ if and only if it holds for $(0, h(j))$ in $P^{\mathbf{R}(m)}$. The function h exists if m is chosen big enough, for this type of specification $m = 4$ is sufficient. One can easily show that for every j, there is a stuttering bisimulation between processes $0, h(j)$ in $P^{\mathbf{R}(m)}$ and processes 0 and j in $P^{\mathbf{R}(n)}$. □

Example 4.6 Verification of Milner's Scheduler.   As mentioned before, Milner's scheduler is supposed to guarantee that all tasks are activated in a round-robin fashion, and that each task can terminate before being activated again (and only terminates after actually being activated). In Figure 4.2, activation of the task is represented by state label A, and termination by state label C. In a uni-directional ring, these requirements can then be expressed in the following parameterized specification:

$$\forall i, j, l : neq(i, j, l), j \in E(i) . \mathsf{AG}\left(A_i \to (\neg A_l \mathsf{U} A_j)\right)$$

$$\forall i . \mathsf{AG}\left((A_i \to (A_i \mathsf{U} \neg A_i \mathsf{U} C_i)) \wedge (C_i \to (C_i \mathsf{U} \neg C_i \mathsf{U} A_i))\right).$$

To verify this specification in systems with an arbitrary number of processes, it is sufficient to verify the first property in systems up to size 5 (by Theorem 4.5 (iv)), and the second property in systems up to size 2 (by Theorem 4.5 (i)). Thus, standard LTL model checking in rings of size up to 5 can be used to decide the PMCP for the given parameterized specification and implementation of Milner's scheduler in uni-directional rings.

Extensions of Cutoff Results for Rings.   Emerson and Namjoshi [1995, 2003] only provide cutoffs for properties with a small number k of index variables, but state that their technique is applicable for all k. Moreover, the original result is based on a strong restriction on process templates, stating that the sequence of actions from $\{in, out\}$ along every infinite path in P strictly alternates between in and out actions. We note that for their proof to work, restriction (†) above suffices.

Aminof et al. [2014a] investigated ways to compute cutoffs in general.

Theorem 4.7 [Aminof et al., 2014a].   *Let $\mathcal{F}_k^*$ be the set of k-CTL*\X formulas with only universal or only existential index quantifiers. Then, for any given k, PMCP($\mathcal{P}_{simp}^u$, $\mathbf{R}$, $\mathcal{F}_k^*$) has cutoff $2k$.*[7]

Proof idea. This result is obtained by applying the general proof technique we will see in the proof of Theorem 4.10 to the special case of uni-directional rings. In this case, we can construct the d-contractions for every k explicitly, and note that for every k and d, the d-contraction is a ring of size at most $2k$.   □

4.2.2   DECIDABILITY FOR SIMPLE TOKEN-PASSING IN GRAPHS

Some of the ideas for simple token-rings have been extended by Clarke et al. [2004] to simple token-passing systems on arbitrary classes of graphs. The main points of difference are: (i) properties are given in prenex ILTL\X, and (ii) the decidability result is non-uniform and non-constructive. That is, the proof only shows that for every given k and parameterized graph $\mathbf{G}$, the PMCP for all formulas from k-LTL\X is decidable. The proof does not supply an effective way to construct this decision procedure, and also makes no statement about the decidability of the PMCP for the full logic ILTL\X.

Theorem 4.8 [Clarke et al., 2004].   PMCP($\mathcal{P}_{simp}^u$, $\mathbf{G}$, k-LTL\X) *is decidable for every parameterized connectivity-graph $\mathbf{G}$ and natural number k. Indeed, every ($\mathcal{P}_{simp}^u$, $\mathbf{G}$, k-LTL\X) has a decomposition.*

Proof idea. Recall that a decomposition is a mapping from inputs of the PMCP to a set of finite model checking problems MC_{fin} and a formula $\Phi_\mathbb{B}$ that combines the results of model checking (see Section 3.2). In this case, MC_{fin} is obtained by considering all so-called k-*topologies* of $\mathbf{G}$. These are graphs of size up to $2k$, obtained by fixing a set of k vertices in some $\mathbf{G}(n)$, and collapsing all other vertices into so-called hub vertices, such that indirect connections between the k fixed vertices are preserved.[8] One can show that for every graph G, evaluating a k-LTL\X-formula ϕ in P^G amounts to a Boolean combination of the model-checking results of ϕ on the k-topologies of $\mathbf{G}$. Thus, the k-topologies, together with the original property, give the first part MC_{fin} of our decomposition. Since there are only finitely many k-topologies, and thus only finitely many Boolean formulas that combine these model checking results, one of them must be the $\Phi_\mathbb{B}$ that is the second part of the decomposition.   □

Looking closely at the decomposition, we note that the Boolean formula $\Phi_\mathbb{B}$ depends on the quantifier structure of ϕ as well as on $\mathbf{G}$. If there are no quantifier alternations, then $\Phi_\mathbb{B}$ is just

---

[7]Khalimov et al. [2013a, Corollary 2] stated that $2k$ is a cutoff for k-LTL\X. Aminof et al. [2014a] noted that this is not the case for formulas with quantifier alternation.

[8]That is, there is a path between vertices v and v' that goes through a hub in the k-topology iff there is a path between v and v' that visits none of the k fixed vertices in the original graph. Note that this is a generalization of the idea by Emerson and Namjoshi [1995, 2003] that one of the main properties that needs to be preserved is whether or not vertices are neighbors.

a big conjunction or disjunction over all model-checking results for the k-topologies of $\mathbf{G}$, and thus we obtain an effective decision procedure whenever we can identify all of these k-topologies. If ϕ contains quantifier alternations, it is in general not known how to obtain $\Phi_{\mathbb{B}}$.[9]

Aminof et al. [2014a] looked at the question whether this proof can be made uniform for arbitrary parameterized graphs $\mathbf{G}$ and specifications in ILTL\X. They show that for certain parameterized connectivity graphs, the (uniform) PMCP is undecidable.

Theorem 4.9 [Aminof et al., 2014a].   *There exists a parameterized connectivity graph $\mathbf{G}$ such that* PMCP$(\mathcal{P}^{\mathsf{u}}_{simp}, \mathbf{G}, \mathsf{ILTL}\backslash\mathsf{X})$ *is undecidable.*

Proof idea.   Define P to be the process template with two states, one with and one without the token. Every transition must change the state, which, in particular, satisfies condition (†) from the definition of TPSs in Section 4.1.2. For $i, j \in \mathbb{N}$ let $L_{i,j}$ be the lasso with prefix of length i, and a loop of length j. Based on some computable ordering on all deterministic Turing machines (for example, lexicographic), let $\mathbf{G}$ consist of all graphs of the form $L_{i,j}$ such that the jth Turing machine halts on the empty word in at most i steps. Note that this is a computable set.

For every $k \in \mathbb{N}$, let φ_k be the formula (in k-LTL\X)

$$\forall i_1, \ldots, i_k : neq(i_1, \ldots, i_k). \neg \left(\mathsf{F}\left(tok_{i_1} \mathsf{U} tok_{i_2} \mathsf{U} \ldots \mathsf{U} tok_{i_k} \mathsf{U} tok_{i_1} \right) \right),$$

where tok_i is a predicate which is true iff process i has the token. Thus, $P^G \models \varphi_k$ if and only if G does not contain a ring of size k as a subgraph.

Now reduce the non-halting problem for Turing Machines to the PMCP:

> the kth TM does not halt
> $\Leftrightarrow$ $\mathbf{G}$ does not contain a graph with a ring of size k as subgraph $\square$
> $\Leftrightarrow$ $P^G \models \varphi_k$ for all $G \in \mathbf{G}$.

For token-passing networks with specifications in ICTL\X, Clarke et al. [2004] showed that decompositions of the form they define cannot exist in general. However, Aminof et al. [2014a] showed that by further refining the construction of Clarke et al. [2004], a non-uniform decidability result can be obtained even for specifications in ICTL*\X. To this end, ICTL*\X is stratified not only with respect to the number k of index quantifiers, but also with respect to the number d of (nested) path quantifiers. In the following, let k-CTL$^*_d$\X be the set of all sentences in k-CTL*\X with nesting depth of path quantifiers at most d.

Theorem 4.10 [Aminof et al., 2014a].   *Let $\mathbf{G}$ be a parameterized connectivity graph. Then for all $k, d \in \mathbb{N}$,* PMCP$(\mathcal{P}^{\mathsf{u}}_{simp}, \mathbf{G}, k\text{-}\mathsf{CTL}^*_d\backslash\mathsf{X})$ *is decidable. Indeed, every* $(\mathcal{P}^{\mathsf{u}}_{simp}, \{\mathbf{G}\}, k\text{-}\mathsf{CTL}^*_d\backslash\mathsf{X})$ *has a decomposition.*

---

[9]Clarke et al. [2004] claimed in the discussion of their theorem that "given k and network graph G, all k-indexed LTL\X-specifications have the same reduction," where a reduction is equivalent to what we call a decomposition. It should be noted that different formulas $\Phi_{\mathbb{B}}$ may be necessary for specifications with different structures of indexed quantifiers.

Proof idea. To show the existence of decompositions, define two graphs G, G' to be (k, d)-equivalent if they cannot be distinguished by formulas in k-CTL$^*_d$\X that use tok_i as the only atomic predicates. The existence of decompositions is proven by two observations: (i) every graph is (d, k)-equivalent to its d-contraction (a certain minimal graph with the same observed behavior), and (ii) there are only finitely many different d-contractions for a given k. By a similar argument as in the proof of Theorem 4.8, the PMCP for a given parameterized graph $\mathbf{G}$, process template P and specification ϕ can thus be reduced to a Boolean combination of checking whether $P^{Con} \models \phi$, for all d-contractions Con of $\mathbf{G}$. □

Note that like Theorem 4.8, this result is non-uniform and non-constructive, and therefore does not supply us with an effective decision procedure for the PMCP with specifications from lCTL*\X. However, for specifications without quantifier alternations and for fixed $\mathbf{G}$ (e.g., $\mathbf{G} \in \{\mathbf{R}, \mathbf{B}, \mathbf{C}\}$), the proof methods can be used to obtain concrete cutoffs for the PMCP.

We have stated before that the uniform PMCP is undecidable for specifications in lLTL\X. For branching-time specifications, undecidability is already obtained with a fixed number of two index quantifiers, as long as the nesting depth of path quantifiers is not bounded.

Theorem 4.11   [Aminof et al., 2014a].   *There exists a parameterized connectivity graph $\mathbf{G}$ such that* PMCP($\mathcal{P}^u_{simp}$, $\mathbf{G}$, 2-CTL*\X) *is undecidable.*

Proof idea.   The proof is a variation of the proof of Theorem 4.9. Again, we define a parameterized graph $\mathbf{G}$ and a sequence of formulas φ_k such that the kth TM does not halt iff φ_k holds in all system instances. The main difference is that now we can use arbitrary nestings of temporal path quantifiers to distinguish these graphs (similar to those used in Clarke et al. [2004, Theorem 5]), and therefore two index variables are sufficient to define all φ_k. □

4.2.3   UNDECIDABILITY RESULTS FOR MULTI-VALUED TOKENS

The decidability results discussed in Sections 4.2.1 and 4.2.2 consider token-passing systems with simple token. Suzuki [1988] and Emerson and Namjoshi [1995, 2003] considered systems where the token can take multiple values.

Theorem 4.12   [Suzuki, 1988].   *Let* 1-Safe *be the safety fragment of* 1-LTL\X. *Then* PMCP($\mathcal{P}^u_T$, $\mathbf{R}$, 1-Safe) *is undecidable for sufficiently large* T.

Proof idea.   (based on Emerson and Namjoshi [2003, Section 6]) The main idea is to simulate n steps of a 2CM in a ring of size n, where one process in the ring will eventually raise a flag "halt" if and only if the 2CM halts in n steps. Given a 2CM $\mathcal{M}$, we describe how the corresponding finite-state process P works.

In the first step, the process that starts with the token moves into a special state with the intention that it will simulate the control-state of $\mathcal{M}$, and it sets a flag to false. We will call this process the *controller*. Each of the remaining processes will be used to store a fixed number of bits—these are called *storage* processes. The values in T represent different commands that the controller can send to the storage processes.

After the first step, the controller sends around the token with an "initialize" command, which makes all other processes go into storage mode. In this mode, each process stores three bit of information, corresponding to the two counters of $\mathcal{M}$, and a "step-counter," respectively. Each counter is stored as a tally in the ring: for every counter, each process (except the controller) stores one bit in unary encoding, and the number of bits in the ring set to 1 is interpreted as the value of that counter. Thus, a ring of size n can store counter values up to $n - 1$. Initially, all counter-bits are set to 0. The controller implements an increment of a counter c by circulating a token with the command "increment c." A process receiving "increment c" will either increment its corresponding counter-bit from 0 to 1 (if possible), and pass a modified token with the "empty" command, or it will not change its internal state and pass the token unchanged (if local increment is not possible). Thus, the value of the token when it returns to the controller indicates whether the command was successful. There are similar commands for decrementing and testing for zero. After the controller implements a step of $\mathcal{M}$, it also increments the step-counter.

The controller proceeds in this way until its "increment step-counter" command returns to it unsuccessful (meaning that n steps of $\mathcal{M}$ have now been simulated). If after n steps the machine $\mathcal{M}$ did not enter a halting state, then the controller sets its flag to true. This completes the description of P. It is a finite-state process that will move into controller mode if it has the token initially, and into storage mode otherwise. The controller sets its flag to true iff $\mathcal{M}$ does not halt in n steps. Since the non-halting problem is undecidable, so is deciding if for all n, the controller in a ring with process implementation P sets the flag to true. This proves that the PMCP is undecidable for uni-directional multi-valued token rings.   □

Binary token.   Emerson and Namjoshi [2003] mentioned a simple way to simulate a multi-valued token with arbitrary set of values T using a binary token, i.e., a token with $\mathsf{T}_\mathbb{B} = \{0, 1\}$. Thus, they obtain another undecidability result.

Theorem 4.13   **[Emerson and Namjoshi, 2003].** $\mathrm{PMCP}(\mathcal{P}^u_{\mathsf{T}_\mathbb{B}}, \mathbf{R}, 1\text{-Safe})$ *is undecidable.*

Proof idea. The general proof idea is the same as in the proof of Theorem 4.12. Additionally, the controller of $\mathcal{M}$ can use the binary token to transmit arbitrary commands from the set of commands T of that proof in a unary encoding: assume commands are numbered, i.e., we have $\mathsf{T} = [n]$ for some $n \in \mathbb{N}$. To encode command $t \in [n]$, the controller sends the token with value 1 for t times, followed by one transmission with value 0. Each storage node internally keeps track of how many 1s it received, say in a variable x. After receiving the token with value 0, every node knows which command should be executed. Now the controller again sends a 1, and every node checks if it can execute the command, i.e., whether its counter can be in- or decremented, or whether it can witness that the overall counter value is not 0. The first node that can actually execute the command (or witness that the overall counter value is not 0) changes the value of the token to 0 (letting the following storage nodes know that they should not execute the command anymore). Regardless of the value of the token in this round, all nodes reset their command variable x to 0 when they pass the token. As before, the value of the token informs the controller whether the command was successful. This procedure can be repeated whenever a command is passed to the storage nodes in the original construction. □

Multi-valued Tokens in General Graphs.   Since rings are a particular form of general graphs, PMCP($\mathcal{P}_{T_{\mathbb{B}}}^u$, $\mathbf{G}$, 1-Safe) is in general undecidable. However, uni-directional rings have the characteriztic property that, from the perspective of a given process, there is exactly one process from which it always receives the token, and exactly one to which it can send it. This is not the case in graphs with in- or out-degree greater than 1. Since the undecidability proof depends on the fact that the token can be used to pass certain commands to all other processes, it is not immediately obvious that it also works for other parameterized graphs. At least for bi-directional rings, we believe this is possible.

Conjecture 4.14   PMCP($\mathcal{P}_{T_{\mathbb{B}}}^u$, $\mathbf{B}$, k-LTL\X) is undecidable.

For general graphs, the problem is mostly open.

Problem 4.15   For which parameterized connectivity graphs $\mathbf{G}$ is PMCP($\mathcal{P}_{T_{\mathbb{B}}}$, $\mathbf{G}$, $\mathcal{F}$) decidable, for $\mathcal{F} \in \{$lLTL\X, lCTL*\X$\}$?

4.3   RESULTS FOR DIRECTION-AWARE TOKEN-PASSING SYSTEMS

In the results considered thus far, if a node has multiple recipients, then it cannot choose which one will receive the token, but one of the possible transitions will fire non-deterministically. In this section, we consider systems that are direction-aware, i.e., where processes can choose who will receive the token and/or from whom they want to receive it. We first give a decidability result for a special class of systems that can be used to model a leader election protocol [Emerson and Kahlon, 2004], and then a general undecidability result.

4.3.1   CUTOFFS FOR CHANGE-BOUNDED TOKENS IN BI-DIRECTIONAL RINGS

Let $\mathbf{B}$ be the parameterized connectivity-graph of bi-directional rings of size n, i.e., $\mathbf{B}(n) = (V, E)$ with $V = [n]$ and $E = \{(i, j), (j, i): j = i + 1 \mod n\}$. Let $Dir_{out} = \{$cw, ccw$\}$, and dir_{out} the function that maps edges $(i, i + 1 \mod n)$ to cw, and edges $(i + 1 \mod n, i)$ to ccw. Let $Dir_{in} = \{$undefined$\}$, and dir_{in} be the function that maps all edges to undefined. Let $\mathbf{B}^{snd}$ be the parameterized bi-directional ring with these direction labels. Let $\mathcal{D}_T^{snd}$ be the set of all deterministic process templates in $\mathcal{P}_T^{snd}$.

We call a parameterized (direction-aware) TPS $(\mathcal{P}_T, \{\mathbf{G}\})$ *change-bounded* if there exists $b \in \mathbb{N}$ such that, for every run of every system instance $\mathcal{P}_T^{\mathbf{G}(n)}$, the value of the token does not change more than b times.[10]

Theorem 4.16   [Emerson and Kahlon, 2004]. $\mathsf{PMCP}(\mathcal{D}_T^{\mathsf{snd}}, \mathbf{B}^{\mathsf{snd}}, 1\text{-}\mathsf{LTL}\backslash\mathsf{X})$ *is decidable if* $(\mathcal{D}_T^{\mathsf{snd}}, \mathbf{B}^{\mathsf{snd}})$ *is change-bounded. Indeed, the cutoff is a polynomial depending on the number of states and the transition graph of process template P.*

Proof idea. The proof is based on the fact that processes are deterministic, and so the token can only make a finite number of moves until the system either deadlocks or runs into a state that it has seen before, entering an infinite loop. The number of steps until the system reaches such a state is independent of the size of the ring, as long as it has a certain minimal size. This size can be computed by constructing the transition graph for the ring, based on the definition of P. It gives a cutoff for $\mathsf{PMCP}(\mathcal{D}_T^{snd}, \mathbf{B}^{snd}, 1\text{-}\mathsf{LTL}\backslash\mathsf{X})$.   □

Note that this result is not displayed in Figure 4.3, since it considers special restrictions to deterministic process templates and change-bounded tokens.

4.3.2   UNDECIDABILITY FOR DIRECTION-AWARE TPSS

Since direction-aware TPSs can degenerate to direction-unaware TPSs, the undecidability results from Section 4.2.3 also hold here, and decidability can only be obtained by adding restrictions.

Note that while Theorem 4.16 gives a cutoff for a system with limited direction-awareness and multi-valued tokens, it is very restricted in the specifications, the processes and the graphs (including direction-awareness) that it can handle. If we consider $|Dir_{in}| > 1$, Aminof et al. [2014a] showed that undecidability follows even for systems with a simple token.

Now, consider the case $Dir_{out} = Dir_{in} = \{\mathsf{cw}, \mathsf{ccw}\}$, and $dir_{out} = dir_{in}$ the function that maps edges in clockwise directions to cw, and edges in counterclockwise direction to ccw. Let $\mathbf{B}^{dir}$ be the parameterized bi-directional ring with these direction labels.

Theorem 4.17   [Aminof et al., 2014a]. $\mathsf{PMCP}(\mathcal{P}_{simp}, \mathbf{B}^{dir}, 1\text{-}\mathsf{LTL}\backslash\mathsf{X})$ *is undecidable.*

Proof idea. The proof goes along the lines of the proofs of Theorems 4.12 and 4.13. The main new idea is that directions can be used to encode the different commands of the controller to the storage nodes, similar to the encoding with a binary token.   □

---

[10]An example is an integer-valued token with fixed starting value b, that can only be decreased, and never become smaller than 0.

Furthermore, undecidability with respect to k-LTL\X has been shown even if only one of $|Dir_{in}| > 1$ or $|Dir_{out}| > 1$ holds, for sufficiently large k.

Theorem 4.18   **[Aminof et al., 2014a]**.   *Assume that $|Dir_{out}| > 1$. Then there exist a parameterized directed connectivity graph* $\mathbf{G}$ *such that* $\mathsf{PMCP}(\mathcal{P}^{\mathsf{snd}}_{simp}, \mathbf{G}, 9\text{-}\mathsf{LTL}\backslash\mathsf{X})$ *is undecidable. Similarly, for* $|Dir_{in}| > 1$ *and suitable* $\mathbf{G}'$, $\mathsf{PMCP}(\mathcal{P}^{\mathsf{rcv}}_{simp}, \mathbf{G}', 9\text{-}\mathsf{LTL}\backslash\mathsf{X})$ *is undecidable.*

Proof idea. The proof is again a reduction from the non-halting problem of 2CMs and requires a parameterized graph with eight special nodes that are directly connected to the controller, and represent the different commands of the 2CM (increment counter, decrement counter, counter is zero, counter is not zero; each for counters 1 and 2). The other nodes are storage nodes, like in the undecidability proofs before.

Consider the case where $|Dir_{out}| = 1$: since all edges have the same outgoing label, processes cannot choose where to send the token. We use a special construction of the parameterized graph and the process template such that every possible path of the token through the graph corresponds to the (partial) execution of one command, represented by the special node that the token visits after leaving the controller. To circumvent the restriction that the controller cannot choose the sending direction, we use a specification that tracks whether the special node that the token is sent to is always the one that the controller intended (represented by the state of the controller). This ensures that we only consider runs of the system that correspond to an execution of the 2CM.

For $|Dir_{in}| = 1$ we can use a similar construction, except that now the controller can issue a certain command, but the storage processes cannot detect which one is intended, and have to guess which command to execute. The special nodes are in this case visited immediately before the token returns to the controller. Again, we use the specification to ensure that only the intended runs are considered.   □

4.4   DISCUSSION

Even in systems with a relatively restricted communication primitive such as passing a valueless token, the PMCP is undecidable if we do not additionally restrict the graph structure or stratify specifications with respect to the number of index and path quantifiers. Undecidability proofs show that such systems can simulate a 2CM, and thus halting of the 2CM could be decided if we could decide the PMCP.

For certain concrete classes of graphs, such as rings, cutoffs can be found by hand. To prove that c is a cutoff for a class of systems and specifications in $\mathsf{ICTL}^*\backslash\mathsf{X}$, it suffices to show that there is a stuttering bisimulation between a system with arbitrarily many components and a system with exactly c components. For specifications that quantify over multiple processes, this needs to take into account whether processes are direct neighbors or not, and consider all possible cases.[11]

[11]In fact, Aminof et al. [2014b] recently showed that cutoffs can be computed automatically for large classes of graphs that are definable either by graph-grammars or in Monadic Second-Order Logic. Examples include rings, cliques, lines, trees,

If tokens can carry values, decidability is lost even in rings. Similarly, if processes can distinguish directions in the graph, we get undecidability in bi-directional rings. Figure 4.3 (on page 37) and Table 4.1 give an overview of decidability results for token-passing systems with these properties, showing that most of the considered cases are undecidable. To recover decidability, additional restrictions on graphs, processes, or specifications, are necessary.

Table 4.1: Decidability results for TPSs and their sources, separated into systems with direction-unaware processes and simple token ($\mathcal{P}^{u}_{simp}$), systems with direction-unaware processes and multi-valued token ($\mathcal{P}^{u}_{T}$, $\mathcal{P}^{u}_{T_{\mathbb{B}}}$), and systems with direction-aware processes

Result	Processes	Graph	Specification	References
a cutoff	$\mathcal{P}^{u}_{simp}$	**R**	fragments of ICTL*\X	[Emerson and Namjoshi 2003] [Aminof et al. 2014a]
decidability for all k	$\mathcal{P}^{u}_{simp}$	∀**G**	k-LTL\X	[Clarke et al. 2004]
decidability for all k, d	$\mathcal{P}^{u}_{simp}$	∀**G**	k-CTL$^{*}_{d}$\X	[Aminof et al. 2014a]
undecidability	$\mathcal{P}^{u}_{simp}$	∃**G**	ILTL\X, 2-CTL*\X	[Aminof et al. 2014a]
undecidability	$\mathcal{P}^{u}_{T}$	**R**	1-Safe	[Suzuki 1988]
undecidability	$\mathcal{P}^{u}_{T_{\mathbb{B}}}$	**R**	1-Safe	[Emerson and Namjoshi 2003]
decidability under bounded change	$\mathcal{D}^{snd}_{T}$	**B**^{snd}	1-LTL\X	[Emerson and Kahlon 2004]
undecidability	$\mathcal{P}_{simp}$	**B**^{dir}	1-LTL\X	[Aminof et al. 2014a]
undecidability for $|Dir_{out}| > 1$, for $|Dir_{in}| > 1$	$\mathcal{P}^{snd}_{simp}$, $\mathcal{P}^{rcv}_{simp}$	∃**G**	9-LTL\X	[Aminof et al. 2014a]

For all of the decidability results in this chapter, a restriction to some notion of fairness is essential. While some of the original results are explicitly restricted to systems or runs where every process receives and sends the token infinitely often, we argue here (and in Aminof et al. [2014a]) that a weaker condition is sufficient, namely that from every state of the process there *exists* a path such that it sends or receives the token—but results are not restricted to runs where such paths

series-parallel graphs, but not grids. From a description (i.e., a grammar or a formula) of such a set of graphs, one can build an algorithm that computes a cutoff for a given formula and thus solves the PMCP for indexed CTL*\X over this set of graphs.

are actually taken. There are no decidability results in the literature that consider systems without any fairness assumption.

4.4.1   VARIATIONS OF THE MODEL

The basic idea behind structuring concurrent applications using a token is that the current holder of the token is privileged, and thus allowed to perform some special action such as entering its critical section. That is, tokens are a means to resolve conflicts over shared resources. However, systems with a single token are based on the assumption that at each time at most one process may be privileged, or equivalently, there is only one shared resource. This severely limits the degree of concurrency in the system.

There are several schemes to increase the degree of concurrency. For instance, any solution to the celebrated dining philosophers problem allows several (non-neighboring) philosophers to eat at the same time. A generalization of dining philosophers are the drinking philosophers [Chandy and Misra, 1984] for general conflict graphs, where again one requires that two neighbors are not drinking at the same time, in case both are currently competing for the same resource. In the extreme case, a completely connected conflict graph then boils down to having at most a single neighbor drinking at a time, and thus to a single token scheme. Intuitively, the dining (or drinking) philosophers on general graphs can thus be interpreted as a token scheme with multiple tokens.

The literature contains results on both areas, access to multiple shared resources and multiple tokens. Regarding multiple shared resources, there are several cutoff results. Ensuring fair access is considered by Emerson and Kahlon [2002], FIFO access is considered by Bouajjani et al. [2008], and strict alternation rules as provided by link reversal algorithms [Barbosa and Gafni, 1989] is considered by Függer and Widder [2012]. Regarding multiple tokens, Emerson and Kahlon [2004] contains a decomposition result that allows to reduce reasoning about 2-indexed properties of uni-directional rings with multiple multi-valued tokens, to reasoning in small rings. To obtain decidability, there are several restrictions on token-passing and the processes: (i) in any run, every multi-valued token can only change its value a bounded number of times, (ii) every token has an "owner" process, and transitions that send or receive a token cannot change the state of a process unless the token is owned by it, and (iii) processes have to be deterministic.

Considering the case with multiple tokens, we conjecture that decidability strongly depends on whether or not processes can distinguish different tokens. If this is the case, then the problem is very similar to a multi-valued token and should quickly become undecidable. For indistinguishable tokens, there is more hope to obtain decidability results.

Problem 4.19   Do any of the decidability results in this chapter still hold for systems with multiple tokens? In particular, do they hold if processes can*not* distinguish different tokens?

Furthermore, all previous work on TPSs only considers prenex ITL. An interesting question is under which circumstances the given results hold if we allow index quantifiers inside of temporal quantifiers.

Problem 4.20   Are there fragments of non-prenex ITL that can express interesting properties that are not in ICTL*\X and still have a decidable PMCP for any of the cases considered in this chapter?

CHAPTER 5

Rendezvous and Broadcast

This chapter considers systems of processes communicating via pairwise rendezvous, asynchronous rendezvous, broadcast, and combinations of these (as defined in Section 2.2.1). We have already seen in Examples 2.1 and 2.2 how pairwise-rendezvous models standard synchronization between exactly two processes. As discussed by Delzanno et al. [2002], asynchronous rendezvous and broadcast also correspond to standard coordination constructs in different programming languages, such as the `notify` and `notifyAll` constructs of the Java programming language.

The specifications considered in this chapter are either action-based, i.e., ωReg(A) and Reg(A), or state-based, i.e., LTL(C) which are LTL formulas whose atoms are indexed by the controller process, and $\forall U$ LTL(U) which are LTL formulas that hold for every user process.

Figure 5.1 and Table 5.1 (on page 53) summarize results taken from the literature [Emerson and Kahlon, 2003b, Esparza et al., 1999, German and Sistla, 1992], including minor extensions. The figure indicates that safety is always decidable, while liveness is decidable for pairwise rendezvous and undecidable for the other communication primitives.

Running example. As the running example of this chapter, we will revisit the simple Client/Server system from Chapter 2, including a number of variants with different communication primitives.

5.1 SYSTEM MODEL

Synchronization constraints. As in Section 2.2.1, pairwise rendezvous is defined by taking card = {1}, asynchronous rendezvous is defined by taking card = {0, 1}, and broadcast is defined by taking card = $\mathbb{N}_0$. Systems with all three primitives, for example, are defined by taking $\overline{\text{card}} = \{\{1\}, \{0, 1\}, \mathbb{N}_0\}$.

Example 5.1 Client/Server (revisited) Recall the simple client/server system from Examples 2.1 and 2.2. Example 2.2 illustrates pairwise rendezvous where the server can synchronize with a single client at a time.

For asynchronous rendezvous, there are two possibilities if a client is ready to take a transition labeled with out_{enter} or out_{leave}. First, the server and the client take a synchronized transition, as in pairwise rendezvous. The second case may occur when the client is ready to effectuate a transition labeled with out_{enter} or out_{leave}, but from the current state of the server there is no outgoing

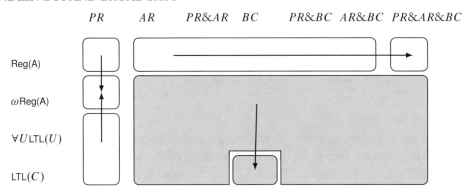

Figure 5.1: PMCP results for systems with a controller, and clique connectivity-graph. The abbreviations PR, AR, BC stand for pairwise rendezvous, asynchronous rendezvous, broadcasts. White boxes are decidability results, dark boxes are undecidability results. An arrow from box A to box B means that the result of A follows from the result, or variation of the proof, of B.

transition labeled with in_{enter} or in_{leave}, respectively. In this case, the client may effectuate its transition alone, that is, without the server. One may view this as the client transmitting information to the server in case the server is ready to receive one, otherwise the message is "lost."

For broadcast, consider the connectivity graph in Figure 5.2(a), and the process templates in Figures 5.2(b) and 5.2(c), where the server has a transition from 0_S labeled with $enter!!$, and all the clients have transitions from 0_C labeled with $enter??$. In this case, the synchronization is initiated by the server, and any client that is ready to take the synchronous step can enter 1_c.

Parameterized connectivity graph.   A graph $G = (V, E)$ is a *clique* if for all distinct $v, w \in V$ it holds that $(v, w) \in E$. The 2-*ary parameterized clique graph* is the sequence $n \mapsto \mathbf{C}_\odot(n)$ where $\mathbf{C}_\odot(n)$ is the clique with $n + 1$ vertices, type$(1) = 1$, and type$(i) = 2$ for all $i \neq 1$. The unique process in $\mathbf{C}_\odot(n)$ of type 1 (it has index 1) is called the *controller*, and all other processes are called *users* and are of type 2.

Example 5.2   Clique topology for Client/Server system   Figure 5.2(a) shows a clique topology with one controller process (modeling the server), and three user processes (modeling the clients). Note that with the process templates defined for server and clients in Figures 2.1(b) and 2.1(c), the behavior of the composed system does not change, since the process templates do not define synchronous transitions between two clients.

Runs and Deadlocks.   In this chapter, system runs are defined as *infinite* paths that start in the initial state (cf. Section 2.2.2). The only exception is Theorem 5.7 about the action-based specification language Reg(A) which is interpreted over finite paths that start in the initial state.

Table 5.1: Decidability results, and their sources, for systems with a controller, using pairwise rendezvous (PR), asynchronous rendezvous (AR), and broadcast (BC)

Result	Processes	Graph	Specification	References
decidability	PR+BC+AR	$\mathbf{C}_\odot$	Reg(A)	[Esparza et al. 1999] [Emerson and Kahlon 2003b]
decidability in EXPSPACE	PR	$\mathbf{C}_\odot$	ωReg(C)	[German and Sistla 1992]
decidability in EXPSPACE	PR	$\mathbf{C}_\odot$	$\forall U\,\omega$Reg(U)	[German and Sistla 1992]
decidability in EXPSPACE	PR	$\mathbf{C}_\odot$	ωReg(A)	[Emerson and Kahlon 2003b] cf. [German and Sistla 1992]
undecidability	BC	$\mathbf{C}_\odot$	ωReg(A)	[Esparza et al. 1999]
undecidability	BC	$\mathbf{C}_\odot$	LTL(C)	[Emerson and Kahlon 2003b] cf. [Esparza et al. 1999]
undecidability	BC	$\mathbf{C}_\odot$	$\forall U$ LTL(U)	cf. [Esparza et al. 1999]
undecidability	AR	$\mathbf{C}_\odot$	ωReg(A)	[Emerson and Kahlon 2003b]
undecidability	AR	$\mathbf{C}_\odot$	LTL(C)	[Emerson and Kahlon 2003b]
undecidability	AR	$\mathbf{C}_\odot$	$\forall U$ LTL(U)	cf. [Emerson and Kahlon 2003b]

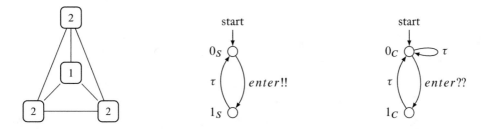

(a) 2-ary clique graph with 3 user vertices and one controller vertex.

(b) Modified process template S' for the server.

(c) Modified process template C for the clients.

Figure 5.2: Clique graph and modified process templates for client/server system.

German and Sistla [1992, Theorem 3.19] proved that deadlock detection is decidable for systems using pairwise rendezvous, by a reduction to the reachability problem for VASS. To the best of our knowledge, this is the only result on parameterized deadlock detection for the systems in this chapter.

Specifications.   Write $\forall U$ LTL(U) for the set of all ILTL sentences of the form $\forall i : type(i) = 2. \, \phi(i)$. The interpretation of such a formula in $\mathbf{C}_\odot(n)$ is that for every process index i of type 2 (i.e., for every "user" process) the projection of every infinite path π onto coordinate i satisfies $\phi(i)$.

Write LTL(C) for the set of all ILTL formulas of the form $\phi(1)$. The interpretation of such a formula in $\mathbf{C}_\odot(n)$ is that the projection of every infinite path π onto the unique controller process satisfies $\phi(1)$.

More generally, denote by ωReg(C) the specification languages of the form $AL(1)$ where L is an ω-regular language over $AP_{pr} \times \{1\}$ (recall the controller has index 1), and denote by $\forall U \, \omega$Reg(U) the specification languages of the form $\forall i : type(i) = 2. \, AL(i)$ where L is an ω-regular language over alphabet $AP_{pr} \times \{i\}$ (recall the users have type 2).

The set of action-based specifications, i.e., Reg(A) and ωReg(A), are defined in Section 2.4.2.

Example 5.3   Specifications for Client/Server system.   An interesting safety property for the clients of the system is mutual exclusion, i.e., no two clients should be in state 1_C at the same time. Note that none of the specification types above allows one to directly express this property. However, as noted by German and Sistla [1992], we can indirectly check for it by modifying the process template: add a state 2_C to the client template that can only be entered from 1_C by synchronizing on a new action fail with another client process that is also in 1_C. In this way, a process can enter 2_C iff we reach a state where at least two processes are in 1_C at the same time. Then, mutual exclusion is expressed by the formula

$$\forall U \; \mathsf{G}\neg 2_C(U),$$

where we use states of a process template as atomic propositions. Alternatively, we can express violation of the property as the regular expression over actions

$$\{a, \mathsf{enter}, \mathsf{leave}\}^* \; \mathsf{fail}.$$

In addition, we can specify liveness properties, e.g., every client should enter 1_C infinitely often. This is expressed by the formula

$$\forall U \; \mathsf{GF}1_C(U).$$

In the following two sections, we will see that the mutual exclusion property can be decided for systems with any combination of pairwise rendezvous, asynchronous rendezvous, and broadcast. In contrast, liveness properties like the one above can in general only be decided in systems that are restricted to pairwise rendezvous.

5.2   DECIDABILITY RESULTS

All the decidability results in this chapter follow the same idea of building a transition system which is a counter representation of the parameterized system and the parameterized specification. In Proposition 5.4 we show that for communication primitives including the ones dealt with in this chapter (namely broadcast, pairwise rendezvous, asynchronous rendezvous) this transition system is a well-structured transition system. The main point to be checked is monotonicity. Moreover, in the case of pairwise rendezvous, this transition system is a vector addition system with states (VASS).

5.2.1   COUNTER REPRESENTATION

The idea of using a counter representation already appears in the work of German and Sistla [1992], and relies quite heavily on the connectivity graph being a clique.

Suppose the process template of the controller has state set Q_C, the process template of the user processes has state set Q_U, and the specification is given by an (finite-state or Büchi) automaton A over the atomic propositions of the controller, and with state set Q_A. Recall from Vardi [1995] that for every LTL formula φ over atomic propositions AP there is a non-deterministic Büchi automaton over alphabet 2^{AP}, of size $2^{O(|\varphi|)}$, that accepts exactly the infinite strings satisfied by φ.

Informally, the counter representation captures the current state of the controller (an element of Q_C), the current state of the automaton (an element of Q_A), and the number of user processes in each state of Q_U (a vector of non-negative integers of dimension $|Q_U|$). Thus, the states of the counter representation are of the form $(q_c, q_a, \bar{v})$, and transitions between these states mimic global transitions in system instances.

Definition of the Counter Representation M.   Suppose $Q_U = \{t_1, \cdots, t_k\}$, and automaton A has initial state $\iota_A \in Q_A$, and accepting state set $F \subseteq Q_A$. Also, suppose $s \in Q_C \times (Q_U)^n$ is a global state of a system instance with n user processes, and q_A is a state of the automaton A. Define the *abstracted state* abs(s, q_A) as the tuple $(q_C, q_A, x_1, \cdots, x_{|Q_U|})$ in $Q_C \times Q_A \times \mathbb{N}_0^{|Q_U|}$ where q_C is $s(1)$ (the local state of the controller process), and for $1 \leq i \leq |Q_U|$, $x_i := \#\{j : s(j) = t_i\}$, i.e., the number of user processes that are in local state t_i in the global state s.

The *counter representation* is a transition system $M = (Q, \Sigma, \Delta)$ defined as follows.

- The *state set* Q of M is defined as $Q_C \times Q_A \times \mathbb{N}_0^{|Q_U|}$, i.e., the set of all abstracted states abs(s, q_A).

- The set of *action labels* Σ of M is the set $\Sigma_{int} \cup \Sigma_{sync}$, i.e., the action labels of the original system.

- The *transitions* Δ of M are of the form abs$(s, q_A) \xrightarrow{a}$ abs(s', q'_A) with $a \in \Sigma$, where

  (i) $s \xrightarrow{a} s'$ is a global transition of the original system, and

(ii) if this transition does not involve the controller then $q'_A = q_A$, else q'_A can be reached from q_A in one step on input $\{p \in AP_{pr} : p \text{ holds in state } q_C\}$. Thus the state q_A evolves according to the label of the state q_C.

If q_A is in the accepting set F then we say that the abstracted transition *hits F*.

- The set of *initial states* consists of all states of the form $(\iota_C, \iota_A, \bar{v})$ where ι_C is an initial state of the controller template, ι_A is the initial state of automaton A, and $\bar{v}$ is an arbitrary vector whose support S (i.e., the set of coordinates with non-zero entries) is non-empty and $s \in S$ iff t_s is an initial state of the user process template. Note that the set of initial states is computable and downward closed, and thus we satisfy the hypothesis of Theorem 3.3(2).

Note that the transition system M, although infinite, is computable, meaning that one can compute the state set and the transition relation.

Properties of the Counter Representation M.   We elaborate on the properties of the counter representation that will later be used in decidability proofs.

Proposition 5.4   If card **is an interval then** M **is a WSTS.**   *Let $\leq$ be the ordering on the states of M defined by $(q_C, q_A, \bar{v}) \leq (q'_C, q'_A, \bar{v}')$ if $q_C = q'_C$, $q_A = q'_A$ and for all i, $v_i \leq v'_i$. If* card *is an interval, namely of the form $[a, b]$ or $[b, \infty)$, then (i) the ordering $\leq$ is monotone with respect to the transition system M and (ii) one can compute, from a basis for an upward closed set C, a basis for $Pred(C)$.*

Proof Sketch. The first item holds under very general computability conditions, namely if card is computable and the global transition relation Δ is computable (see computablity assumption 2.5.1). Indeed: if B is a basis for C, then a basis $Pred(C)$ consists of all configurations $\bar{v}$ such that there is some action label a and a global transition from $\bar{v}$ to some element of B on action a.

For the second item we fix some notation. Define an operation $+$ on states of M that have the same first two coordinates, namely, $(q, r, \bar{v}) + (q, r, \bar{w}) := (q, r, \bar{v} + \bar{w})$ where addition is componentwise. From now on we drop all mention of the first two coordinates. The states of U are $\{t_1, \cdots, t_k\}$. For $i \leq k$, write e_i for the vector $\bar{v}$ such that $v_i = 1$ and $v_j = 0$ for all $j \neq i$.

For the second item, suppose $\bar{v} \xrightarrow{a} \bar{w}$ is a transition of M induced by a local transition $t_i \xrightarrow{a_{out}} t_j$. Then we may write $\bar{v} = e_i + \bar{c}$ and $\bar{w} = e_j + \bar{d}$ for some vectors $\bar{c}, \bar{d}$. Suppose that exactly N processes synchronize with the initiating process in this transition. Then $N \in$ card and either $N = \max(\text{card})$; or $N < \max(\text{card})$ and $N + 1 \in$ card (because card is an interval) and, by condition (MAX), there are no more processes in the state represented by $\bar{v}$ that can synchronize on an a-action (†).

Now, to establish monotonicity, suppose $\bar{v} \leq \bar{y}$. We should prove that there is an a-transition from $\bar{y}$ to some $\bar{z} \geq \bar{w}$. It is enough to consider the case that $\bar{y} = \bar{v} + e_l$ for some l.

If $N = \max(\text{card})$ then we may define $\bar{z} := \bar{w} + e_l$ (i.e., mimic the transition $\bar{v} \overset{a}{\to} \bar{w}$, and the new process in state t_l does not synchronize).

Now assume $N < \max(\text{card})$. There are two cases.

First case: action a is not enabled from state t_l, i.e., the local state t_l has no outgoing transition labeled a_{in}. In this case we may define $\bar{z} := \bar{w} + e_l$ (i.e., mimic the transition $\bar{v} \overset{a}{\to} \bar{w}$, and the new process in state t_l does not, in fact cannot, synchronize)

Second case: action a is enabled from state t_l, say $t_l \overset{a_{in}}{\to} t_m$ is a local transition. In this case we may define $\bar{z} := \bar{w} + e_m$. Indeed, in the transition from $\bar{y}$ to $\bar{z}$ exactly $N + 1 \in$ card processes synchronize with the initiating process, and if it were possible that more than $N + 1$ were available to synchronize, then more than N would have been available to synchronize in the transition from $\bar{v}$, contrary to (†).   □

In other words, the combined system in which card is an interval and the specification is given by an automaton is a WSTS. Note that card is an interval for pairwise rendezvous ($\{1\}$), asynchronous rendezvous ($\{0, 1\}$), and broadcast ($\mathbb{N}_0$). The next lemma allows one to combine WSTS from different communication primitives into a single WSTS.

Lemma 5.5   *If $M_i = (Q, \Sigma_i, \Delta_i)$ ($i = 1, 2$) are two transition systems over the same state set Q, and with disjoint sets of action labels Σ_i, and $\leq$ is an ordering on Q, and both M_1 and M_2 are WSTS with respect to $\leq$, then the transition system $M_1 \cup M_2 := (Q, \Sigma_1 \cup \Sigma_2, \Delta_1 \cup \Delta_2)$ is a WSTS with respect to $\leq$.*

Sketch. First, $M := M_1 \cup M_2$ is computable since the M_i are. Second, $\leq$ is monotonic with respect to M since the sets of action labels of the M_is are disjoint. Third, $Pred_M(C) = Pred_{M_1}(C) \cup Pred_{M_2}(C)$. From a basis for C compute a basis B_i for $Pred_{M_i}(C)$. Then $B_1 \cup B_2$, which is certainly computable, is a basis for $Pred_M(C)$.   □

Corollary 5.6   *Let M be the counter representation of the parameterized system $n \mapsto \text{sys}(\overline{P}, \mathbf{G}(n), \text{card})$ where $\overline{P}$ consists of the set of all 2-ary system templates, $\text{card} = \{\{1\}, \{0, 1\}, \mathbb{N}_0\}$ and $\mathbf{G}$ is the 2-ary clique graph of size n. Then M is a WSTS.*

Aside.   If card is not an interval then M may not be a WSTS under $\leq$. This is due to the (MAX) item in the definition of synchronous transition (p. 8). For instance, suppose $\text{card} = \{1, 3\}$ and the process template has transitions $q \overset{a_{out}}{\to} q$ and $s \overset{a_{in}}{\to} s'$. Let c be the configuration in which one process is in state q and *two* processes are in state s. Then there is a synchronous transition to configuration c' in which *one* process is in state q, one process is in state s, and one process is in state q'. Now, consider configuration d in which one process is in state q and *three* processes are in state s. Then $c \leq d$. However the only synchronous transition from d results in a configuration d' in which one process in state q, and *none* in state s — this is because the (MAX) item forces all three processes in state s to receive the broadcast. But it is not the case that $c' \leq d'$, and so $\leq$ is not monotone.

On the other hand, if synchronous transitions are defined without the (MAX) item then M is a WSTS for every card (since in the proof of Proposition 5.4 we may simply take $\bar{z} = \bar{w} + e_l$).

5.2.2 DECIDABILITY FOR ALL THREE PRIMITIVES

We justify the decidability entry in the PR&AR&BC column of Figure 5.1.

Theorem 5.7 *[Esparza et al., 1999, Section 4] [Emerson and Kahlon, 2003b, Section 4.1] If synchronization is by pairwise rendezvous, asynchronous rendezvous, and broadcast, then* $\mathsf{PMCP}(\mathcal{P}, \mathbf{C}_\odot, \mathsf{Reg}(A))$ *is decidable.*

Proof. Let A be an automaton for the complement of the specification ϕ, and build the WSTS M as above. By Corollary 5.6, M is a WSTS. Let C be the finite set $Q_P \times F_A \times (0, \cdots, 0)$, where F_A are the final states of the automaton A. There is a path from $(\iota_P, \iota_A, 0, \cdots, 0)$ to $\uparrow C$ iff the specification ϕ fails on some system instance of the parameterized system. Now use the fact that coverability is decidable for WSTS (Theorem 3.3). □

5.2.3 DECIDABILITY FOR PAIRWISE RENDEZVOUS

We discuss the decidability results in the PR column of Figure 5.1.

Theorem 5.8 *[German and Sistla, 1992, Section 3.2] If synchronization is by pairwise rendezvous then* $\mathsf{PMCP}(\mathcal{P}, \mathbf{C}_\odot, \omega\mathsf{Reg}(C))$ *and* $\mathsf{PMCP}(\mathcal{P}, \mathbf{C}_\odot, \mathsf{LTL}(C))$ *are decidable in EXPSPACE.*

Sketch. Let A be a Büchi automaton over the atomic propositions of the controller. We build the WSTS M as above, except that we introduce a unique initial state $init$, with transitions to all states of the form $(\iota_C, \iota_A, (0, \cdots, 0))$ where ι_C is an initial state of the controller and ι_A is the initial state of the automaton, as well as transitions from $(\iota_C, \iota_A, \bar{v})$ to $(\iota_C, \iota_A, \bar{w})$ where $\bar{w}$ is equal to $\bar{v}$ except that at some coordinate, say i, $w_i = v_i + 1$ and t_i is an initial state of the user process, and from each of the states $(\iota_C, \iota_A, \bar{v})$ there are transitions which begin the simulation of the original system. Informally, M first loads the size of the system and then simulates it. In addition, one has to make sure that global transitions with no effect on the counters are correctly simulated. This is done by splitting each transition into two: first the coordinates of the source-states are decremented by 1 and then the coordinates of the target-states are incremented by 1.

By Corollary 5.6, M is a WSTS. It is not hard to show that M is the configuration space of a vector addition system with states (VASS). The reason for this is that transitions of the original system (internal transitions and pairwise-rendezvous) translate to adding constant vectors to states of M. Actually, one has to make sure that global rendezvous transitions with no net-effect on the counters do not result in extra behaviors. This is done by splitting each VASS transition into two: first the co-ordinates of the source-states are decremented by 1 (recall that a decrement transition can only be taken in a VASS if the co-ordinates being decremented are non-zero) and then the co-ordinates of the target-states are incremented by 1.

The problem "is there an $n \in \mathbb{N}$ and an infinite run in the system with n users that is accepted by automaton A" is equivalent to the problem of whether some path of the VASS M hits F infinitely often. This is a control state repeated reachability problem, which is decidable in EXPSPACE for VASS (Theorem 3.4).

Note that if the specification is given as an LTL formula ϕ over the controller then the first step is to translate the formula into a non-deterministic Büchi automaton L of size $2^{O(|\phi|)}$. In this case the VASS is $O(|U|)$-dimensional and has state set of size $|Q_C| \times 2^{O(|\phi|)}$. Thus, by Theorem 3.4 we can solve PMCP in space polynomial in $|Q_C| \times 2^{O(|\phi|)}$ and exponential in $|U|$, thus in EXPSPACE. □

By simulating a user process in the controller and using the fact that each user has the same set of neighbors, one gets the following.

Theorem 5.9   *[German and Sistla, 1992, Section 3.2] If synchronization is by pairwise rendezvous then* PMCP$(\mathcal{P}, \mathbf{C}_\odot, \forall U\ \omega\mathrm{Reg}(U))$ *is decidable in EXPSPACE. In particular, the result holds for* $\forall U$ LTL(U).

A proof of the following theorem is hinted at by Emerson and Kahlon [2003b]. It can be proven in a similar way to Theorem 5.8.

Theorem 5.10   *[Emerson and Kahlon, 2003b, Section 5.2] If synchronization is by pairwise rendezvous then* PMCP$(\mathcal{P}, \mathbf{C}_\odot, \omega\mathrm{Reg}(\mathsf{A}))$ *is decidable in EXPSPACE.*

5.3   UNDECIDABILITY RESULTS

We discuss the undecidability results in the BC and AR columns of Figure 5.1. The rest of the undecidability results are then immediate. The basic idea is to reduce the non-halting problem of 2CMs to the PMCP by simulating the states of the 2CM in the controller and distributing the counters over the users.

5.3.1   UNDECIDABILITY FOR BROADCAST

We discuss the undecidability results in the BC column of Figure 5.1. The proofs of the following results are all similar, and follow Esparza et al. [1999, Section 5].

Theorem 5.11   *Suppose synchronization is by broadcast. Then:*

1. PMCP$(\mathcal{P}, \mathbf{C}_\odot, \mathrm{LTL}(C))$ *is undecidable;*

2. PMCP$(\mathcal{P}, \mathbf{C}_\odot, \omega\mathrm{Reg}(\mathsf{A}))$ *is undecidable; and*

3. PMCP$(\mathcal{P}, \mathbf{C}_\odot, \forall U\ LTL(U))$ *is undecidable.*

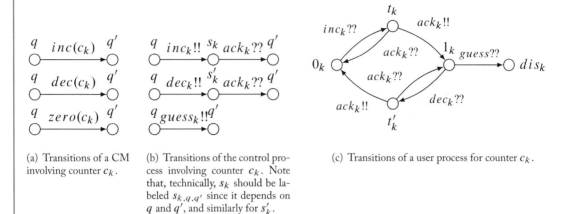

(a) Transitions of a CM involving counter c_k.

(b) Transitions of the control process involving counter c_k. Note that, technically, s_k should be labeled $s_{k,q,q'}$ since it depends on q and q', and similarly for s'_k.

(c) Transitions of a user process for counter c_k.

Figure 5.3: Simulating a CM using broadcasts.

Proof idea. We explain the first item. The second is similar, and we remark at the end how to deal with the third item. Suppose M is a 2CM with a halting location m, and without loss of generality the starting location 1 cannot be reached by a transition from any location. We build a new 2CM M' that simulates M but if the halting location m is reached then both counters are drained to zero and then there is a transition to the initial location. Thus, M' never stops and has the following property: M has a computation that enters location m if and only if M' has a computation that enters the location m infinitely often. The protocol in Figure 5.3 simulates M' using broadcasts. We will see that although such faithful simulations cannot always be ensured (simulating the zero-test is the problem), they can be ensured from some point on.

The controller process stores the current location of M', while the users collectively store the values of counters. In a system instance of size $n + 1$, there are n user processes each of which is the product of two copies of the state diagram in Figure 5.3(c) (instantiated with $k = 1, 2$). Thus, the state of a user process is of the form (x_1, x_2) where the x_ks are the vertices pictured in Figure 5.3(c).

- If $x_k = 0_k$ then we say that the process' kth counter is set to zero;

- if $x_k = 1_k$, that its kth counter is set to one;

- if $x_k = dis_k$, that its kth counter is disabled; and

- if $x_k = t_k$ or t'_k, that its counter is in an intermediate state.

Ideally, the number of user processes with $x_k = 1$ is equal to the value of counter k.

In Figure 5.3 we see that increments and decrements are achieved as follows: to increment counter 1 the controller broadcasts this intention ($inc_k!!$) and goes to an intermediate state s_1

while the memory processes with kth counter set to zero (if any) respond and go to an intermediate state t_1; then exactly one memory process broadcasts that it has set its counter 1 bit from zero to one, and all the other processes, including the controller process, leave their intermediate state. It is an invariant of the simulation that if there is a user whose kth counter is in an intermediate state, say t_k, then (a) every process whose kth counter is in an intermediate state is in fact in state t_k, and (b) the controller process is also in an intermediate state, i.e., s_k (see Figure 5.3(b)). In this case the only possible next step is for some user process to broadcast an acknowledgement. Decrements are similar. On the other hand, if no process has a kth counter set to 0 (i.e., the memory storing the counter is full) and the controller broadcasts inc_k!! then the simulation hangs. Similarly, if no process has a kth counter set to 1 and the controller broadcasts dec_k!! then the simulation hangs. Thus, in an infinite run of a system instance, increments and decrements are faithfully simulated (†), i.e., every time the controller tries to increment (or decrement) a counter, it does so successfuly.

Zero transitions are more subtle—the controller may broadcast a "guess counter k is zero" command. If the kth counter of every user is set to zero, then the simulation proceeds faithfully, i.e., the control of the counter machine proceeds as if the counter is zero and indeed the total value of the counter stored in the users is zero; otherwise, every user whose kth counter is set to one enters a special state dis_k (thus permanently disabling it from being used as storage for counter k). In the second scenario the simulation is no longer faithful, i.e., the control of the counter machine proceeds as if the counter is zero but the value of the counter stored by the user processes is not zero. However, we will see that from some point on the simulation is faithful. To this end, let N_k be the number of processes whose kth counter is not disabled, and note that the sum $N_1 + N_2$ is non-increasing (††).

Now, if the 2CM M' enters the halting location m infinitely often, then the 2CM M has a (finite) run that enters the halting location m, and thus there is a run in a large enough system instance in which the control process enters m infinitely often.

Conversely, suppose that in some system instance there is a run such that the control process enters m infinitely often. By (†), every time the controller tries to increment (or decrement) a counter, it does successfuly. By (††), from some point in time t onwards, the sum $N_1 + N_2$ is constant. Thus, at all later points $t' > t$ that the controller broadcasts "guess counter k is zero," the kth counter of every process is equal to zero. Thus, the simulation after time t is faithful. Let $t'' \geq t$ be a time in which the controller is in the initial location. Then the run from this time onwards witnesses that M' enters the halting state m infinitely often.

In summary, the 2CM M halts if and only if there is a system instance that satisfies EGFh_1 where h_1 is the indexed atomic proposition that holds if the controller is in state m.

For the third item repeat the proof above except that initially the first scheduled process sends a broadcast message declaring itself a controller (it now acts as the controller and all the other processes act as users). $\square$

5.3.2   UNDECIDABILITY FOR ASYNCHRONOUS RENDEZVOUS

We discuss the undecidability results in the AR column of Figure 5.1. The proofs of the following undecidability results are similar and follow Emerson and Kahlon [2003b, Section 4].

Theorem 5.12   *Suppose synchronization is by asynchronous rendezvous. Then:*

1. $\mathsf{PMCP}(\mathcal{P}, \mathbf{C}_\odot, \mathsf{LTL}(C))$ *is undecidable;*

2. $\mathsf{PMCP}(\mathcal{P}, \mathbf{C}_\odot, \omega\mathsf{Reg(A)})$ *is undecidable; and*

3. $\mathsf{PMCP}(\mathcal{P}, \mathbf{C}_\odot, \forall U\ LTL(U))$ *is undecidable.*

Proof Sketch.   In the proof of Theorem 5.11 for $\mathsf{LTL}(C)$, replace broadcast by asynchronous rendezvous. The only difference in behavior of the two simulations is that previously, if more than one process received a broadcast message, now, exactly one process receives the asynchronous-rendezvous message. The proof proceeds verbatim, except that one should note that at most one user is in an intermediate state at a time, and the phrase "every user whose kth counter is set to one enters a special state dis_k," should change to "at least one user whose kth counter is set to one enters a special state dis_k."

The case of $\omega\mathsf{Reg(A)}$ is similar.

To extend this proof to the case $\forall U\ LTL(U)$ we proceed differently from the broadcast case. The controller's first move should be to synchronize, once and for all, with a single user, say v, and then to move into a special state where it is no longer used. On synchronizing the user v enters a special component of its state set and plays the role of the controller. The specification is of the form "for all users U, for all runs, if U initially synchronizes with the controller then it infinitely often satisfies h_1." □

5.4   DISCUSSION

In contrast to the token-passing systems of Chapter 4, the literature has focused on the more symmetric case of clique topologies for systems with communication by broadcast, pairwise rendezvous, or asynchronous rendezvous. One reason for this is that already in uni-directional rings the PMCP for these systems is undecidable, even for safety properties. This is because such systems can simulate a binary-valued token (as in Section 4.1.2 and Section 4.2.3).

However, even in a clique topology there are many undecidability results due to the fact that in a system of size n one can simulate the run of a 2CM as long as the counters do not exceed n. Common techniques to do this simulation include:

- using broadcast to elect a unique "controller" process (if needed) that simulates the control of the 2CM, while all the others are "memory" processes;

- using pairwise rendezvous between the controller and user processes to ensure that exactly one process increments/decrements the counter; and

- using broadcast (or asynchronous rendezvous) to reduce the number of active memory processes when the controller incorrectly "guesses" that a counter is zero.

We briefly discuss how the results of this chapter are affected under the assumption that there is no controller (i.e., all processes have the same type and are in a clique). Decidability proofs are not affected. Undecidability proofs in the case of no controller typically proceed as follows: first elect a controller using broadcast, and then proceed as in the case with a controller. Although broadcast is powerful enough to elect a controller, asynchronous rendezvous only seems powerful enough to elect a temporary controller.

Problem 5.13   Is the PMCP undecidable for systems communicating by asynchronous rendezvous, without a controller and for liveness specifications?

In summary, looking at Figure 5.1, all the entries (in the first three rows) are known to hold also for the case without controller, except for the columns AR and PR&AR and liveness specifications (i.e., the second and third rows).

Decidability results are typically proven using counter representations: since every process in a clique can communicate with every other process, it is enough to store the number of processes in every state. Pairwise rendezvous leads to a vector addition system with states, and thus certain safety and liveness properties are decidable. In contrast, broadcast and asynchronous rendezvous lead to well-structured transition systems, and thus safety is decidable, whereas it turns out that liveness is in general undecidable.

We note that the literature has only a few exact bounds on the complexity of the PMCP. We enumerate them here.

1. For broadcast protocols, Schmitz and Schnoebelen [2013] proved that the complexity of PMCP for coverability specifications is $\mathbf{F}_\omega$-complete (the class $\mathbf{F}_\omega$ of Ackermannian problems is closed under primitive-recursive reductions).

2. For pairwise-rendezvous protocols:

   (a) Esparza [2014, Section 3.3] reported that the complexity of PMCP for the coverability problem and pairwise rendezvous is EXPSPACE-complete.

   (b) Aminof et al. [2014b] showed that PMCP is undecidable for pairwise rendezvous and 1-index CTL*\X specifications.

   (c) Aminof et al. [2014b] proved that for topologies that generalize cliques and stars (but not rings) that PMCP for 1-index LTL\X is EXPSPACE-complete (and PSPACE-complete without a controller), and that the program complexity (i.e., the formula is fixed) is EXPSPACE-complete (and in PTIME without a controller).

5.4.1 VARIATIONS OF THE MODEL

One variation are systems without a controller process. Here the connectivity graph is a clique, and all processes have the same type, i.e., all are user processes. The known results are summarized in Figure 5.1 (on page 52).

As a rule of thumb, systems with a unique controller are more difficult to verify than systems with only one process template, or systems with a constant number of process templates, but requiring that there is no bound on the number of processes instantiating each template. For instance, the PMCP for coverability specifications and pairwise-rendezvous synchronization is in PTIME if there is no controller (this follows immediately from German and Sistla [1992, Lemma 4.5]), while it is EXPSPACE-complete if there is a controller [Esparza, 2014, Section 3.3].

The proofs of decidability typically yield *cutoffs* that depend on both the template and the formula. For instance, for pairwise rendezvous with a controller, there is a cutoff (on the number of user processes) that is, roughly, doubly exponential in the size of the user template and the formula [German and Sistla, 1992, p. 687]. Since PMCP of liveness with broadcast is undecidable, there is no way to effectively compute cutoffs. However, the following restricted broadcast system has cutoffs for the specification language which is an extension of the universal fragment of CTL*\X by the epistemic operator K, see Kouvaros and Lomuscio [2013a]: for every two local states q, q' and broadcast action label a, it holds that $(q, a!!, q')$ is a local transition if and only if $(q, a??, q')$ is a local transition. Such a broadcast transition may be called *symmetric broadcast*. Systems that communicate with symmetric broadcast and pairwise rendezvous are, in the presence of a controller, quite expressive, e.g., Kouvaros and Lomuscio [2015] modeled a swarm aggregation algorithm. In the restricted case of a single symmetric broadcast action and pairwise rendezvous (or, more generally, k-wise rendezvous for some k), both safety and liveness are decidable [Aminof et al., 2015].

Ad hoc networks (Chapter 7) are concurrent systems in which the connectivity graphs are *general graphs* (not necessarily cliques), and the communication primitive is broadcast. Although the PMCP for general graphs and safety specifications is undecidable, one regains decidability by restricting the class of graphs (e.g., to graphs of bounded diameter).

The decidability results in the PR column of Figure 5.1 still hold if one only considers runs satisfying the following *fairness* condition: a run of a system instance is *fair* (following German and Sistla [1992, p. 680]) if every process that is enabled infinitely often is scheduled infinitely often. Here, a process is *enabled* in a global state if it can make an internal transition or synchronize with another process. However, the complexity is at least as hard as reachability for VASS.

The *Token-passing systems* that we see in Chapter 4 can be defined in terms of pairwise rendezvous, and there various fairness notions are used to get cutoff results. A similar "no-blocking" idea is used to get cutoffs for broadcast systems in the presence of a controller on cliques; see Kouvaros and Lomuscio [2013b, Definition 4.3].

CHAPTER 6

Guarded Protocols

In this chapter we extend the computational model of Section 2.2 with a new means of coordination. Until now processes coordinated with synchronized transitions and we have used transition labels to express which transitions should be taken together. In this chapter, we introduce guards, which are conditions on the global state and determine whether a specific local transition may be fired. We review results on systems with guards that contain quantifiers over all processes except the one evaluating the guard. Hence, the current state of other processes may restrict the control flow of a process. In contrast to synchronized transitions that, intuitively, link transitions of different processes, guards link transitions to the state of other processes.

Most of the models we discuss here contain two types of process templates, a single coordinator C, and user processes U. The systems are parameterized in the number of processes of type U.

The (un)decidability results we review here depend on the form of the guards as well as on the logic fragments used to formalize the specifications. Figure 6.1 and Table 6.1 give an overview of the results that we discuss in this chapter. In addition, in Section 6.7 we review restrictions of guards which ensure decidability, and are used to model cache-coherence protocols [Emerson and Kahlon, 2003a,c].

The undecidability results are proven by reduction to the non-halting problem of two-counter machines (cf. Section 3.1). The decidability proofs are based on the cutoff results by Emerson and Kahlon [2000], who construct runs in a small cutoff system from runs of bigger systems and vice versa.

6.1 MOTIVATING EXAMPLE

Consider a multi-threaded program, composed of n threads that are concurrently accessing or modifying a shared doubly linked list. Figure 6.2 shows an example of such a list. As is typical, we assume that a single update of a pointer in the list is atomic, that is, a thread reads an old pointer value, if another thread is currently writing to that pointer. However, our list is a non-atomic data structure, that is, while one process is updating several pointers in the list, the other processes may access the list. Figure 6.3 shows the list in an inconsistent state, when one thread started to delete the second element. To avoid such scenarios, we need a protocol that ensures that no other thread accesses the list in an inconsistent state. Such a protocol is usually called "multiple readers/single writer protocol."

Table 6.1: Decidability results for Guarded Protocols and their sources, separated into systems with boolean guards ($\mathcal{P}_{\text{bool}}$), conjunctive guards ($\mathcal{P}_{\text{conj}}$), init-conjunctive guards ($\mathcal{P}_{\text{init-conj}}$), and disjunctive guards ($\mathcal{P}_{\text{disj}}$)

Result	Protocol	Graph	Specification	References
undecidability	$\mathcal{P}_{\text{bool}}$	clique (**C**)	LTL(C)	[Emerson and Namjoshi 1996] (proof idea)
undecidability	$\mathcal{P}_{\text{init-conj}}$	clique (**C**)	LTL(C), Reg(A), ωReg(A)	[Emerson and Kahlon 2003b]
a cutoff for $\ell \in \{1, 2\}$	$\mathcal{P}_{\text{init-conj}}[2]$	clique (**C**)	1-LTL\X(P^ℓ), 1-ELTL\X(P^ℓ), LTL\X(C)	[Emerson and Kahlon 2000]
a trivial cutoff for deadlock-free instances	$\mathcal{P}_{\text{init-conj}}$	clique (**C**)	as above	[Emerson and Kahlon 2000]
a trivial cutoff for finite-path properties	$\mathcal{P}_{\text{init-conj}}$	clique (**C**)	as above	[Emerson and Kahlon 2000]
a cutoff $\ell \in \{1, 2\}$	$\mathcal{P}_{\text{disj}}[2]$	clique (**C**)	1-LTL\X(P^ℓ), 1-ELTL\X(P^ℓ), LTL\X(C)	[Emerson and Kahlon 2000]
a cutoff	$\mathcal{P}_{\text{disj}}$	clique (**C**)	2-LTL\X($P^\ell, P^{\ell'}$), 2-ELTL\X($P^\ell, P^{\ell'}$), LTL\X(C)	[Emerson and Kahlon 2000]
decidability	$\mathcal{P}_{\text{disj}}$	clique (**C**)	Reg(A), ωReg(A)	[Emerson and Kahlon 2003b]
decidability	$\mathcal{P}_{\text{disj\&rdvz}}$	clique (**C**)	Reg(A), ωReg(A), LTL(C), 1-LTL\X(P^ℓ)	[Emerson and Kahlon 2003b]
decidability	$\mathcal{P}_{\text{disj\&ardvz}}$	clique (**C**)	Reg(A)	[Emerson and Kahlon 2003b]
undecidability	$\mathcal{P}_{\text{disj\&ardvz}}$	clique (**C**)	ωReg(A)	[Emerson and Kahlon 2003b]
decidability	$\mathcal{P}_{\text{disj\&bcast}}$	clique (**C**)	Reg(A)	[Emerson and Namjoshi 1998], [Emerson and Kahlon 2003b]
undecidability	$\mathcal{P}_{\text{disj\&bcast}}$	clique (**C**)	ωReg(A)	[Esparza et al. 1999], [Emerson and Kahlon 2003b]
undecidability	$\mathcal{P}_{\text{conj\&disj}}$ $\mathcal{P}_{\text{conj\&[a]rdvz}}$ $\mathcal{P}_{\text{conj\&bcast}}$	clique (**C**)	all above	[Emerson and Kahlon 2003b], [Esparza et al. 1999]

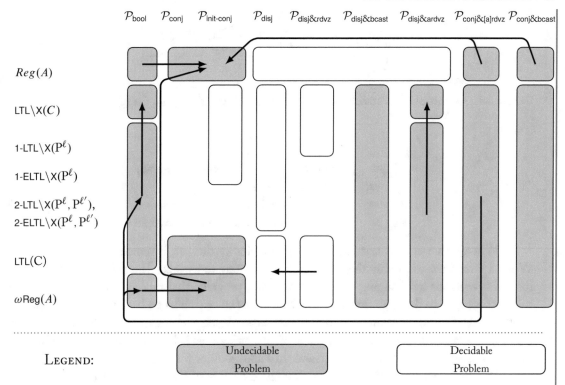

Figure 6.1: Decidability results for guarded protocols. An arrow from box A to box B means that the result of A follows from the result, or variation of the proof, of B. Blank entries are those not covered in the literature. The guarded protocols are defined over process templates $P^1, \ldots, P^d$, and $1 \leq \ell, \ell' \leq d$. In case of LTL\X($C$) and LTL($C$), we assume that template $C = P^1$, and there is only one process of type C.

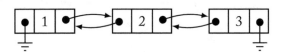

Figure 6.2: A doubly linked list shared by n threads.

To prevent several threads from simultaneously modifying the list or accessing the list that is being modified by another thread, we introduce a multiple readers/single writer protocol that is shown in Figure 6.4. The guards $\phi_1, \ldots, \phi_4$ are defined in Equations 6.1–6.4. The formal syntax and semantics of guards follows in Section 6.2.

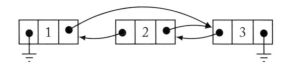

Figure 6.3: An inconsistent state of the list when one thread is deleting the second element.

$$\phi_1 \;\equiv\; [\forall \text{ other } j]\, \text{neutral}_j \vee \text{try-write}_j \vee \text{try-read}_j \qquad (6.1)$$
$$\phi_2 \;\equiv\; [\exists \text{ other } j]\, \text{lock-write}_j \qquad (6.2)$$
$$\phi_3 \;\equiv\; [\forall \text{ other } j]\, \text{neutral}_j \vee \text{try-read}_j \vee \text{lock-read}_j \qquad (6.3)$$
$$\phi_4 \;\equiv\; [\forall \text{ other } j]\, \text{neutral}_j \vee \text{try-read}_j \vee \text{lock-read}_j \qquad (6.4)$$

When a thread does not have to access or modify the list, it remains in the neutral state. When a thread has to modify the list, it changes its state to try-write. The thread can lock the list for exclusive access by changing its state to lock-write, provided that no other thread resides in the state lock-write, or in the state lock-read. The thread has an option to go back to the state neutral, if another thread has already entered the state lock-write. When the thread enters the state lock-write, it can iterate over the list and modify its elements; as soon as it finishes with the modifications, the thread goes back to the neutral state and thus allows other threads to access the list.

When a thread is going to iterate over the elements of the list without modifying it, the thread changes its state to try-read. The thread can lock the list for shared access by changing its state to lock-read, provided that there is no other thread in state try-write or lock-write, that is, no other thread has exclusively locked the list, or is trying to do so. Multiple processes can reside in the state lock-read and therefore can concurrently read the contents of the list. A thread must leave the state lock-read, as soon as it has finished reading its contents, or another thread has entered the state try-write.

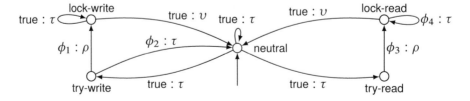

Figure 6.4: A process template modeling a multiple readers/single writer protocol. The circles represent local states labeled with state names, e.g., neutral. The edges represent transitions labeled with guards and actions, e.g., $\phi_1 : \rho$ for a guard ϕ_1 and an action ρ.

The protocol enforces the readers to have a lower priority than the writer. Moreover, the readers are preempted by a thread that is going to modify the list. When writes happen rarely, multiple readers can efficiently access the list. On the other hand, when the writes occur frequently, the readers might starve, without ever accessing the list.

Note that, in order to lock the list, a thread has to make sure that there are no other threads in certain states. Although the exclusive access to the list can be enforced with a token-passing protocol (see Section 4), it is not easy to model the locking mechanism by multiple readers with token passing. The protocol can be modeled using broadcasts (see Section 5) by introducing auxiliary states and enforcing the threads to "listen" to the broadcasts by the threads locking and unlocking the list. This modeling, however, is closer to hardware rather than to multi-threaded programs, because the threads have to perform steps synchronously. Guarded protocols is a natural computational model for our example.

6.2   SYSTEM MODEL

To formalize guarded protocols, we slightly specialize the notion of process template, as we require specific atomic propositions to define guards. From this specialized process template, we obtain a system template in the usual way. Then, for a given system template we can define guards. In this way, we collect all ingredients to define guarded system instances: we associate to each *local* transition a guard, and restrict the *global* transition relation in a way that only admits global transitions that are built from local transitions whose guards evaluate to true in the current global state.

Identity-labeled process templates.   We specialize the definition of a process template from Section 2.2 in that we identify atomic propositions with the local states, and restrict the label of a local state to be the singleton containing the state itself. That is, given d disjoint sets of local states $Q^1, \ldots, Q^d$, we specialize AP_{pr} to be $Q^1 \cup \cdots \cup Q^d$. An *identity-labeled process template* P^ℓ is a process template $P^\ell = (Q^\ell, Q_0^\ell, \Sigma_{pr}, \delta^\ell, \lambda^\ell)$, where for all $q \in Q^\ell$ it holds that $\lambda^\ell(q) = \{q\}$. Then, a tuple $(P^1, \ldots, P^d)$ of identity-labeled process templates is an *identity-labeled d-ary system template*.

Example 6.1   In our example in Figure 6.4, there is one process template P^1 with the set of local states $Q^1 = \{$neutral, try-read, try-write, lock-read, lock-write$\}$. The set of atomic propositions AP_{pr} equals to the set of local states Q^1. The set of actions is $\Sigma_{pr} = \Sigma_{int} = \{\rho, \upsilon, \tau\}$. Every local state is labeled with itself, e.g., $\lambda^1($neutral$) = \{$neutral$\}$.

Guards.   We start by restricting the syntax of formulas that will be used in guards. In what follows, we will write $\phi(j)$ to denote a boolean formula over $AP_{pr} \times \{j\}$. In other words, $\phi(j)$ is a boolean formula over atomic propositions AP_{pr} of a process, indexed with a free index variable j. When j is instantiated with a constant $w \in V(G)$, the formula $\phi(w)$ becomes a boolean formula over AP_{sys}. Given $w \in V(G)$, the formula $\phi(w)$ is evaluated inductively at a state $s = (q_1, \ldots, q_{|V|}) \in S$ of a system instance $\overline{P}^G$ as follows: for $p \in \mathrm{AP}_{\mathrm{pr}}$, it holds that $(\overline{P}^G, s) \models (p, w)$ if and only if $(p, w) \in \Lambda(s)$; The boolean connectives are interpreted as usual. We define disjunctive, conjunctive, and boolean guards as follows.

- Let $\phi(j)$ be a disjunction over $\mathrm{AP}_{\mathrm{pr}} \times \{j\}$. Then,

  - $[\forall \, \mathrm{other} \, j] \, \phi(j)$ is a *conjunctive guard*, and
  - $[\exists \, \mathrm{other} \, j] \, \phi(j)$ is a *disjunctive guard*.

- Conjunctive and disjunctive guards are *boolean guards*. If f and g are boolean guards, then $\neg f$, $f \vee g$, and $f \wedge g$ are boolean guards as well.

To simplify notation, we write p_j to denote a proposition $(p, j) \in \mathrm{AP}_{\mathrm{pr}} \times \{j\}$.

Example 6.2   In the protocol in Figure 6.4, the guard $\phi_1 \equiv [\forall \, \mathrm{other} \, j] \, \mathrm{neutral}_j \vee \mathrm{try\text{-}write}_j \vee \mathrm{try\text{-}read}_j$ is an example of a conjunctive guard, whereas the guard $\phi_2 \equiv [\exists \, \mathrm{other} \, j] \, \mathrm{lock\text{-}write}_j$ is an example of a disjunctive guard.

One can see from the definition that the quantifiers $[\forall \, \mathrm{other} \, j]$ and $[\exists \, \mathrm{other} \, j]$ are never nested, but the boolean connectives can introduce subformulas with several quantifiers.

Intuitively, if one fixes a process v, then $[\forall \, \mathrm{other} \, j] \, \phi(j)$ means that ϕ should evaluate to true on *all processes* other than v, and $[\exists \, \mathrm{other} \, j] \, \phi(j)$ means that ϕ should evaluate to true on *at least one* process other than v. Formally, given a system instance $\overline{P}^G$, its global state s, a process $v \in V(G)$, and a guard f, we evaluate f in s with respect to v (in symbols, $(\overline{P}^G, s) \models_v f$) as follows.

- If f has the form $[\forall \, \mathrm{other} \, j] \, \phi(j)$, then $(\overline{P}^G, s) \models_v f$ if and only if for *every* process $w \in V(G) \setminus \{v\}$ it holds $(\overline{P}^G, s) \models \phi(w)$, where $\phi(w)$ is obtained from $\phi(j)$ by substituting all instances of j with w.

- Similarly, if f has the form $[\exists \, \mathrm{other} \, j] \, \phi(j)$, then $(\overline{P}^G, s) \models_v f$ if and only if there *exists* a process $w \in V(G) \setminus \{v\}$ with the property $(\overline{P}^G, s) \models \phi(w)$.

- If f is constructed using boolean connectives $\neg$, $\vee$, and $\wedge$, then $(\overline{P}^G, s) \models_v f$ is defined as usual via evaluation of the subformulas of f.

Consider a boolean formula $\mathit{all\_states}(i) = \bigvee_{q \in Q^1 \cup \cdots \cup Q^d}(q, i)$. Observe that the formula evaluates to true on every local state $q \in Q^1 \cup \cdots \cup Q^d$ of a process i. Using $\mathit{all\_states}(i)$, one can construct the conjunctive guard "$[\forall \, \mathrm{other} \, i] \, \mathit{all\_states}(i)$" and the disjunctive guard "$[\exists \, \mathrm{other} \, i] \, \mathit{all\_states}(i)$" that both evaluate to true on *every* global state. We abbreviate either of these guards with true: the form $[\forall \, \mathrm{other} \, i] \, \mathit{all\_states}(i)$ is used when the class of protocols is restricted to the protocols with conjunctive guards; the form $[\exists \, \mathrm{other} \, i] \, \mathit{all\_states}(i)$ is used when the class of protocols is restricted to the protocols with disjunctive guards.

Guarded protocols.   A guarded protocol is an identity-labeled d-ary system template equipped with an assignment of a guard to each transition. Formally, a *guarded protocol* is a pair $((P^1, \ldots, P^d), \mathsf{gd})$, where $(P^1, \ldots, P^d)$ is an identity-labeled d-ary system template with $P^\ell = (Q^\ell, Q_0^\ell, \Sigma_{pr}, \delta^\ell, \lambda^\ell)$, and gd maps every transition from $\bigcup_{1 \leq \ell \leq \mathsf{d}} \delta^\ell$ to a guard.

Example 6.3   The protocol in Figure 6.4 has 10 transitions, each labeled with a guard. For instance, the transition $t = (\text{try-read}, \rho, \text{lock-read})$ is labeled with the guard ϕ_3, or, formally, $\mathsf{gd}(t) = \phi_3$.

   When we consider guarded protocols with synchronization actions, a standard assumption is that receive actions are always enabled. More formally, for every $\mathsf{in}_a \in \mathrm{AP}_{pr}$ and every $t = (q, \mathsf{in}_a, q') \in \delta^\ell$, we require that $\mathsf{gd}(t) = \mathsf{true}$. For instance, if in_a is a broadcast receive $a??$, then every transition with action label $a??$ is guarded by true.

Connectivity graphs.   In this chapter we restrict d-ary connectivity graphs to cliques. Let $\mathbf{C} : \mathbb{N}^{\mathsf{d}} \mapsto \mathbf{C}(n)$ be a sequence of graphs that associates a d-ary connectivity graph with a size vector $n = (n_1, \ldots, n_{\mathsf{d}}) \in \mathbb{N}^{\mathsf{d}}$. We require that each $\mathbf{C}(n)$ is a clique of size n, i.e., if $\mathbf{C}(n) = (V, E, \text{type})$, then $E = V \times V$ and for all $\ell \in [\mathsf{d}]$, it holds $|\{v \in V : \text{type}(v) = \ell\}| = n_\ell$. We also introduce notation $\mathbf{I}(n)$ for the set of indices $\{i : 1 \leq i \leq n_1 + \cdots + n_{\mathsf{d}}\}$.

Example 6.4   The protocol in Figure 6.4 has one process template, that is, $\mathsf{d} = 1$. Then, $\mathbf{C}(n) : \mathbb{N} \to \mathbb{N}$ is a function that for each $n \geq 1$, returns a clique of size n, which corresponds to a system of n processes created from the template P^1.

Guarded system instances.   We construct a guarded system instance $\overline{P}^{\mathbf{C}(n)}$ of a guarded protocol $((P^1, \ldots, P^d), \mathsf{gd})$ by restricting the global transition relation. In particular, we restrict internal and synchronous transitions—defined in Section 2.2—to guarded internal transitions and guarded synchronous transitions.

   A *guarded internal transition* of $\overline{P}^{\mathbf{C}(n)}$ is a triple $(s, a, s') \in S \times \Sigma_{int} \times S$ for which there exists a process index $v \in V$ fulfilling the conditions (INT-STEP), (INT-FRAME), and

(INT-GUARD) The guard of the process transition $t_v = (s(v), a, s'(v))$ is satisfied in the global state s, that is, $(\overline{P}^{\mathbf{C}(n)}, s) \models_v \mathsf{gd}(t_v)$.

   A *guarded synchronous transition* is $(s, a, s') \in S \times \Sigma_{sync} \times S$ for which there exists a process index $v \in V$ and a set $\mathcal{I} \subseteq \{w \in V : E(v, w)\}$ of recipients of v in $\mathbf{C}(n)$ satisfying (CARD), (STEP), ($\mathcal{I}$-STEP), (FRAME), (MAX), and the following condition:

(GUARD) The guard of the process transition $t_v = (s(v), \mathsf{out}_a, s'(v))$ of process v is satisfied in the global state s, that is, $(\overline{P}^{\mathbf{C}(n)}, s) \models_v \mathsf{gd}(t_v)$. (Recall that input actions are labeled with true.)

Finally, the global transition relation Δ of $\overline{P}^{\mathbf{C}(n)}$ consists only of guarded internal and synchronous transitions.

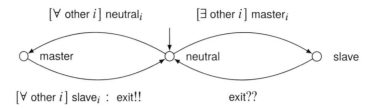

Figure 6.5: A barrier synchronization protocol. The first process enters the barrier as a master, and all other processes enter the barrier later as slaves. Once all processes gather in the states slave and master, the master broadcasts the action exit!! and all processes go to the state neutral synchronously. The guards of unlabeled edges are equal to true, and the actions of unlabeled edges are equal to τ.

Example 6.5 Consider a system instance $P_{RW}^{\mathbf{C}(3)}$ of three processes following the template P_{RW} that is shown in Figure 6.4. Let s and t be the states (neutral, try-read, try-read) and (neutral, lock-read, try-read), respectively. Then, the transition (s, τ, t) is a guarded internal transition of the system instance $(P_{RW})^{\mathbf{C}(3)}$. Indeed, the condition (INT-GUARD) is satisfied, as the guard ϕ_3 holds true in the global state s and therefore process 3 can perform its internal transition (try-read, τ, lock-read).

Example 6.6 Consider the process template P_B shown in Figure 6.5. The processes following the template P_B implement a barrier synchronization protocol: the processes enter the barrier and, as soon as all processes gather at the barrier, leave it synchronously. Let s and t be the states (master, slave, slave) and (neutral, neutral, neutral), respectively. Then, the transition (s, τ, t) is a guarded transition of the system instance $P_B^{\mathbf{C}(3)}$. Indeed, the condition (GUARD) is satisfied, as the guard [∀ other i] slave$_i$ holds true for process 1 in the global state s, and therefore process 1 performs the transition (master, x!!, neutral). Moreover, according to the conditions (CARD) and (MAX), processes 2 and 3 must perform the transition (slave, x??, neutral).

Deadlocks.   In this chapter, we require that the transition relation of a system instance is total. If there is a deadlock in a system, then the deadlocked run is extended to an infinite one with the deadlock state repeated at the end (cf. discussion in Section 2.2.2).

In contrast to most other systems considered in the literature, the parameterized deadlock detection problem for guarded protocols has been studied extensively, and decidability results for PMCP often extend to parameterized deadlock detection. This is the case for Theorems 6.22, 6.25, and 6.30 in this chapter.

6.2.1 CLASSES OF GUARDED PROTOCOLS

There are several important classes of guarded protocols in the literature. The following classes restrict the form of guards, and assume that only *internal transitions* occur, that is, $\Sigma_{sync} = \emptyset$:

$\mathcal{P}_{bool}$: guarded protocols with boolean guards [Emerson and Namjoshi, 1996];

$\mathcal{P}_{disj}$: guarded protocols using only disjunctive guards [∃ other j] $\phi(j)$ [Emerson and Kahlon, 2000];

$\mathcal{P}_{conj}$: guarded protocols using only conjunctive guards [∀ other j] $\phi(j)$ [Emerson and Kahlon, 2003b];

$\mathcal{P}_{init\text{-}conj}$: the subclass of $\mathcal{P}_{conj}$ with the following restrictions [Emerson and Kahlon, 2000]:

- each process template P^ℓ has $init^\ell$ as the only initial state, i.e., $Q_0^\ell = \{init^\ell\}$; and
- every guard is satisfiable by the initial states, i.e., the guard can be written in the form [∀ other j] $(init^1 \vee \cdots \vee init^d \vee \psi(j))$.

Although both $\mathcal{P}_{conj}$ and $\mathcal{P}_{init\text{-}conj}$ are usually called protocols with conjunctive guards, we differentiate $\mathcal{P}_{init\text{-}conj}$ from $\mathcal{P}_{conj}$, as they differ in decidability. In particular, the former have remarkable decidability results.

Example 6.7 Consider the guarded protocol (P, gd) shown in Figure 6.4. As it contains both conjunctive and disjunctive guards, the protocol belongs to the class $\mathcal{P}_{bool}$. Let (P', gd') be the protocol obtained from (P, gd) by removing the transition that is labeled with ϕ_2. Then, the resulting protocol belongs to the class $\mathcal{P}_{conj}$. Moreover, as the guards ϕ_1, ϕ_3, and ϕ_4 contain the initial state neutral, the guarded protocol (P', gd') belongs to the class $\mathcal{P}_{init\text{-}conj}$.

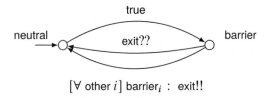

$$\text{[∀ other } i] \text{ barrier}_i : \text{ exit!!}$$

Figure 6.6: A simplified version of the barrier synchronization protocol shown in Figure 6.5. Every process may enter the state barrier. Once all processes gather in the state barrier, one of them broadcasts the action exit!! and all processes go to the state neutral synchronously. The guards of unlabeled edges are equal to true, and the actions of unlabeled edges are equal to τ.

Further, when synchronous transitions are allowed, we consider the classes of the form $\mathcal{P}_{g\&z}$. Each such a class contains guards of type $g \in \{\text{conj}, \text{disj}\}$, internal guarded transitions, and guarded transitions with the synchronization primitives of type $z \in \{\text{bcast}, \text{rdv}, \text{ardv}\}$, where conj and disj stand for conjunctive and disjunctive guards, while bcast, rdv, and ardv denote broadcast, pairwise rendezvous, and asynchronous rendezvous, respectively (Section 2.2.1). For instance, $\mathcal{P}_{\text{disj\&bcast}}$ and other combinations of disjunctive guards with synchronization primitives have been investigated by Emerson and Kahlon [2003a,b,c]. We revisit the results on combinations of guards with synchronization primitives in Section 6.6.

Example 6.8   The guarded protocol shown in Figure 6.5 belongs to the class $\mathcal{P}_{\text{bool\&bcast}}$. Figure 6.6 shows a simplified version of the barrier protocol that belongs to the class $\mathcal{P}_{\text{conj\&bcast}}$.

In what follows, by $\mathcal{P}[\mathsf{d}]$ we denote guarded protocols from class $\mathcal{P}$ with exactly d process templates.

One can find two syntactically different forms of disjunctive guards in the literature. The first paper on guarded systems [Emerson and Namjoshi, 1996][1] introduces disjunctive guards as expressions $[\exists\,\mathsf{other}\ j]\,\phi(j)$, where $\phi(j)$ is a boolean formula over $\text{AP}_{\text{pr}} \times \{j\}$. Recall that in this book we consider $\phi(j)$ only in restricted form, namely, $\phi(j)$ is a disjunction over propositions from $\text{AP}_{\text{pr}} \times \{j\}$; cf. Emerson and Kahlon [2000, 2003a,b,c]. In fact, both definitions of guarded systems have the same expressive power. Indeed, every global state of a system instance is labeled with exactly one local state of every process, and thus it is easy to prove the following observation.

Observation 6.9   Consider a guarded d-ary system template $(P^1, \ldots, P^{\mathsf{d}})$. Let $\phi(j)$ be a boolean formula over $\text{AP}_{\text{pr}} \times \{j\}$. Then there exists a formula $\psi(j) = p_1 \vee \cdots \vee p_k$ with $\{p_1, \ldots, p_k\} \subseteq \text{AP}_{\text{pr}} \times \{j\}$ with the following property:

For every clique $\mathbf{C}(n)$, for every global state s of system instance $\overline{P}^{\mathbf{C}(n)}$, and for every process $v \in V(\mathbf{C}(n))$, it holds $\overline{P}^{\mathbf{C}(n)}, s \models \phi(v)$ if and only if $\overline{P}^{\mathbf{C}(n)}, s \models \psi(v)$ is true.

6.2.2   SPECIFICATIONS

Indexed formulas on guarded protocols restrict the scope of indexed variables to a single process template. Recall that the notation $\forall i\!:\!\text{type}(i) = \ell.\,\phi(i)$ denotes that i ranges only over the indices of processes instantiated from template P^ℓ.

In what follows, we consider several classes of specifications met in the literature.

- *Classes* 1-LTL\X$(P^\ell)$ and 1-ELTL\X$(P^\ell)$ contain *one-index* formulas over the atomic propositions of processes having the same fixed process template P^ℓ. If $\phi(i)$ is an $\{A, E\}$-free 1-CTL*\X path formula over $Q^\ell \times \{i\}$, then "$\forall i\!:\!\text{type}(i) = \ell.\,A\phi(i)$" and "$\forall i\!:\!\text{type}(i) = \ell.\,E\phi(i)$" are 1-LTL\X$(P^\ell)$ and 1-ELTL\X$(P^\ell)$ formulas, respectively.[2]

---

[1]We do not include the results by Emerson and Namjoshi [1996] in this book, as they consider synchronous systems, that is, the systems where all processes make a step at once.

[2]In the nonparameterized case, one can reduce the problem of checking an ELTL-formula $E\neg\psi$ on a Kripke structure M to $M \not\models A\psi$. This, however, does not work in the parameterized case: a straightforward negation of PMCP for 1-LTL\X$(P^\ell)$, that is, $\neg(\forall n \geq (1, \ldots, 1).\ \overline{P}^n \models \forall i\!:\!\text{type}(i) = \ell.\,A\phi(i))$ is not equivalent to PMCP for 1-ELTL\X$(P^\ell)$, that is, $\forall n \geq (1, \ldots, 1).\ \overline{P}^n \models \forall i\!:\!\text{type}(i) = \ell.\,E\neg\phi(i)$.

- *Classes* LTL(C) and LTL\X(C) contain LTL and LTL\X formulas, respectively, over the states of the sole controller process of type 1. This only process is created from a process template P^1 and is usually called the *controller*, while the other processes are created from a process template P^2 and are usually called the *users*. In what follows, we will use C to denote the controller process template P^1 and U to denote the user process template P^2. One can see LTL\X(C) as a subclass of 1-LTL\X(C), where the process type is compared to 1, that is, a specification is of the form $\forall i: \text{type}(i) = 1. \varphi(i)$, and there is only one process of type 1. The properties from these classes are also discussed in Section 5.

- *Classes* 2-LTL\X($P^\ell, P^{\ell'}$) and 2-ELTL\X($P^\ell, P^{\ell'}$) are similar to 1-LTL\X(P^ℓ) and 1-LTL\X(P^ℓ), but they contain *two–index* formulas over the states of processes created from process templates P^ℓ and $P^{\ell'}$. That is, the formulas have the form

  - $\forall i: \text{type}(i) = \ell. (\forall j: \text{type}(j) = \ell'. A\phi(i, j))$ or
  - $\forall i: \text{type}(i) = \ell. (\forall j: \text{type}(j) = \ell'. E\phi(i, j))$.

- *Classes* Reg(A) and ωReg(A) are regular and ω-regular languages over actions Σ_{int} as defined in Section 2.4.2.

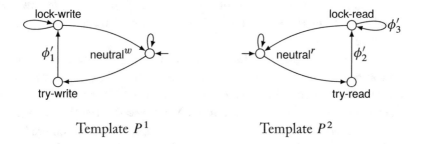

Template P^1 Template P^2

Figure 6.7: Another modeling of multiple readers/single writer protocol using two process templates: template P^1 models a writer in the system; template P^2 models a reader in the system. The guards ϕ'_1, ϕ'_2, and ϕ'_3 are defined in Equations 6.5–6.7. The guards of unlabeled edges are equal to true, and the actions of unlabeled edges are equal to τ.

Example 6.10 Consider the guarded protocol shown in Figure 6.4.

The specification $\forall i: \text{type}(i) = 1. AG(\text{try-write}_i \rightarrow F(\text{lock-write}_i \vee \text{neutral}_i))$ states that in every execution, every process that is trying to obtain the write lock will eventually do so, or will fall back to the state neutral. This specification belongs to the class 1-LTL\X(P^1).

The specification $\forall i: \text{type}(i) = 1. EG(\text{try-write}_i \rightarrow F \text{lock-write}_i)$ states that there is at least one execution, where every process that is trying to obtain the write lock will do so. This specification belongs to the class 1-ELTL\X(P^1). The specification $(\rho \tau^* \upsilon)^*$ states that locking action ρ

and unlocking action υ alternate; the specification belongs to the class Reg(A). Similarly, the specification $(\rho \tau^* \upsilon)^\omega$ states that locking and unlocking actions alternate infinitely often; it belongs to the class ωReg(A).

Example 6.11   Consider the guarded protocol shown in Figure 6.7. The guards ϕ_1', ϕ_2', and ϕ_3' are defined as follows:

$$\phi_1' \equiv [\forall \text{ other } j] \text{ neutral}_j^r \vee \text{neutral}_j^w \vee \text{try-read}_j \vee \text{try-write}_j \tag{6.5}$$
$$\phi_2' \equiv [\forall \text{ other } j] \text{ neutral}_j^r \vee \text{neutral}_j^w \vee \text{try-read}_j \vee \text{lock-read}_j \tag{6.6}$$
$$\phi_3' \equiv [\forall \text{ other } j] \text{ neutral}_j^r \vee \text{neutral}_j^w \vee \text{try-read}_j \vee \text{lock-read}_j \tag{6.7}$$

The specification $\forall i : \text{type}(i) = 1. \; (\forall j : \text{type}(j) = 2. \; \text{AG}(\neg\text{lock-write}_i \vee \neg\text{lock-read}_j))$ states that in every execution, no reader and writer can lock the critical section simultaneously. This specification belongs to the class 2-LTL$\backslash$X(P^1, P^2).

The specification $\forall i : \text{type}(i) = 1. \; (\forall j : \text{type}(j) = 2. \; \text{EG}((\text{try-write}_i \wedge \text{lock-read}_j) \rightarrow \text{lock-write}_i))$ states that there is an execution, in which a writer eventually obtains the lock, when a reader holds a lock. This specification belongs to the class 2-ELTL$\backslash$X(P^1, P^2).

Example 6.12   Consider the guarded protocol shown in Figure 6.7. Denote with C process template P^1 and with U process template P^2. Further, assume that every system instance contains exactly one instance of P^1.

The specification G(try-write $\rightarrow$ F lock-write) states that in every execution, the controller—the only writer in the system—eventually obtains the write lock, whenever it tries to enter the critical section. This specification belongs to the classes LTL$\backslash$X(C) and LTL(C).

The specification G(try-write $\rightarrow$ X (lock-write $\vee$ X lock-write)) states that in every execution the controller obtains the write lock in at most two system steps, after it has entered the state try-write (this specification is violated on a system instance with at least three readers). This specification belongs to the class LTL(C), but not to the class LTL$\backslash$X(C).

6.3   UNDECIDABILITY: BOOLEAN AND CONJUNCTIVE GUARDS

We start by showing that PMCP with boolean guarded protocols is undecidable in Theorem 6.13. For conjunctive guarded protocols, we review results from Emerson and Kahlon [2003b, Propositions 3.1, 3.2, 3.3] that show that PMCP is undecidable for Reg(A), ωReg(A), and LTL(C). We will see that the same proofs apply to the class $\mathcal{P}_{\text{init-conj}}$.

Theorem 6.13   PMCP$(\mathcal{P}_{\text{bool}}, \mathbf{C}, \text{LTL}(C))$ *is undecidable. The non–halting problem for two–counter machines can be reduced to* PMCP$(\mathcal{P}_{\text{bool}}, \mathbf{C}, \{\text{G}\neg\text{halt}_C\})$ *with* d $= 2$, *where* halt$_C$ *is a local state of the controller* C.

Proof. This proof is based on the idea mentioned by Emerson and Namjoshi [1996] in the conclusions.

Recall the notation from Section 3.1. Let $\mathcal{M}$ be a 2CM with locations $[m]$, the initial state 1, the halting state m, and a set of commands $\Delta \subseteq [m] \times \mathcal{A} \times [m]$. We denote the two counters of M by A and B. Given such a machine, we construct two process templates: Template C for the coordinator emulating the control flow of Δ; Template U for the user processes. Each user process is either storing a single unary digit of A or B, or staying in the standby state $init_U$. Given $N \geq 1$, the system $(C, U)^{C(2N+1)}$ simulates at least N steps of $\mathcal{M}$.

The construction ensures that whenever the controller of type C begins to execute a command a, exactly one user process of type U performs a unary increment or decrement as prescribed by a. This is ensured by the controller and the user processes using conjunctive and disjunctive guards as follows.

- Using either a conjunctive or a disjunctive guard, the controller tests the counters for zero by observing the local states of the user processes.

- The controller tests with a disjunctive guard, whether at least one user process heard the command by C and started to execute it.

- A user process tests with a conjunctive guard that no other user process has started to execute the command issued by the controller.

We construct template C such that it has three kinds of states.

- The initial state $init_C$.

- A state $i \in [m]$ for each location i of the counter machine.

- A state $\langle i, a, i' \rangle$ representing a transition $(i, a, i') \in \Delta$. We need this state to record that the machine is in the middle of executing a command $a \in \{inc(A), dec(A), inc(B), dec(B)\}$. When C moves from $\langle i, a, i' \rangle$, the system has finished to simulate the command a at location i and is continuing with the command at location i'.

Template U has the following states.

- The initial state $init_U$, where the process contributes neither to A, nor to B.

- Storage states A_1 and B_1 reflecting that the process contributes a unary 1 to A and B, respectively.

- Temporary states A_{01} and B_{01} meaning that the process is in the middle of adding a unary 1 to A or B, respectively.

- Temporary states A_{10} and B_{10} meaning that the process is in the middle of subtracting a unary 1 from A or B, respectively.

Table 6.2: The guards of the transitions that simulate the commands over counter A. The sets Δ_A^+ and Δ_A^- are defined as follows: $\Delta_A^+ = \{(i,a,i') \in \Delta \mid a = inc(A)\}$ and $\Delta_A^- = \{(i,a,i') \in \Delta \mid a = dec(A)\}$. To obtain the case for B, swap A and B

C's transition	Guard
$(init_C, \tau, 1)$	$[\forall \text{ other } j]\, init_U$
$(i, inc(A), \langle i, inc(A), i'\rangle)$	$[\forall \text{ other } j]\, init_U \vee A_1 \vee B_1$
$(i, dec(A), \langle i, dec(A), i'\rangle)$	$[\forall \text{ other } j]\, init_U \vee A_1 \vee B_1$
$(\langle i, inc(A), i'\rangle, end(A), i')$	$[\exists \text{ other } j]\, A_{01}$
$(\langle i, dec(A), i'\rangle, end(A), i')$	$[\exists \text{ other } j]\, A_{10}$
$(i, zero(A), i')$	$[\forall \text{ other } j]\, init_U \vee B_1$
U's transition	**Guard**
$(init_U, inc(A), A_{01})$	$[\forall \text{ other } j]\, init_U \vee A_1 \vee B_1 \vee \bigvee\limits_{t \in \Delta_A^+} \langle t\rangle$
(A_{01}, τ, A_1)	$[\forall \text{ other } j]\, init_U \vee A_1 \vee B_1 \vee \bigvee\limits_{k=1}^{m} k$
$(A_1, dec(A), A_{10})$	$[\forall \text{ other } j]\, init_U \vee A_1 \vee B_1 \vee \bigvee\limits_{t \in \Delta_A^-} \langle t\rangle$
$(A_{10}, \tau, init_U)$	$[\forall \text{ other } j]\, init_U \vee A_1 \vee B_1 \vee \bigvee\limits_{k=1}^{m} k$

Figure 6.8 depicts the transitions of template C, and Figure 6.9 depicts the transitions of template U. Table 6.2 assigns the guards to the transitions of C and U.

When a user process observes at least one process at state $\langle i, a, i'\rangle$—this can be only the controller—it starts to execute the command a by moving to one of temporary states $\{A_{01}, A_{10}, B_{01}, B_{10}\}$. After that the controller waits until one of U's leaves its intermediate state. To prevent several user processes from executing the same command, the transition guards ensure that no other user process has started to execute the command. For instance, two user processes cannot both move to A_{01} after seeing $\langle i, inc(A), i'\rangle$, because as soon as the first of them moved to A_{01}, the guard of the second process becomes false, as the first process violates $[\forall \text{ other } j]\, init_U \vee A_1 \vee B_1 \vee \bigvee_{(i,inc(A),i')\in\Delta} \langle i, inc(A), i'\rangle$. Note that we are exploiting the interleaving semantics in this argument.

Given $N \geq 1$, the system instance of $2N$ processes of type U and one process of type C simulates at least N steps of the two counter machine $\mathcal{M}$. By identifying proposition $halt_C$ with the state m of the controller, we specify the non-halting property as $G\neg m$ over the state of C. As we have encoded the undecidable non-halting problem of an arbitrary two-counter machine $\mathcal{M}$ as $\mathsf{PMCP}(\{C, U\}, \mathbf{C}, (G\neg m))$, we have proven the claim. $\square$

From Theorem 6.13, we know that $\mathsf{PMCP}(\mathcal{P}_{\mathsf{bool}}, \mathbf{C}, \mathsf{LTL}(C))$ is undecidable. So, we immediately have undecidability for the following specification classes.

- As the LTL-formula in the proof does not use the next-time operator X, the proof applies to LTL\X(C) without modification.

- As LTL\X(C) is subclass of 2-LTL\X($P^\ell, P^{\ell'}$), the proof applies to 2-LTL\X($P^\ell, P^{\ell'}$) and 2-ELTL\X($P^\ell, P^{\ell'}$) as well.

- One can encode a non-deterministic choice whether a process takes the role of the controller or the user. Using conjunctive guards one assures that the first process to take a step becomes the controller, and all other processes become user processes. Then Theorem 6.13 applies to 1-LTL\X(P^ℓ) and 1-ELTL\X(P^ℓ).

Corollary 6.14   PMCP($\mathcal{P}_{bool}, \mathbf{C}, \mathcal{F}$) *is undecidable for every specification class $\mathcal{F}$ from the list:* LTL\X*(C)*, LTL*(C)*, 1-LTL\X(P^ℓ), 1-ELTL\X(P^ℓ), 2-LTL\X($P^\ell, P^{\ell'}$), 2-ELTL\X($P^\ell, P^{\ell'}$).

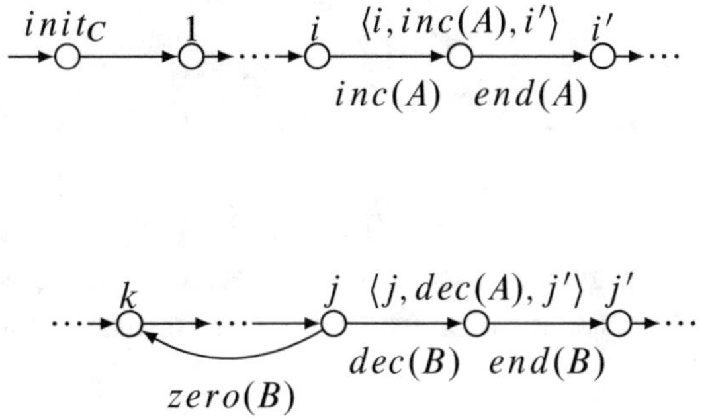

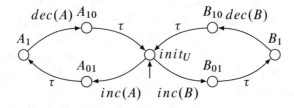

Figure 6.8: Template C simulating the control flow of a 2CM over counters A and B. The edges are labeled with actions; if an edge is not labeled, then the action is τ.

Figure 6.9: Template U of user processes that together simulate two integer counters A and B. An instance of U contributes a unary 1 to A (resp. B), when in A_1 (resp. in B_1). The edges are labeled with actions; if an edge is not labeled, then the action is τ.

We now turn our attention to conjunctive guards. The case of conjunctive guards is undecidable for LTL(C), as shown by Emerson and Kahlon [2003b, Propositions 3.1–3.2]. We re-use the

Table 6.3: The guards of the transitions simulating the 2CM's commands labeled with actions $a \in \{inc(A), dec(A)\}$ and $zero(A)$. To obtain the case for B, swap A and B

C's transition	Guard
$(init_C, \tau, 1)$	$[\forall \text{ other } j]\, init_U$
$(i, a, \langle i, a, i' \rangle)$	$[\forall \text{ other } j]\, init_U \vee A_1 \vee B_1$
$(\langle i, a, i' \rangle, end(A), i')$	$true$
$(i, zero(A), i')$	$[\forall \text{ other } j]\, init_U \vee B_1$
U's transition	**Guard**
$(init_U, inc(A), A_{01})$	$[\forall \text{ other } j]\, init_U \vee A_1 \vee B_1 \vee \bigvee\limits_{t \in \Delta_A^+} \langle t \rangle$
$(A_1, dec(A), A_{10})$	$[\forall \text{ other } j]\, init_U \vee A_1 \vee B_1 \vee \bigvee\limits_{t \in \Delta_A^-} \langle t \rangle$
(A_{01}, τ, A_1)	$[\forall \text{ other } j]\, init_U \vee A_1 \vee B_1 \vee \bigvee\limits_{k=1}^{m} k$
$(A_{10}, \tau, init_U)$	$[\forall \text{ other } j]\, init_U \vee A_1 \vee B_1 \vee \bigvee\limits_{k=1}^{m} k$

construction of C and U from the proof of Theorem 6.13. As we cannot use disjunctive guards anymore, we replace several guards with $true$ as reflected in Table 6.3. Rather, we encode the interlocking behavior in the specification using the next-time operator X.

Theorem 6.15 $\mathsf{PMCP}(\mathcal{P}_{\text{conj}}, \mathbf{C}, \mathsf{LTL}(C))$ *is undecidable. The non–halting problem for two-counter machines can be reduced to* $\mathsf{PMCP}(\mathcal{P}_{\text{conj}}, \mathbf{C}, \{\mathsf{G}\neg halt_C\})$ *with* $\mathsf{d} = 2$, *where* $halt_C$ *is a local state of the controller C.*

Proof. We change the commands from Table 6.2 of the proof of Theorem 6.13, as shown in Table 6.3. The guards of the transitions $(\langle i, inc(A), i' \rangle, end(A), i')$ and $(\langle i, dec(A), i' \rangle, end(A), i')$ are replaced with $true$. With the new guards the reachability of location m in a family $\{(C, U)^{\mathbf{C}(1,n)}\}_{n \geq 1}$ does not simulate the two-counter machine anymore, as the process C may invoke $inc(A)$ and then immediately proceed to the next control location without waiting for a user process performing the operation. Indeed, the guard is $true$, so C can jump out of $\langle i, inc(A), i' \rangle$ earlier than it could with the disjunctive guards in Table 6.2. To deal with that issue, we only consider restricted runs. This can be done by constructing a specification that uses the X operator, and is thus represented with $\mathsf{LTL}(C)$ instead of $\mathsf{LTL}\backslash \mathsf{X}(C)$. Formally, given an action $a \in \{inc(A), dec(A), dec(B), dec(B)\}$ of the counter machine, we introduce an LTL formula $yield_a$:

$$yield_a = \mathsf{G} \left(\bigwedge_{(i, a, i') \in \Delta} \left((\neg \langle i, a, i' \rangle \wedge \mathsf{X} \langle i, a, i' \rangle) \to \mathsf{XX} \langle i, a, i' \rangle \right) \right).$$

Observe that in runs in which $yield_{inc(A)}$ holds, C cannot make the next step immediately after going to $\langle i, inc(A), i' \rangle$. As a consequence, the formula can be used to filter out only the executions, where a process of type U makes a step right after C moved to $\langle i, inc(A), i' \rangle$.

Finally, the $yield_a$ formulas are combined with the non-halting property. Thus, we arrive at the parameterized model checking problem, where a system instance with $2N$ user processes is simulating at least N steps of the two counter machine $\mathcal{M}$:

$$\forall n \geq 1. (C, U)^{\mathbf{C}(1,n)} \models \left(yield_{inc(A)} \wedge yield_{inc(B)} \wedge yield_{dec(A)} \wedge yield_{dec(B)} \right) \rightarrow \mathsf{G}(\neg halt_C).$$

As this problem is an instance of $\mathsf{PMCP}(\mathcal{P}_{\text{conj}}, \mathbf{C}, \mathsf{LTL}(C))$, we conclude that the latter is undecidable.

Note carefully that the constructed specification is not a safety property, as its negated normal form is using temporal operators G and F. $\square$

In fact, the guarded protocol constructed in the proof of Theorem 6.15 uses only init-conjunctive guards, that is, all the guards in Table 6.3 contain $init_U$. Thus, we immediately arrive at the conclusion that PMCP is undecidable for $\mathcal{P}_{\text{init-conj}}$, which is a subclass of $\mathcal{P}_{\text{conj}}$:

Corollary 6.16   *The problem* $\mathsf{PMCP}(\mathcal{P}_{\text{init-conj}}, \mathbf{C}, \mathsf{LTL}(C))$ *is undecidable.*

As noted by Emerson and Kahlon [2003b, Proposition 3.3], the proof of Theorem 6.15 can be also applied to regular and ω-regular action-based specifications.

Theorem 6.17 $\mathsf{PMCP}(\mathcal{P}_{\text{conj}}, \mathbf{C}, \mathsf{Reg}(A))$ *and* $\mathsf{PMCP}(\mathcal{P}_{\text{conj}}, \mathbf{C}, \omega\mathsf{Reg}(A))$ *are undecidable.*

Proof. We re-use the proof from Theorem 6.15, except that the *yield* constraints have to be expressed as a regular language over actions, rather than an LTL formula. We show how to express $yield_{inc(A)}$ and $yield_{dec(A)}$; the formulas for B are obtained similarly.

Let letter i denote an action $inc(A)$ or $dec(A)$ of C, letter e denote the action $end(A)$, and expression X be the regular expression that recognizes the complement $\Sigma_{pr} \setminus \{i, e\}$ of i and e. Then $yield_i$ can be written as the following regular expression:

$$yield_i = (i\, i\, e \mid X)^*.$$

As the parameterized model checking problem is undecidable for regular properties, so it is for ω-regular properties. $\square$

6.4   DECIDABILITY: INIT-CONJUNCTIVE AND DISJUNCTIVE GUARDS

In contrast to the classes of boolean and conjunctive guards of the previous section, the PMCP over indexed LTL\X formulas and LTL\X(C) is decidable for the classes of init-conjunctive and disjunctive guards [Emerson and Kahlon, 2000]. In this section, we present the results from a

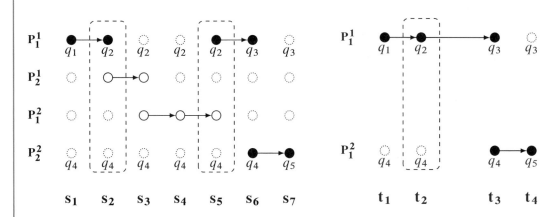

Figure 6.10: Illustration of path reduction. Processes 1 and 4 of $(P^1, P^2)^{(2,2)}$ are projected onto Processes 1 and 2 of $(P^1, P^2)^{(1,1)}$ using $pr_{idx} : \{1 \mapsto 1, 4 \mapsto 2\}$. Thus, the run $s_1 \ldots s_7$ becomes the sequence $t_1 \ldots t_4$ by collapsing $s_2 \ldots s_5$ to t_2 and hiding the local states of processes 2 and 3 on the left. Observe that $t_1 = pr_{st}(s_1)$ and $t_4 = pr_{st}(s_7)$.

slightly different angle than the original work by Emerson and Kahlon [2000]: we give a general proof schema that structures cutoff proofs for the disjunctive and init-conjunctive guards; and we explain why both types of guards preserve their satisfiability when the system has "enough" processes. We have to pay attention to deadlocked computations in all cases. Here, we give the proofs of the cutoff results as instances of two general proof schemas: namely, *bounding* shows how to reduce a run in a "large" system to a run in "small" cutoff system; *monotonicity* constructs an equivalent run (a term we make precise later) of a large system from a run of a small system. Together, bounding and monotonicity prove equivalence of large systems to the cutoff system with respect to the formulas from 1-LTL\X, 1-ELTL\X(P^ℓ), and LTL\X(C).

6.4.1   PRELIMINARIES

We start with the ingredients of the schemas: the counting function, path reduction, and symmetry argument.

Counting function.   Given a system instance $(P^1, P^2)^{C(n_1, n_2)}$ with the set of global states S, we define the *counting function* $\kappa : S \times (Q^1 \cup Q^2) \to \mathbb{N}_0$. For every global state $s \in S$ and a local state $q \in Q^1 \cup Q^2$, the number of times q occurs in s is given by $\kappa(s, q)$. When it is clear from context, we apply the same symbol κ to different system instances.

Path reduction.   Intuitively, given a path (a sequence of global states) in a large system, we project the global states onto a subset of the processes. Steps in the original path performed by the processes that are not in the subset result in stuttering in the projection. In path reduction we remove stuttering that is due to this effect. See Figure 6.10 for an illustration.

Formally, consider two system instances $(P^1, P^2)^{\mathbf{C}(n_1, n_2)}$ and $(P^1, P^2)^{\mathbf{C}(m_1, m_2)}$ with $n_1 \geq m_1$ and $n_2 \geq m_2$. An *index projection* is a bijective partial function pr_{idx} from $V(\mathbf{C}(n_1, n_2))$ to $V(\mathbf{C}(m_1, m_2))$. For $v \in V(\mathbf{C}(n_1, n_2))$, we write $pr_{idx}(v) = \bot$ to denote that pr_{idx} is undefined on v. Using pr_{idx}, we define a state projection pr_{st}. Namely, given a state s of $(P^1, P^2)^{\mathbf{C}(n_1, n_2)}$, state $t = pr_{st}(s)$ of $(P^1, P^2)^{\mathbf{C}(m_1, m_2)}$ is defined as follows: For every $i \in \mathbf{I}((n_1, n_2))$, if $pr_{idx}(i) \neq \bot$, then the local state $t(pr_{idx}(i))$ is defined as $s(i)$.

Given the functions pr_{idx} and pr_{st}, we define a function pr_{path} that maps a run $\pi = s_1 s_2 \ldots$ of $(P^1, P^2)^{\mathbf{C}(n_1, n_2)}$ to a sequence of states of $(P^1, P^2)^{\mathbf{C}(m_1, m_2)}$. Note that it is part of the framework to prove that the latter sequence is actually a run. To this end, we partition π into (finitely or infinitely many) paths $\Pi_1, \Pi_2, \ldots$ with the following properties for every $k \geq 1$.

- The last state of Π_k and the first state of Π_{k+1} form a transition of a process whose index i satisfies $i \in \mathbf{I}((n_1, n_2))$ and $pr_{idx}(i) \neq \bot$.

- Every pair of successive states in Π_k forms a transition of a process whose index i satisfies $i \in \mathbf{I}((n_1, n_2))$ and $pr_{idx}(i) = \bot$.

Let $s_{j(1)} s_{j(2)} \ldots$ be the sequence of the first states of $\Pi_1, \Pi_2, \ldots$. Then $pr_{path}(\pi)$ is defined as follows.

- If the sequence $\Pi_1 \Pi_2 \ldots$ is infinite, then $pr_{path}(\pi) = pr_{st}(s_{j(1)}) pr_{st}(s_{j(2)}) \ldots$.

- If the sequence $\Pi_1 \Pi_2 \ldots$ has length k, then $pr_{path}(\pi) = pr_{st}(s_{j(1)}) pr_{st}(s_{j(2)}) \ldots pr_{st}(s_{j(k)}) (pr_{st}(s_{j(k)}))^{\omega}$.

Given a path π, $pr_{path}(\pi)$ is a sequence, not necessarily a run. As pr_{st} and pr_{path} remove processes, the sequence $pr_{path}(\pi)$ is not immediately a path of $(P^1, P^2)^{\mathbf{C}(m_1, m_2)}$. The partitioning of $pr_{path}(\pi)$ implies that $pr_{path}(\pi)$ is *stuttering equivalent* to π; a state s_i of $pr_{path}(\pi)$ forms its own partition that is equivalent to partition Π_i. Similarly to [Baier and Katoen, 2008, Theorem 7.92], one can prove the following.

Observation 6.18   Let $(P^1, P^2)^{\mathbf{C}(n_1, n_2)}$ and $(P^1, P^2)^{\mathbf{C}(m_1, m_2)}$ be two system instances of a guarded protocol (P^1, P^2) such that $n_2 \geq m_2$ and $n_1 \geq m_1$. Let pr_{idx} be an index projection from $\mathbf{C}(n_1, n_2)$ to $\mathbf{C}(m_1, m_2)$ and $c \in V(\mathbf{C}(n_1, n_2))$ a process index.

Consider an LTL\X-formula φ over atomic propositions $Q^{\text{type}(c)} \times \{c\}$ and an LTL\X-formula φ' that is the result of substitution of c with $pr_{idx}(c)$. For each run π of $(P^1, P^2)^{\mathbf{C}(n_1, n_2)}$, the following holds:

$(P^1, P^2)^{\mathbf{C}(n_1, n_2)}, \pi \models \varphi$ if and only if $(P^1, P^2)^{\mathbf{C}(m_1, m_2)}, pr_{path}(\pi) \models \varphi'$.

Of course, we are interested only in an index projection pr_{idx} that actually generates runs, that is, it turns every run π of $(P^1, P^2)^{\mathbf{C}(n_1, n_2)}$ into a *run* $pr_{path}(\pi)$ of $(P^1, P^2)^{\mathbf{C}(m_1, m_2)}$. We call such a projection a *proper index projection*.

An index projection removes processes, and thus it cannot increase the number of processes in a local state. This intuition is formulated in the following proposition, which is easy to prove.

Proposition 6.19   *Let $(P^1, P^2)^{\mathbf{C}(n_1, n_2)}$ be a system instance with the set of global states S and pr_{idx} an index projection. For every global state $s \in S$ and every local state $q \in Q^1 \cup Q^2$, it holds that $\kappa(s, q) \geq \kappa(pr_{st}(s), q)$.*

Symmetry argument.   Similarly to parameterized token rings (cf. Emerson and Namjoshi [1995]), it was noticed by Emerson and Kahlon [2000] that model checking of a guarded protocol with a fixed number of processes against a formula from 1-ELTL\X(P^ℓ) or 1-LTL\X(P^ℓ) can be reduced to model checking against an ELTL\X formula over the states of a fixed process:

Observation 6.20
For a system instance $(P^1, P^2)^{\mathbf{C}(m_1, m_2)}$ of a guarded protocol, process type $\ell \in \{1, 2\}$, index c of a process of type ℓ, and an indexed $\{A, E, X\}$-free path formula $\varphi(i)$, the following holds.

1. $(P^1, P^2)^{\mathbf{C}(m_1, m_2)} \models \forall i : \text{type}(i) = \ell. \; E\varphi(i)$ if and only if $(P^1, P^2)^{\mathbf{C}(m_1, m_2)} \models E\varphi(c)$.

2. $(P^1, P^2)^{\mathbf{C}(m_1, m_2)} \models \forall i : \text{type}(i) = \ell. \; A\varphi(i)$ if and only if $(P^1, P^2)^{\mathbf{C}(m_1, m_2)} \not\models E\neg\varphi(c)$.

When having guarded protocols with one controller C and many user processes U, Observation 6.20(2) leads to the following corollary.

Corollary 6.21
For a system instance $(C, U)^{\mathbf{C}(1, m_2)}$ of a guarded protocol (C, U), and an $\{A, E, X\}$-free path formula φ over the states of controller C, the following holds: $(C, U)^{\mathbf{C}(1, m_2)} \models A\varphi$ if and only if $(C, U)^{\mathbf{C}(1, m_2)} \not\models E\neg\varphi$.

6.4.2   PROOF SCHEMAS

Based on counting function, path reduction, and symmetry argument, we can define the two proof schemas that are used to prove cutoff results for disjunctive and init-conjunctive guards.

Bounding schema

i. Estimate the cutoff size (c_1, c_2) based on the number of local states in P^1 and P^2 and the types of guards (disjunctive, init-conjunctive). Typically, one gives an arithmetic expression for c_1 and c_2 over $|Q^1|$ and $|Q^2|$, respectively. Fix system size $(n_1, n_2) \geq (c_1, c_2)$ and an arbitrary run $\pi = s_1 s_2 \ldots$ of $(P^1, P^2)^{\mathbf{C}(n_1, n_2)}$, which we use in the rest of the proof. In case of disjunctive guards, we require an intermediate step and π actually is a representative run with a special structure.

ii. Based on point (i), construct an index projection pr_{idx} from $\mathbf{C}(n_1, n_2)$ to $\mathbf{C}(c_1, c_2)$. This leads to the mapping pr_{path}, as discussed in the path reduction.

iii. Show that the guards of π are not locked in $pr_{path}(\pi)$. From this follows that the pairs of consecutive states in $pr_{path}(\pi)$ form a transition, and thus that the sequence $pr_{path}(\pi)$ is a path of $(P^1, P^2)^{\mathbf{C}(c_1,c_2)}$. If π is a deadlocked run, then prove that $pr_{path}(\pi)$ is also a deadlocked run.

This actually constitutes the core of the proof. One shows that if a guard evaluates to true in a state s of $(P^1, P^2)^{\mathbf{C}(n_1,n_2)}$, then it is also true in state $pr_{st}(s)$ of $(P^1, P^2)^{\mathbf{C}(c_1,c_2)}$. Typically, if one underestimates (c_1, c_2) at point (i), then the proof breaks at this point.

iv. Apply Observation 6.18 to conclude that for every index k with $pr_{idx}(k) \neq \perp$ it holds that $(P^1, P^2)^{\mathbf{C}(n_1,n_2)} \models \mathrm{E}\varphi(k)$ implies $(P^1, P^2)^{\mathbf{C}(c_1,c_2)} \models \mathrm{E}\varphi(pr_{idx}(k))$.

Monotonicity schema

i. Fix system sizes (m_1, m_2) and $(m_1 + d_1, m_2 + d_2)$ with $d_1 + d_2 = 1$ and $d_1, d_2 \in \{0, 1\}$. Pick an arbitrary run $\pi = t_1 t_2 \ldots$ of $(P^1, P^2)^{\mathbf{C}(m_1,m_2)}$. The goal of the next steps is to construct a corresponding run σ of system instance $(P^1, P^2)^{\mathbf{C}(m_1+d_1,m_2+d_2)}$.

ii. Construct a sequence $\sigma = s_1 s_2 \ldots$ of global states of $(P^1, P^2)^{\mathbf{C}(m_1+d_1,m_2+d_2)}$ by mapping every pair of states (t_i, t_{i+1}) of π on a sequence of states in $(P^1, P^2)^{\mathbf{C}(m_1+d_1,m_2+d_2)}$. Typically, the pair of states is replaced by one or two transitions that mimic (t_i, t_{i+1}).

iii. Show that the guards of the transitions in σ evaluate to true. Thus, the pairs of consecutive states in σ form a transition, and the sequence σ is a run of $(P^1, P^2)^{\mathbf{C}(m_1+d_1,m_2+d_2)}$. If π is a deadlocked run, then prove that σ is also a deadlocked run.

iv. Construct an index mapping pr_{idx} from $\mathbf{C}(m_1 + d_1, m_2 + d_2)$ to $\mathbf{C}(m_1, m_2)$ as follows: $pr_{idx}(m_1 + d_1 + m_2 + d_2) = \perp$; for all $i \leq m_1 + m_2$, $pr_{idx}(i) = i$. Conclude that $pr_{path}(\sigma) = \pi$.

v. From $pr_{path}(\sigma) = \pi$, conclude that for every index $k \leq m_1 + m_2$ it holds that $(P^1, P^2)^{\mathbf{C}(m_1,m_2)} \models \mathrm{E}\varphi(pr_{idx}(k))$ implies $(P^1, P^2)^{\mathbf{C}(m_1+d_1,m_2+d_2)} \models \mathrm{E}\varphi(k)$.

In the following sections, we instantiate the bounding and monotonicity proof schemas for init-conjunctive and disjunctive guards. Figures 6.11, 6.12, 6.13, 6.14, and 6.15 illustrate these proofs.

Cutoff argument.   Assume that the bounding schema works for a cutoff size (c_1, c_2). By applying inductively the monotonicity schema and Observation 6.20, we conclude that the following holds for every $n_1 \geq c_1$ and $n_2 \geq c_2$ and every formula ψ from 1-LTL\X and 1-ELTL\X:

$$(P^1, P^2)^{\mathbf{C}(n_1,n_2)} \models \psi \text{ if and only if } (P^1, P^2)^{\mathbf{C}(c_1,c_2)} \models \psi.$$

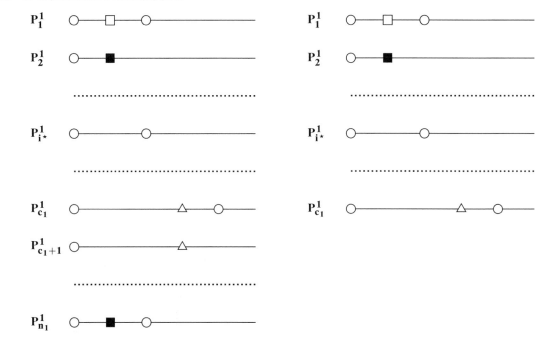

Figure 6.11: Illustration of the bounding schema for the init-conjunctive guards. For simplicity, we left out the processes instantiated from the template P^2. Local states of the processes are depicted with $\bigcirc$, $\square$, $\blacksquare$, and $\triangle$. The processes in the shaded area are hidden by the index projection function pr_{idx}, and thus only the processes $P_1^1, \ldots P_{c_1}^1$ are left after the bounding schema has been applied. The process $P_{i\star}^1$ makes infinitely many transitions, unless the original execution is deadlocked. (If the process $P_{i\star}^1$ has an index above c_1, we first apply the symmetry argument and swap it with an arbitrary process having an index below c_1, e.g., process P_2^1.)

6.4.3   INIT-CONJUNCTIVE GUARDS

Here we instantiate the bounding and monotonicity schemas to arrive at the following theorem for init-conjunctive guarded protocols [Emerson and Kahlon, 2000, Theorem 7].

Theorem 6.22

    For number $\ell \in \{1, 2\}$ and a specification class $\mathcal{F}$ from $1\text{-LTL}\backslash X(P^\ell)$, $1\text{-ELTL}\backslash X(P^\ell)$, or $\text{LTL}\backslash X(C)$, the problem $\text{PMCP}(\mathcal{P}_{\text{init-conj}}[2], \mathbf{C}, \mathcal{F})$ is decidable.

    Moreover, for every init-conjunctive guarded protocol (P^1, P^2), there exists a cutoff of size (c_1, c_2), that is for every formula $\varphi \in \mathcal{F}$, the following two statements are equivalent.

    1. *For every clique $\mathbf{C}(n_1, n_2)$ it holds $(P^1, P^2)^{\mathbf{C}(n_1, n_2)} \models \varphi$.*

    2. *For every clique $\mathbf{C}(m_1, m_2)$ with $m_1 \leq c_1$ and $m_2 \leq c_2$, it holds $(P^1, P^2)^{\mathbf{C}(m_1, m_2)} \models \varphi$.*

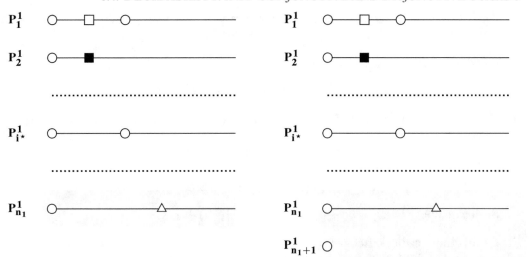

Figure 6.12: Illustration of the monononicity schema for init-conjunctive guards. For simplicity, we left out the processes instantiated from the template P^2. Local states of the processes are depicted with $\bigcirc$, $\square$, $\blacksquare$, and $\triangle$. The additional process $P^1_{n_1+1}$ never leaves the initial state $\bigcirc$.

The cutoff size is defined by $c_\ell = 2|Q^\ell| + 1$ and $c_{3-\ell} = 2|Q^{3-\ell}|$.

For the rest of the section, we fix a guarded protocol (P^1, P^2) with init-conjunctive guards and a $\{A, E, X\}$-free formula $\varphi(1)$ over the states of process 1. As in Theorem 6.22, we fix cutoff size to be $c_1 = 2|Q^1| + 1$ and $c_2 = 2|Q^2|$.

For bounding schema we consider two cases: (1) a run is free of deadlocks; and (2) a run has a deadlock.

(1) Bounding schema for deadlock-free runs:

  i. Let $\pi = s_1 s_2 \ldots$ be a deadlock-free run of $(P^1, P^2)^{\mathbf{C}(n_1, n_2)}$. This implies that there is a process that performs infinitely many steps in π. Let $i^\star$ be the index of such a process.

 ii. Construct an index projection pr_{idx} from $\mathbf{C}(n_1, n_2)$ to $\mathbf{C}(c_1, c_2)$ that has the following properties: (a) $pr_{idx}(1) = 1$; (b) $pr_{idx}(i^\star) \neq \bot$. Note carefully that by the definition of index projection, exactly $c_1 + c_2$ indices of $\mathbf{C}(n_1, n_2)$ are mapped on $\mathbf{C}(c_1, c_2)$.

iii. We have to show that for every $i \geq 1$, the guard of the transition from s_i to s_{i+1} is evaluated to true in $pr_{st}(s_i)$. Consider the transition from s_i to s_{i+1} made by process p. Let its guard g_i be $[\forall \text{ other } p]\ q_1 \vee \cdots \vee q_k$. As $s_i \models_p g_i$, all processes are in a state from $\{q_1, \ldots, q_k\}$, and for every $q \in Q^1 \cup Q^2 \setminus \{q_1, \ldots, q_k\}$ it holds that $\kappa(s_i, q) = 0$. Hence, from Proposition 6.19, it immediately follows that $\kappa(pr_{st}(s_i), q) = 0$. From the latter we conclude that $pr_{st}(s_i) \models_{pr_{idx}(p)} g_i$. Thus, $pr_{path}(\pi)$ constitutes a run of $(P^1, P^2)^{\mathbf{C}(c_1, c_2)}$.

iv. Apply Observation 6.18 to conclude that for every index k with $pr_{idx}(k) \neq \bot$ it holds that $(P^1, P^2)^{\mathbf{C}(n_1, n_2)} \models \mathrm{E}\varphi(k)$ implies $(P^1, P^2)^{\mathbf{C}(c_1, c_2)} \models \mathrm{E}\varphi(pr_{idx}(k))$.

(2) Bounding schema for deadlocked runs:

i. Let $\pi = s_1 s_2 \ldots s_d (s_d)^\omega$ be a deadlocked run of $(P^1, P^2)^{\mathbf{C}(n_1, n_2)}$.

ii. We construct an index projection pr_{idx} from $\mathbf{C}(n_1, n_2)$ to $\mathbf{C}(c_1, c_2)$ with the following properties:

- (a) $pr_{idx}(1) = 1$; and
- (b) for every $q \in Q^1 \cup Q^2$, $\kappa(pr_{st}(s_d), q) \geq min(\kappa(s_d, q), 2)$.

Such a mapping exists, as $c_1 + c_2 = 2 \cdot (|Q^1| + |Q^2|) + 1$.

iii. As in the deadlock-free case, for every $i \geq 1$ and every $q \in Q^1 \cup Q^2$, $\kappa(s_i, q) \geq \kappa(pr_{path}(s_i), q)$. It follows that for every $i : 1 \leq i < d$ and every process index $p : 1 \leq p \leq n_1 + n_2$, $s_i \models_p g_i \Rightarrow s_i \models_{pr_{idx}(p)} g_i$.

It remains to prove that $pr_{st}(s_d)$ is a deadlock state, that is, for every guard g and some process index p, it holds $s_d \not\models_p g \Rightarrow pr_{st}(s_d) \not\models_{pr_{idx}(p)} g$. Let us fix g to be $[\forall \text{ other } p] q_1 \vee \cdots \vee q_k$ and a process index p. As $s_d, p \not\models g$, there is a state $q \in Q^1 \cup Q^2 \setminus \{q_1, \ldots, q_k\}$ with the following properties:

- *(a)* if $s_d(p) = q$, then $\kappa(s_d, q) \geq 2$; and
- *(b)* if $s_d(p) \neq q$, then $\kappa(s_d, q) \geq 1$.

From point (ii) we have $\kappa(pr_{st}(s_d), q) \geq min(\kappa(s_d, q), 2)$. Hence, in case (a), we have $\kappa(pr_{st}(s_d), q) \geq 2$. In case (b), we have $\kappa(pr_{st}(s_d), q) \geq 1$. In both cases we conclude that $pr_{st}(s_d) \not\models_{pr_{idx}(p)} g$. Thus, $pr_{st}(s_d)$ is a deadlock state, as required.

iv. Apply Observation 6.18 to conclude that for every index k with $pr_{idx}(k) \neq \bot$ it holds that $(P^1, P^2)^{\mathbf{C}(n_1, n_2)} \models \mathrm{E}\varphi(k)$ implies $(P^1, P^2)^{\mathbf{C}(c_1, c_2)} \models \mathrm{E}\varphi(pr_{idx}(k))$.

Monotonicity schema:

i. Fix system sizes (m_1, m_2) and $(m_1 + d_1, m_2 + d_2)$ for $\ell \in \{1, 2\}$ and $d_1 = \ell \cdot (2 - \ell)$ and $d_2 = \ell \cdot (\ell - 1)$. Pick an arbitrary run $\pi = t_1 t_2 \ldots$ of $(P^1, P^2)^{\mathbf{C}(m_1, m_2)}$.

ii. Map every pair (t_i, t_{i+1}) on a pair (s_i, s_{i+1}), where for all $j : 1 \leq j \leq m_1 + m_2$, $s_i(j) = t_i(j)$, $s_{i+1}(j) = t_{i+1}(j)$ and $s_i(m_1 + m_2 + d_1 + d_2) = s_{i+1}(m_1 + m_2 + d_1 + d_2) = init^\ell$.

iii. We have to show that for every guard g, every process index p, and every $i \geq 1$, if $t_i \models_p g$, then $s_i \models_{pr_{idx}(p)} g$. This is immediate, as, by the definition, every init-conjunctive guard contains $init^\ell$, which is the only state the added process resides in.

iv. Construct an index mapping pr_{idx} from $\mathbf{C}(m_1 + d_1, m_2 + d_2)$ to $\mathbf{C}(m_1, m_2)$ as follows: $pr_{idx}(m_1 + d_1 + m_2 + d_2) = \bot$; for all $i \leq m_1 + m_2$, $pr_{idx}(i) = i$. Conclude that $pr_{path}(\sigma) = \pi$.

v. From $pr_{path}(\sigma) = \pi$, conclude that for every index $k \leq m_1 + m_2$ it holds that $(P^1, P^2)^{\mathbf{C}(m_1, m_2)} \models \mathbf{E}\varphi(pr_{idx}(k))$ implies $(P^1, P^2)^{\mathbf{C}(m_1 + d_1, m_2 + d_2)} \models \mathbf{E}\varphi(k)$.

Figure 6.11 illustrates the bounding schema, and Figure 6.12 illustrates the monotonicity schema.

By applying the bounding and monotonicity schemas, we finish the proof of Theorem 6.22.

Further Results.   As one can see from the proof of Theorem 6.22, if the system instances are deadlock-free, there is a trivial cutoff.

Theorem 6.23 [Emerson and Kahlon, 2000].   *Consider a guarded protocol $(P^1, \ldots, P^d)$ with conjunctive guards and a formula φ from 1-LTL\X(P^ℓ), 1-ELTL\X(P^ℓ), or LTL\X(C) for some $\ell \in [d]$. If every instance $(P^1, \ldots, P^d)^{\mathbf{C}(n)}$ does not have deadlocked runs, then there is a cutoff system of size $(1, \ldots, 1, 2, 1, \ldots, 1)$, i.e., the following two statements are equivalent.*

1. *For each $(n_1, \ldots, n_d) \geq (1, \ldots, 1)$, it holds $(P^1, \ldots, P^d)^{\mathbf{C}(n_1, \ldots, n_d)} \models \varphi$.*

2. *The cutoff instance of size $(c_1, \ldots, c_d)$, where $c_\ell = 2$ and $\forall k \neq \ell. c_k = 1$, satisfies the formula: $(P^1, \ldots, P^d)^{(c_1, \ldots, c_d)} \models \varphi$.*

A similar argument works for properties that require only finite paths, e.g., reachability and safety.

Theorem 6.24 [Emerson and Kahlon, 2000].   *Consider a d-ary conjuctive system template $(P^1, \ldots, P^d)$ and a formula φ from 1-LTL\X(P^ℓ), 1-ELTL\X(P^ℓ), or LTL\X(C) for some $\ell \in [d]$. If φ can be verified on finite computations, then the system of size $(1, \ldots, 1)$ is a cutoff: for each $(n_1, \ldots, n_d) \geq (1, \ldots, 1)$, it holds $(P^1, \ldots, P^d)^{\mathbf{C}(n_1, \ldots, n_d)} \models \varphi$ if and only if $(P^1, \ldots, P^d)^{\mathbf{C}(1, \ldots, 1)} \models \varphi$.*

6.4.4   DISJUNCTIVE GUARDS

Emerson and Kahlon [2000] obtained the following cutoff result for systems with disjunctive guards.

Theorem 6.25   *For number $\ell \in \{1, 2\}$ and a specification class $\mathcal{F}$ from 1-LTL\X(P^ℓ), 1-ELTL\X(P^ℓ), or LTL\X(C), the problem PMCP($\mathcal{P}_{disj}[2], \mathbf{C}, \mathcal{F}$) is decidable.*

Moreover, for every disjunctive guarded protocol (P^1, P^2), there exists a cutoff of size (c_1, c_2), that is for every formula $\varphi \in \mathcal{F}$, the following two statements are equivalent.

1. *For every clique $\mathbf{C}(n_1, n_2)$ it holds $(P^1, P^2)^{\mathbf{C}(n_1, n_2)} \models \varphi$.*

2. *For every clique* $\mathbf{C}(m_1, m_2)$ *with* $m_1 \leq c_1$ *and* $m_2 \leq c_2$, *it holds* $\overline{P}^{\mathbf{C}(m_1,m_2)} \models \varphi$.

The cutoff size is defined by $c_\ell = |Q^\ell| + 2$ *and* $c_{3-\ell} = |Q^{3-\ell}| + 1$.

To prove Theorem 6.25, we instantiate the bounding and monotonicity schemas. The most important part of the proof, however, is established in the "Unlocking" lemma that follows after the technical definition of a local computation of a process in a run of a system instance. In the following definition, we project a run on one process and remove stuttering introduced by the other processes.

Definition 6.26 Let $\pi = s_1, \ldots, s_k$ be a run of a guarded system instance $(P^1, P^2)^{\mathbf{C}(n_1,n_2)}$ and p be the index of a process of type $\ell \in \{1, 2\}$. Further, let $i(1), \ldots, i(m)$ be a sequence of numbers in $[k]$ with the following properties:

- $i(1) = 1$;

- for all $j : 1 \leq j < m, i(j) < i(j+1)$ and $(s_{i(j)}(p), s_{i(j+1)}(p)) \in \delta^\ell$; and

- for all $j : 1 \leq j < m$, for all $h : 1 \leq h < i(j)$, it holds $(s_{i(j)+h}(p), s_{i(j)+h+1}(p)) \notin \delta^\ell$.

We call the sequence $s_{i(1)}(p), \ldots, s_{i(m)}(p)$ a *local computation* of p in $s_1, \ldots, s_k$ and denote it as $(s_1, \ldots, s_k) \downarrow p$.

Definition 6.27 Let π be run $s_1 s_2 \ldots$ of a guarded instance $(P^1, P^2)^{\mathbf{C}(n_1,n_2)}$. We define the set of local reachable states as $Reach(\pi) = \{q \mid \exists i \geq 1, \exists p : 1 \leq p \leq n_1 + n_2. s_i(p) = q\}$.

In the following lemma, we assign a unique process to each local state from $Reach(\pi)$. That local state is called a *goal state*.

Lemma 6.28 Unlocking Let π be a run $s_1 s_2 \ldots$ of a guarded system instance $(P^1, P^2)^{\mathbf{C}(n_1,n_2)}$ that has only disjunctive guards. There exists a run π' of $(P^1, P^2)^{\mathbf{C}(n_1+|Q^1|,n_2+|Q^2|)}$ organized as follows: π' has a prefix, where each of the at most $|Q^1| + |Q^2|$ processes runs into its unique goal state from $Reach(\pi)$ and remains there; the prefix is followed by transitions of $n_1 + n_2$ processes as in π. The run π' is stuttering equivalent to π w.r.t. to $n_1 + n_2$ processes.

Proof. We construct π' and then exploit that the transitions have only disjunctive guards to show that π' is a run. To this end, for each $q \in Q^1 \cup Q^2$, we define the distance of q from the initial state in π as $dist(q) = min\{i \mid \exists p : 1 \leq p \leq n_1 + n_2, s_i(p) = q\}$, if $q \in Reach(\pi)$, and ∞ otherwise.

Let $q_1, \ldots, q_k$ be the sequence of all local states from $Reach(\pi)$, ordered with respect to $dist$. Due to interleaving semantics, only one process takes a step at a time. Hence, for every $q, q' \in Reach(\pi), q \neq q'$, it holds $dist(q) \neq dist(q')$. Due to this fact, we can define a function $first : Reach(\pi) \rightarrow [n_1 + n_2]$ that maps a reachable state q to the index of the process that performed the transition $dist(q)$. As all processes are initially either in $init^1$ or $init^2$, we define $first(init^1) = n_1$

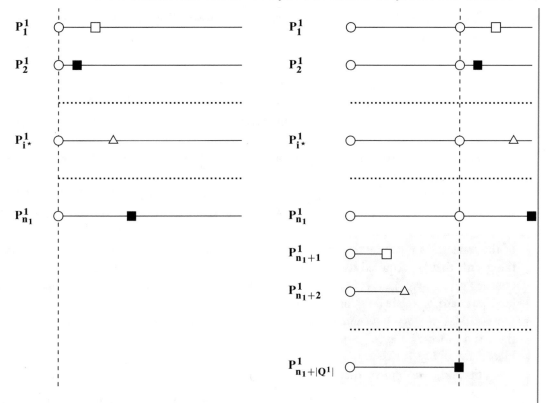

Figure 6.13: Illustration of the unlocking lemma (Lemma 6.28) for the disjunctive guards. For simplicity, we left out the processes instantiated from the template P^2. Local states of the processes are depicted with $\bigcirc$, $\square$, $\blacksquare$, and $\triangle$. The shaded area on the right highlights the processes added by the unlocking lemma. Each of these processes halts after reaching its designated state.

and $first(init^2) = n_2$. Note that $first$ does not have to be an injection, that is, it maps several local states to the index of the same process, if the process is the first one to visit these states.

We construct a set of local computations $\{\rho_i \mid 1 \le i \le k\}$ with $\rho_i = (s_1, \ldots, s_{dist(q_i)}) \downarrow first(q_i)$ for each $i : 1 \le i \le k$. Now we define a set of paths $\{y_1^i, \ldots, y_{|\rho_i|}^i \mid 1 \le i \le k\}$ that belong to the system instance $(P^1, P^2)^{C(n_1 + |Q^1|, n_2 + |Q^2|)}$. For each $i : 1 \le i \le k$, each $j : 1 \le j \le |\rho_i|$, and each process index $p : 1 \le p \le n_1 + |Q^1| + n_2 + |Q^2|$ we define a local state $y_j^i(p)$ of process p as follows:

$$y_j^i(p) = \begin{cases} \rho_i[j] & \text{if } p = n_1 + n_2 + i, 0 \le i \le |Reach(\pi)| \\ \rho_i[|\rho_{i'}|] & \text{if } dist(q_{i'}) < dist(q_i), p = n_1 + n_2 + i', 0 \le i' \le |Reach(\pi)| \\ init^{\text{type}(p)} & \text{otherwise.} \end{cases}$$

Then we extend the global states $s_1, s_2, \ldots$ with the halting states of the new $|Q^1| + |Q^2|$ processes, that is, for each $j \geq 1$:

$$
s'_j(p) = \begin{cases} s_j(p) & \text{if } p \leq n_1 + n_2 \\ \rho_i[|\rho_i|] & \text{if } p = n_1 + n_2 + i, 0 \leq i \leq |Reach(\pi)| \\ init^{\text{type}(p)} & \text{otherwise.} \end{cases}
$$

Finally, we construct a sequence π' as a $(y_1^1, \ldots, y_{|\rho_1|}^1), \ldots, (y_1^k, \ldots, y_{|\rho_k|}^k), s'_1, s'_2 \ldots$. Now we show that π' is actually a run.

First, we show that the suffix $s'_1, s'_2 \ldots$ forms a path of $(P^1, P^2)^{\mathbf{C}(n_1 + |Q^1|, n_2 + |Q^2|)}$. As the transitions have only disjunctive guards, and the states of the processes with indices below $n_1 + n_2$ remain as in π, the processes with the indices above $n_1 + n_2$ do not disable the guards of the transitions made by the processes with the indices below $n_1 + n_2$. On the contrary, all the guards that are required to fire the transitions of π become enabled after executing the sequence $(y_1^1, \ldots, y_{|\rho_1|}^1), \ldots, (y_1^k, \ldots, y_{|\rho_k|}^k)$. Formally, let $g \equiv [\exists \text{ other } j] \, q_1 \vee \cdots \vee q_m$ be a disjunctive guard, s_i a state on π, and $p \leq n_1 + n_2$ a process index such that $s_i \models_p g$. Then there is a process index $p' \leq n_1 + n_2$ and a local state $q \in \{q_1, \ldots, q_m\}$ with $s_i(p') = q$. As $q \in Reach(\pi)$, there is a process index $p'' > n_1 + n_2$ with $y_{n_k}^k(p'') = q$, moreover, for all $i \geq 1$, $s'_i(p'') = q$. Hence, for all $i \geq 1$, $s'_i \models_p g$.

Second, we prove that the prefix $(y_1^1, \ldots, y_{|\rho_1|}^1), \ldots, (y_1^k, \ldots, y_{|\rho_k|}^k)$ is a run of $(P^1, P^2)^{\mathbf{C}(n_1 + |Q^1|, n_2 + |Q^2|)}$. As we define each ρ_i as a local computation, the sequent states are related with δ^1 or δ^2. The guards in $y_1^i, \ldots, y_{|\rho_i|}^i$ are enabled, as we ordered $q_1, \ldots, q_k$ by $dist$, and π witnessed the shortest local computations $\rho_1, \ldots, \rho_k$, leading to the local states in $Reach(\pi)$.

The run $(y_1^1, \ldots, y_{|\rho_1|}^1), \ldots, (y_1^k, \ldots, y_{|\rho_k|}^k)$ does not change the local states of the processes with the indices below $n_1 + n_2$. Thus, π' is stuttering equivalent to π w.r.t. the indices below $n_1 + n_2$.

Hence, π' is the required run of $(P^1, P^2)^{\mathbf{C}(n_1 + |Q^1|, n_2 + |Q^2|)}$. □

Figure 6.13 illustrates application of the unlocking lemma.

We are now in the position to prove Theorem 6.25 according to the proof schema.

Bounding schema:

i. Let $\pi = s_1 s_2 \ldots$ be a run of $(P^1, P^2)^{\mathbf{C}(n_1, n_2)}$. If π is a deadlock-free run, then let $i^\star$ be the index of a process that fires infinitely many transitions in π, otherwise $i^\star$ is an arbitrary index different from 1. Construct a stuttering equivalent run π' of $(P^1, P^2)^{\mathbf{C}(n_1 + |Q^1|, n_2 + |Q^2|)}$ as stated in Lemma 6.28.

ii. Construct an index projection pr_{idx} from $\mathbf{C}(n_1 + |Q^1|, n_2 + |Q^2|)$ to $\mathbf{C}(c_1, c_2)$ as follows:

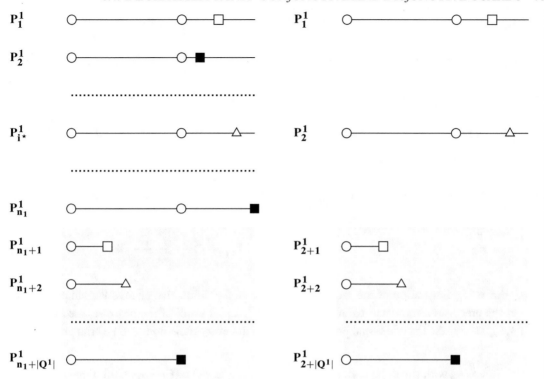

Figure 6.14: Illustration of the bounding schema applied together with the unlocking lemma (Lemma 6.28). For simplicity, we left out the processes instantiated from the template P^2. Local states of the processes are depicted with $\bigcirc$, $\square$, $\blacksquare$, and $\triangle$. Process P_1^1 is kept as is, because its behavior is observed by the specification. Process $P_{i^\star}^1$ is mapped to process P_2^1, as it makes infinitely many transitions (if the execution is deadlock-free). Every process $P_{n_1+i}^1$ is mapped to process P_{2+i}^1 for $1 \le i \le |Q^1|$.

$$pr_{idx}(i) = \begin{cases} 1 & \text{if } i = 1 \\ 2 & \text{if } i = i^\star \\ 2 + (i - (n_1 + n_2)) & \text{if } n_1 + n_2 < i \le n_1 + n_2 + |Q_1| + |Q_2| \\ \bot & \text{otherwise.} \end{cases}$$

iii. As we keep the processes with the indices above $n_1 + n_2$, and they fire transitions before the processes with the indices below $n_1 + n_2$, their guards remain enabled. The guards of the transitions by the processes with the indices 1 and $i^\star$ are enabled by the local states of the

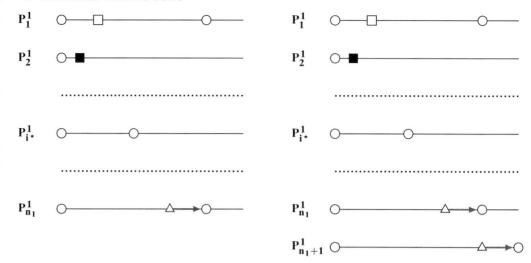

Figure 6.15: Illustration of the monononicity schema for disjunctive guards. For simplicity, we left out the processes instantiated from the template P^2. Local states of the processes are depicted with $\bigcirc, \square, \blacksquare$, and $\triangle$. The additional process $P^1_{n_1+1}$ mimics every transition made by the process $P^1_{n_1}$.

processes with the indices above $n_1 + n_2$, as constructed in Lemma 6.28. Hence, $pr_{path}(\pi')$ is a run of $(P^1, P^2)^{\mathbf{C}(c_1, c_2)}$.

iv. From stuttering equivalence of π and π' and Observation 6.18, we conclude that for every index k with $pr_{idx}(k) \neq \perp$ it holds that $(P^1, P^2)^{\mathbf{C}(n_1, n_2)} \models E\varphi(k)$ implies $(P^1, P^2)^{\mathbf{C}(c_1, c_2)} \models E\varphi(pr_{idx}(k))$.

Figure 6.14 illustrates application of the bounding schema together with the unlocking lemma.

Remark 6.29   In the proof of Lemma 6.28, we move specific processes to cover all states in *Reach*. Thus, if the run π has a deadlock state s_d, it might happen that s'_d is not a deadlock state. To repair this, similar to Unlocking lemma, one can introduce a suffix that moves the processes with indices above $n_1 + n_2$ out of $Reach(\pi) \setminus \{q \mid \exists p. \, s_d(p) = q\}$ states.

Monotonicity schema:

i. Fix system sizes (m_1, m_2) and $(m_1 + d_1, m_2 + d_2)$ with $d_1, d_2 \in \{0, 1\}$ and $d_1 + d_2 = 1$. Pick an arbitrary run $\pi = t_1 t_2 \ldots$ of $(P^1, P^2)^{\mathbf{C}(m_1, m_2)}$.

ii. By N we abbreviate the index $m_1 + m_2$. Then $N + 1 = m_1 + d_1 + m_2 + d_2$. Map every pair t_i, t_{i+1} as follows.

Case 1. If (t_i, t_{i+1}) is a transition by process with index N, then we map it on a triple s_i, s'_i, s_{i+1}, where $\forall p : 1 \leq p < m_1 + m_2$. $s_i(p) = t_i(p)$, $s'_i(p) = t_i(p)$, $s_{i+1}(p) = t_{i+1}(p)$ and $s_i(N) = t_i(N)$, $s'_i(N) = s_{i+1}(N) = t_{i+1}(N)$ and $s_i(N+1) = s'_i(N+1) = t_i(N)$, $s_{i+1}(N+1) = t_{i+1}(N+1)$. Informally, the process with index $N+1$ copies the transition of the process with index N.

Case 2. If (t_i, t_{i+1}) is a transition by process $p \neq N$, then we map it on a pair s_i, s_{i+1}, where $\forall p : 1 \leq p \geq m_1 + m_2$. $s_i(p) = t_i(p)$, $s_{i+1}(p) = t_{i+1}(p)$ and $s_i(N+1) = t_i(N)$, $s_{i+1}(N+1) = t_{i+1}(N)$.

iii. In case (ii.1), we have to show that for every guard g and every process index $p < m_1 + m_2$, if $t_i \models_p g$ holds then $s_i \models_p g$ and $s'_i \models_p g$ also hold. Let g be $[\exists \text{ other } q_1 \vee \cdots \vee q_k]$. From $t_i \models_p g$ we conclude that there is a process $p' \leq m_1 + m_2$ and $p' \neq p$ with $t_i(p') \in \{q_1, \ldots, q_k\}$. From (ii), $s_i(p') = s'_i(p') = t_i(p')$. Hence, $s_i \models_p g$ and $s'_i \models_p g$. In case (ii.2), we immediately obtain that guards are preserved in every state s_i.

iv. Apply Observation 6.18 to conclude that for every index k with $pr_{idx}(k) \neq \bot$ it holds that $(P^1, P^2)^{\mathbf{C}(m_1, m_2)} \models \mathrm{E}\varphi(pr_{idx}(k))$ implies $(P^1, P^2)^{\mathbf{C}(m_1 + d_1, m_2 + d_2)} \models \mathrm{E}\varphi(k)$.

Figure 6.15 illustrates application of the monotonicity schema.

The unlocking lemma, the bounding schema, and the monotonicity schema applied together finish the proof of Theorem 6.25.

Further Results.   Emerson and Kahlon [2000] also extended the cutoff result on two index specifications:

Theorem 6.30   *Let ℓ and ℓ' be process types and $\mathcal{F}$ be one of 2-LTL\X($P^\ell, P^{\ell'}$) and 2-ELTL\X($P^\ell, P^{\ell'}$). The problem* PMCP($\mathcal{P}_{\mathsf{disj}}, \mathbf{C}, \mathcal{F}$) *is decidable. Moreover, there is a cutoff of size $(c_1, \ldots, c_d)$, where $c_\ell = |Q^\ell| + 1$ and $c_{\ell'} = |Q^{\ell'}| + 1$ and for all other $k \in [d] \setminus \{\ell, \ell'\}$, $c_k = |Q^k|$.*

The estimates of cutoffs in Theorems 6.25 and 6.30 require model checking of quite large systems containing at least $|Q^\ell|$ processes of each type ℓ. Emerson and Kahlon [2000] gave an efficient solution for universal-path-quantified formulas. We do not give details here.

Emerson and Kahlon [2003b] noted that the PMC problem for protocols with disjunctive guards is decidable for regular and ω-regular properties over actions.

Theorem 6.31   PMCP($\mathcal{P}_{\mathsf{disj}}, \mathbf{C}, \mathcal{F}$) *is decidable for $\mathcal{F} = Reg(A)$ and $\mathcal{F} = \omega Reg(A)$.*

Proof Sketch.   The intuition is that the behavior of all the systems instantiated from a disjunctive system template $(P^1, \ldots, P^d)$ can be encoded as a Petri net $\mathcal{P}$. The language of $\mathcal{P}$ is checked for intersection with the specification, i.e., the language of either a Büchi automaton, or a finite automaton over actions. This problem is known to be decidable [Esparza and Nielsen, 1994, Theorem 8].

The constructed Petri net $\mathcal{P}$ has one place per local state from $Q^1 \cup \cdots \cup Q^d$; the number of tokens in a place q encodes the number of processes in local state q. If a process makes a transition from one local state to another, then the number of tokens in the source place and the target places are decremented and incremented, respectively. A disjunctive guard $[\exists$ other $i]\, q_1 \vee \cdots \vee q_k$ is then encoded as k transitions—one per local state q_i—fetching a token from q_i and then returning it back to q_i. $\square$

6.5   DISJUNCTIVE GUARDS VS. RENDEZVOUS

In this section we consider the relation between systems with disjunctive guards and pairwise rendezvous. We review results by Emerson and Kahlon [2003b] who showed that the systems with disjunctive guards and the systems with pairwise rendezvous are reducible to each other in the sense that the reduction preserves properties from Reg(A) and ωReg(A) (formally defined below).

For LTL$\backslash$X(C) properties, we show that the given reductions (designed for Reg(A) and ωReg(A)) work only in one direction: the provided reduction from disjunctive guards to pairwise rendezvous preserves LTL$\backslash$X(C) properties. However, for the other direction, the provided reduction from pairwise rendezvous to disjunctive guards is not conservative with respect to LTL$\backslash$X(C).

First, we introduce the notions of ξ-reducibility (Emerson and Kahlon [2003b] denoted it via $\prec_\phi$) and a special case of stuttering trace equivalence. Let us fix AP and two LTSs $M_i = (Q_i, Q_i^0, \Sigma_i, \delta_i, \lambda_i)$ for $i = 1, 2$. Furthermore, let $\xi : \Sigma_1 \to \Sigma_2^+$ be an action mapping; as common we extend ξ to a language $L \subseteq \Sigma_1^* \cup \Sigma_1^\omega$ as $\xi(L) = \{\xi(w) : w \in L\}$.

We say that M_1 is ξ-reducible to M_2 if for every regular language $L \subseteq \Sigma_1^*$ and every ω-regular language $L_\omega \subseteq \Sigma_1^\omega$ the following holds.

- Properties of *finite* action-labeled runs of M_1 and M_2 are indistingushable by L and $\xi(L)$, i.e., $\mathcal{L}(M_1) \cap L = \emptyset$ iff $\mathcal{L}(M_2) \cap \xi(L) = \emptyset$.

- Properties of *infinite* action-labeled runs of M_1 and M_2 are indistingushable by L_ω and $\xi(L_\omega)$, i.e., $\xi(\mathcal{L}_\omega(M_1)) \cap L_\omega = \emptyset$ iff $\mathcal{L}_\omega(M_2) \cap \xi(L_\omega) = \emptyset$.

Thus, if M_1 is ξ-reducible to M_2, then one can reduce model checking of an action-based property of M_1, which is using one kind of synchronization primitives, to model checking of the corresponding property of M_2, which is using another set of synchronization primitives. Note carefully that ξ-reducibility does not require the languages of M_1 and M_2 to be equivalent (up to ξ), hence, the language of M_2 may contain action runs that are not in $\xi(\Sigma_1)$.

Furthermore, for a (finite or infinite state-labeled) path $\pi : i \mapsto q_i$ we call the sequence $tr(\pi) : i \mapsto \lambda(q_i)$ the *trace* of π. Let *stutter$_k$* be the function defined as $stutter_k(w_1 w_2 \dots) = (w_1)^k (w_2)^k \dots$ for any word $w_1 w_2 \cdots \in \text{AP}^* \cup \text{AP}^\omega$, i.e., every letter of the word is repeated k times. We say that M_1 is k-*equivalent* to M_2, if the traces of the systems coincide up to proposition stuttering, i.e., $\{stutter_k(tr(\pi)) : \pi \text{ is a run of } M_1\} = \{tr(\pi') : \pi' \text{ is a run of } M_2\}$.

One can see that k-equivalence implies stutter trace equivalence. Thus, using the well-known fact about preservation of LTL\X properties by stutter trace equivalent systems (cf. Baier and Katoen [2008, Theorem 7.92]), we obtain: *For k-equivalent LTSs M_1 and M_2 and for LTL\X-formula ψ, the following holds: $M_1 \models \psi$ iff $M_2 \models \psi$.*

Now we prove an interesting fact: Every system with disjunctive guards is ξ-reducible and 2-equivalent to a system with pairwise rendezvous (shown by Emerson and Kahlon [2003b, Section 5]):

Theorem 6.32   *For every guarded system template $(P^1, \ldots, P^d)$ there exists a system template $(\tilde{P}^1, \ldots, \tilde{P}^d)$ using pairwise rendezvous such that for every clique $\mathbf{C}(n)$, the system instance $(P^1, \ldots, P^d)^{\mathbf{C}(n)}$ is ξ-reducible and 2-equivalent to the system instance $(\tilde{P}^1, \ldots, \tilde{P}^d)^{\mathbf{C}(n)}$.*

Proof. Let every process template P^ℓ be $(Q^\ell, Q_0^\ell, \Sigma^\ell, \delta^\ell, \lambda^\ell)$. Following Emerson and Kahlon [2003b], we assume that the set of actions Σ_{pr} is a disjoint union $\delta^1 \cup \cdots \cup \delta^d$, and every transition is labeled with a unique action from Σ_{pr}. For every $\ell \in [d]$, we construct a process template $\tilde{P}^\ell = (\tilde{Q}^\ell, \tilde{Q}_0^\ell, \tilde{\Sigma}^\ell, \tilde{\delta}^\ell, \tilde{\lambda}^\ell)$ as follows.

- Set of states $\tilde{Q}^\ell$ is the disjoint union of the original states Q^ℓ and of a set of auxiliary states defined by $\{syn(t) : t \in \delta^\ell\} \cup \{cosyn(c, t) : c \in Q^1 \cup \cdots \cup Q^d \text{ and } t \in \delta^\ell\}$.

- Initial states stay the same: $\tilde{Q}_0^\ell = Q_0^\ell$.

- State labels $\tilde{\delta}^\ell$ are assigned as follows: Original states $q \in Q^\ell$ are labeled with $\{q\}$; Synchronization states $syn((q, a, q')) \in Q^\ell$ are labeled with their predecessor $\{q\}$; Co-synchronization states $cosyn(c, t) \in Q^\ell$ are labeled with their predecessor $\{c\}$.

- $\tilde{\Sigma}^\ell = \{req(t)! : t \in \delta^\ell\} \cup \{ack(t)? : t \in \delta^\ell\} \cup \{ack(t)! : t \in \bigcup_{k \in [d]} \delta^k\} \cup \{req(t)? : t \in \bigcup_{k \in [d]} \delta^k\}$.

- For every transition $t = (q, a, q')$ from δ^ℓ one adds to $\tilde{\delta}^\ell$ two transitions $(q, req(t)!, syn(t))$ and $(syn(t), ack(t)?, q')$. Furthermore, for every proposition c_i of the disjunctive guard $gd(t) = [\exists \text{ other } j] \ c_1 \vee \cdots \vee c_k$, one adds two transitions $(c_i, req(t)?, cosyn(t))$ and $(cosyn(t), ack(t)!, c_i)$ to the corresponding transition relation $\tilde{\delta}^{\ell'}$ of the process template containg the state c_i.

It is easy to see that every transition $t = (q, a, q')$ of P^ℓ is translated to a sequence of transitions $q \xrightarrow{req(t)!} syn(t) \xrightarrow{ack(t)?} q'$ made by a process of type ℓ; this sequence is synchronized with a sequence $c_i \xrightarrow{req(t)?} cosyn(c_i, t) \xrightarrow{ack(t)!} c_i$ executed by a process residing in state c_i. The intermediate state $cosyn(c_i, t)$ stores its predecessor c_i to return back to it later.

By construction, the intermediate states $syn(t)$ and $cosyn(c_i, t)$ preserve the labels of their predecessors. Thus, every letter in a trace of $(P^1, \ldots, P^d)^{\mathbf{C}(n)}$ is doubled in $(\tilde{P}^1, \ldots, \tilde{P}^d)^{\mathbf{C}(n)}$.

Define a mapping $\xi(t)$ as $req(t)! \cdot ack(t)?$. Now it is easy to see that every system instance $(P^1, \ldots, P^d)^{\mathbf{C}(n)}$ is ξ-reducible and 2-equivalent to the system instance $(\tilde{P}^1, \ldots, \tilde{P}^d)^{\mathbf{C}(n)}$.   □

Emerson and Kahlon [2003b, Section 5] showed a reduction of systems with pairwise rendezvous to systems with disjunctive guards, while preserving ξ-reducibility.

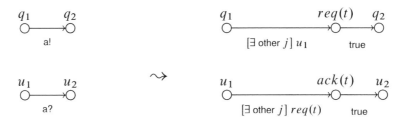

Figure 6.16: Reducing *with caveat* pairwise rendezvous (left) to transitions with disjunctive guards (right).

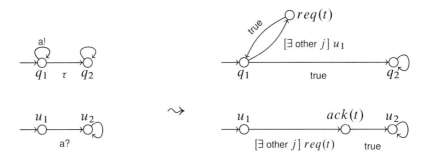

Figure 6.17: An example showing that the reduction on Figure 6.16 does not preserve formulas from LTL\X(C).

Theorem 6.33   *For each system template $(P^1, \ldots, P^d)$ with pairwise rendezvous there is a guarded protocol $(\tilde{P}^1, \ldots, \tilde{P}^d)$ with disjunctive guards having the following property: For every clique $\mathbf{C}(n)$, system instance $(P^1, \ldots, P^d)^{\mathbf{C}(n)}$ is ξ-reducible to system instance $(\tilde{P}^1, \ldots, \tilde{P}^d)^{\mathbf{C}(n)}$.*

Proof idea. The proof similar to the proof of Theorem 6.32. Figure 6.16 shows how a pair of synchronized transitions $t = (q_1, a!, q_2)$ and $(u_1, a?, u_2)$ is translated to four transitions with disjunctive guards. The intermediate states $req(t)$ and $ack(t)$ keep the labels of their predecessors, i.e., of q_1 and u_1. Given process templates, such a translation is done for every pair of transitions carrying synchronization actions of the same type.

Let b, c, d, and e be the actions assigned to the transitions $q_1 \to req(t)$, $req(t) \to q_2$, $u_1 \to ack(t)$, $ack(t) \to u_2$, respectively. Then the mapping ξ of $a!$ is defined as $\xi(a!) = bcde$.

Thus, a finite (or Büchi) automaton checking a specification has to recognize the sequence $bcde$ instead of letter $a!$, which corresponds to handshake of two processes issuing actions $a!$ and $a?$. □

In contrast to action-based properties, state-based properties are not preserved by the reduction in the proof of Theorem 6.33.

Observation 6.34   The reduction provided in the proof of Theorem 6.33 does not preserve LTL\X(C) properties.

Proof. Figure 6.17 shows a system template (C, U) with rendezvous (left-hand side) and its reduction to a guarded protocol (C', U') with disjunctive guards (righthand-side). Fix an arbitrary $n \in \mathbb{N}$. For the system with rendezvous, it holds that $(C, U)^{\mathbf{C}(1,n)} \models \mathsf{F}q_2$, as n processes of type U, allow C to fire $(q_1, a!, q_1)$ finitely many times, that is, every user process moves from u_1 to u_2 once. In the system with disjunctive guards, C' can fire $(q_1, [\exists \text{ other } j] \, u_1, req(t))$ infinitely often, without a single process of type U' moving. Hence, $(C', U')^{\mathbf{C}(1,n)} \not\models \mathsf{F}q_2$.   □

6.6   VARIATIONS ON THE MODEL: GUARDS AND SYNCHRONIZATION PRIMITIVES

The protocols we considered so far had guarded internal transitions only. Emerson and Kahlon [2003a,b,c] investigated the cases of guarded systems with broadcast actions, pairwise rendezvous, and asynchronous rendezvous. These combined systems allow one to model, e.g., cache coherence protocols.

Most of the results for the combined models are obtained using reduction techniques by Emerson and Kahlon [2003b]. The results are summarized in Figure 6.1. Here we briefly discuss the ideas behind the results. Most of the proofs are based on the undecidability results for (rendezvous and broadcast) systems without guards, and the reduction provided in Section 6.5.

Disjunctive guards and rendezvous $\mathcal{P}_{\text{disj\&rdvz}}$.   Decidability of the PMCP for $\mathcal{P}_{\text{disj\&rdvz}}$ (disjunctive guards and pairwise rendezvous) depends on the specification class. Decidability for Reg(A) is given by Emerson and Kahlon [2003b]; the result relies on backward reachability in well-structured systems, which is decidable [Abdulla et al., 1996]. Further, as the systems with disjunctive guards are reducible to systems with pairwise rendezvous (see Theorem 6.32) one can re-use the decidability proof for rendezvous by German and Sistla [1992] (cf. Section 5). Namely, the PMCP is also decidable for the classes of LTL\X(C), LTL(C), 1-LTL\X(P^ℓ), and ωReg(A) properties.

Disjunctive guards and broadcast $\mathcal{P}_{\text{disj\&bcast}}$.   In the case of $\mathcal{P}_{\text{disj\&bcast}}$ (disjunctive guards and broadcasts), none of the specification classes mentioned in this section are decidable except Reg(A). As disjunctive guards are reducible to pairwise rendezvous, and systems with pairwise rendezvous and broadcasts are reducible to systems with broadcasts (see Section 5 and Esparza et al. [1999]), we can reduce systems in $\mathcal{P}_{\text{disj\&bcast}}$ to systems with broadcast. As Esparza et al. [1999] showed, the PMCP is undecidable for all classes except Reg(A); in the case of Reg(A), the construction of a coverability graph by Emerson and Namjoshi [1998] applies.

Disjunctive guards and asynchronous rendezvous $\mathcal{P}_{disj\&ardvz}$. The PMCP for $\mathcal{P}_{disj\&ardvz}$ (disjunctive guards and asynchronous rendezvous) is also undecidable, except for the case of Reg(A), which is similar to the result for $\mathcal{P}_{disj\&rdvz}$. As shown by Emerson and Kahlon [2003b], the PMCP of LTL\X(C) properties is undecidable for systems with both pairwise rendezvous and asynchronous rendezvous. Due to this and reducibility of disjunctive guards to pairwise rendezvous, it immediately follows that the PMCP is undecidable for all specification classes that include LTL\X(C).

Conjunctive guards and synchronization. Disjunctive guards are reducible to pairwise rendezvous (see Theorem 6.32). Thus, PMCP for $\mathcal{P}_{conj+disj}$ (in other words, PMCP for boolean guards, $\mathcal{P}_{bool}$) can be reduced to PMCP for $\mathcal{P}_{conj+rdvz}$ (conjunctive guards and pairwise rendezvous). As PMCP is undecidable for boolean guards and every class of specifications (see Theorem 6.13), PMCP for $\mathcal{P}_{conj+rdvz}$ and every class of specifications is undecidable as well.

Furthermore, as shown by Emerson and Kahlon [2003b], pairwise rendezvous is reducible to asynchronous rendezvous. As we have just shown that PMCP for $\mathcal{P}_{conj+rdvz}$ is undecidable for every class of specifications, it follows that PMCP for $\mathcal{P}_{conj+ardvz}$ (conjunctive guards and asynchronous rendezvous) is also undecidable for every class of specifications. Similarly, PMCP is undecidable for $\mathcal{P}_{conj\&bcast}$ (conjunctive guards and broadcasts). Again, this is due to reducibility of disjunctive guards to pairwise rendezvous and of pairwise rendezvous to broadcast [Esparza et al., 1999]. Together with the undecidability results for boolean guards, this shows undecidability for all considered classes of specifications.

6.7   DISCUSSION

In this chapter, we introduced the results on guarded protocols in the unified framework. This allows us to present different computational models from the literature as instances of our definitions. We re-structure the proofs of the cutoff theorems for disjunctive and init-conjuctive guards, which highlight central arguments of these important results. Emerson and Kahlon [2003b] claimed in their discussions that there is a decidability result for conjunctive guards. However, the reference they give is based on init-conjunctive guards [Emerson and Kahlon, 2000]. As the proofs use the fact that an init-conjunctive guard cannot be disabled by a process at the initial state, it is not straightforward to generalize these proofs to conjunctive guards. Hence, to the best of our understanding, decidability for system with *conjunctive guards* and specifications from 1-LTL\X(P^ℓ), 1-ELTL\X(P^ℓ), or LTL\X(C) are open problems.

We clarified that the reduction of disjunctive guards to rendezvous presented in Emerson and Kahlon [2003b] is limited to action-based specifications. In particular, we showed that disjunctive guards are not powerful enough to capture rendezvous with respect to LTL(C) properties.

Guarded protocols are interesting not only from a theoretical point of view, but are also useful in modeling cache coherence protocols—an important concept for hardware designs. The following papers discuss applications of guarded protocols in modeling and verification of cache coherence protocols. There are two notable papers by Emerson and Kahlon [2003a,c] showing how guarded protocols with broadcasts can be applied to modeling of cache coherence protocols. In the mentioned papers, the authors consider restrictions of guarded systems with one process template U.

- The conjunctive guards have the form $[\forall \text{ other } i]\ init$.

- The disjunctive guards have the form $[\exists \text{ other } i]\ \neg init$.

- Apart from guards, processes use broadcasts.

- The transitions of process templates have various structural restrictions, e.g., from every state the process is able to go to $init$.

Emerson and Kahlon [2003a,c] modeled eight cache coherence protocols with the framework of guarded systems. As the PMCP for guarded systems with broadcast is undecidable, the authors had to develop special abstraction and cutoff techniques for the protocols with the restrictions mentioned above. As the results seem to be considerably tailored to the special structure of cache coherence protocols, we do not give details in this survey. An interested reader finds a detailed exposition in the original papers.

Some lower bounds are known for disjunctively guarded systems: PMCP is undecidable for 1-index CTL*\X specifications Aminof et al. [2014b]; for systems with or without a controller the complexity of the PMCP is PSPACE-complete (the upper bound is from Emerson and Kahlon [2000] and the lower bound is from Aminof et al. [2014b]); for systems with a controller the program complexity (i.e., the formula is fixed and not part of the input) is coNP-complete Aminof et al. [2014b], whereas for systems without a controller the program complexity is in PTIME (the upper bound is from Emerson and Kahlon [2000] and the lower bound is from Aminof et al. [2014b]).

From a theoretical point of view, we observe from the discussions in this chapter that there are the following open problems.

Problem 6.35   Is the PMCP with conjunctive guards and the following specifications decidable: 1-LTL\X(P^ℓ), 2-LTL\X($P^\ell, P^{\ell'}$), LTL(C)? Is there a cutoff, similar to Theorem 6.22?

Problem 6.36   Is the PMCP with disjunctive guards and the following specifications decidable: prenex lLTL\X, prenex lCTL*\X, lLTL\X?

CHAPTER 7

Ad Hoc Networks

In ad hoc networks, processes communicate via broadcasts. Recall from Section 2.2.1 that in transitions synchronized by broadcast, all immediate neighbors of a sender simultaneously take a transition with the sender, and the sender is not blocked if there are no recipients that are ready to synchronize. This chapter summarizes the results by Delzanno et al. [2010, 2011, 2012b] and Abdulla et al. [2013a].

The literature studies ad hoc networks arranged in different classes of connectivity graphs that try to model typical topologies met in practice (see Section 7.4), and also networks in which broadcast messages can be lost and thus not received by some of the sender's neighbors. In case of (non-lossy) ad hoc networks (AHN), parameterized model checking problems, even for safety properties, are undecidable for systems with general connectivity graphs, but become decidable for certain classes of graphs. In case of lossy ad hoc networks (LAHN), the additional non-determinism of whether or not a message is lost for a receiving process makes all parameterized model checking problems considered in this chapter decidable. However, it is well known that important problems cannot been solved in the presence of lossy links, e.g., the two generals paradox [Gray, 1978]. A related model is that of *mobile* ad hoc networks, in which the structure of the communication graph can change during execution. It has been shown by Delzanno et al. [2012b] that such networks are equivalent to a certain class of lossy ad hoc networks. Generally, the models discussed in this section, though inspired by ad hoc networks (cf. Karl [2005]), have not yet found their practical applications, so that in the next section we provide a toy example to help us to illustrate the theoretical results.

7.1   RUNNING EXAMPLE

Consider the process template in Figure 7.1. Processes start in the initial state $init$. Processes that are in state u will be called "user" processes, processes in l are "leader" processes, processes in hub are "hub" processes, and processes in err are "error" processes. Figure 7.2 gives two connectivity graphs with reachable global states of the system in AHNs or LAHNs, respectively. For AHNs composed of processes running this protocol, the following holds:

(i) in AHNs arranged on any undirected graph, state err is unreachable;

(ii) in AHNs arranged in cliques, state hub is unreachable; and

(iii) in AHNs arranged on any undirected graph, any process adjacent to a leader is not a leader (and will eventually be either a hub or a user process).

Consider the first item. Let process p_{err} be one of the processes that reach state err first (hypothetically, there may be several processes that reach err at the same time). Let us assume that p_{err} reaches err via transition $l' \overset{req??}{\to} err$. Also, wlog. assume p_{err} is the first among the error processes that reaches l'. Just before getting into l' the process sends $req!!$ which makes it impossible for any adjacent process to send $req!!$. The last fact implies that p_{err} cannot reach err from l'. Contradiction. In a similar way, we can derive a contradiction for the case of reaching err via transition $l \overset{req??}{\to} req$. Later in this chapter, in Example 7.20 we prove this formally by applying an algorithm that can answer reachability questions of this kind.

The items (i)–(iii) do not hold for LAHNs, namely: on cliques, states err and hub are reachable, and leader processes can be adjacent. Later in this chapter, Example 7.22 proves item (i) adapted to LAHNs on cliques formally. An example of the protocol execution that falsifies (iii) for LAHNs is in Figure 7.2.

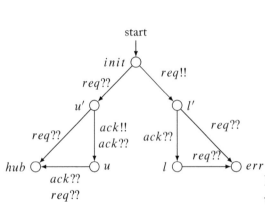

Figure 7.1: Process template for the running example.

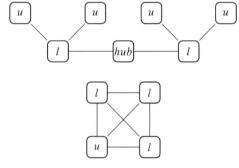

Figure 7.2: On top: reachable global state after executing the protocol in an AHN. Processes are labeled with their local state. On the bottom: reachable global state after executing the protocol in a LAHN.

7.2 SYSTEM MODEL

Process and system template. The only communication primitive allowed is a broadcast as defined in Section 2.2.1, i.e., the synchronization constraint is card $= \mathbb{N}_0$. In the literature, only systems with a single process template P are considered, i.e., $d = 1$. Denote by $\mathcal{P}_{bcast}$ the set of all process templates that communicate via broadcasts.

1-ary parameterized connectivity graph $\mathbf{G}$. In this chapter, we consider 1-ary parameterized connectivity graphs $\mathbf{G}$ as a *set* of 1-colored connectivity graphs, rather than a sequence as defined in Section 2.2. This is simply a matter of convenience, as the order of graphs will not matter.

AHN system instance P^G. The definition of AHN system instance P^G follows that of Section 2.2.

LAHN system instance P^G_{lossy}. To define LAHN system instance we introduce a *lossy broadcast transition* by dropping the (MAX) requirement from the definition in Section 2.2.1. Recall that the (MAX) requirement forces all processes that can take a "receive" broadcast transition to take it. Dropping the (MAX) requirement allows a process to "ignore" it: for every process that is a recipient of the initiator and can take a transition labeled with some b??, whether it actually takes it is chosen non-deterministically. Informally, this may be viewed as a "message loss." Denote by P^G_{lossy} a system instance with all broadcast transitions being lossy.

Mobile AHNs. In *mobile ad hoc networks*, the underlying connectivity graph can change during a run of the system. We will not include such changes of the connectivity graph into our system model. However, it has been shown by [Delzanno et al., 2012b, Proposition 1] that mobile ad hoc networks are equivalent to LAHNs on cliques, and therefore the decidability results for LAHNs on cliques also apply to mobile ad hoc networks.

Example 7.1 Figure 7.1 illustrates a process template from $\mathcal{P}_{\text{bcast}}$. Figure 7.2 gives global states that can be reached in an AHN and a LAHN, respectively, after execution of the protocol.

Deadlocks. In this chapter, a run is a finite or infinite maximal path that starts in the initial state, i.e., we handle finite paths directly and neither extend nor ignore deadlocked system runs. Note that the problem of ensuring the absence of deadlocks in parameterized AHNs is undecidable already for AHNs on cliques; this can be proven using a modified construction from Theorem 5.11. In contrast, this problem for LAHNs and AHNs is decidable for parameterized cliques and general graphs, since we can reduce it to the deadlock detection problem in Petri nets, which is decidable [Cheng et al., 1993].

7.3   PMC PROBLEMS FOR AD HOC NETWORKS

For ad hoc networks, three special PMC problems were studied in the literature—COVER, REPEAT, and TARGET.

- COVER$_\mathbf{G}$, or *control state reachability*:
  input: process template $P = (Q, Q_0, \Sigma, \delta, \lambda) \in \mathcal{P}_{\text{bcast}}$, control states $C \subseteq Q$
  output: "Yes" if there exists $G = (V, E) \in \mathbf{G}$ such that system P^G has a run $s_0, s_1, \ldots$ (finite or infinite) where for some process index $i \in V$ and some state s_n of the run: $s_n(i) \in C$. That is, there is a system where some process reaches a control state. "No" otherwise.

- REPEAT$_\mathbf{G}$, or *repeated control state reachability*:
  input: process template $P = (Q, Q_0, \Sigma, \delta, \lambda) \in \mathcal{P}_{\text{bcast}}$, control states $R \subseteq Q$
  output: "Yes" if there exists $G = (V, E) \in \mathbf{G}$ such that P^G has an infinite run $\sigma = s_0, s_1, \ldots$

where for some process index $i \in V$ the set $\{k \mid s_k(i) \in R\}$ is infinite. That is, there is a system where some process can visit a control state infinitely often. "No" otherwise.

- TARGET$_\mathbf{G}$, or *target reachability*:
  input: process template $P = (Q, Q_0, \Sigma, \delta, \lambda) \in \mathcal{P}_{\mathsf{bcast}}$, control states $T \subseteq Q$
  output: "Yes" if there exists $G = (V, E) \in \mathbf{G}$ such that system P^G has a run $\sigma = s_0, s_1, \ldots$ (finite or infinite) where for all process indices $i \in V$ $s_n(i) \in T$. That is, there is a system that reaches a global state with all processes being in a control state (the control state may be different for different processes). "No" otherwise.

Under certain conditions (for example, in systems where all runs infinite), these PMC problems can be expressed in indexed temporal logic[1]. In particular:

- any instance of COVER$_\mathbf{G}$ can be expressed as a negation of an instance of the PMCP with respect to a 1-indexed safety property;

- any instance of REPEAT$_\mathbf{G}$—with respect to a universal 1-index persistence property; and

- any instance of TARGET$_\mathbf{G}$—with respect to a safety property in non-prenex fragment.

The PMC problems for LAHNs are defined similarly, except that P^G is replaced with P^G_{lossy}. Delzanno et al. [2012b] studied PMC problems for LAHN arranged in cliques. We write $P^\mathbf{C}_{lossy}$ for such parameterized systems, where $\mathbf{C}$ is a parameterized clique. To the best of our knowledge, the case of LAHN on other parameterized connectivity graphs was not studied in the literature.

Table 7.1 (on page 128) gives an overview of the results that we discuss in this chapter.

Example 7.2   Now we can relate instances of PMCPs from Section 7.1 with COVER with fixed inputs. Denote the process template from the running example by P_{re}. Then:

- PMC in (i) is equivalent to COVER$_{\mathbf{All}}$ with $C = \{err\}$ and $P = P_{re}$, where **All** is the set of all undirected connected graphs;

- PMC in (ii) is equivalent to COVER$_\mathbf{C}$ with $C = \{hub\}$ and $P = P_{re}$, where $\mathbf{C}$ is the set of all cliques; and

- PMC (iii) cannot be expressed directly via an instance of COVER, TARGET or REPEAT. But in case of AHNs we can express the PMC in (iii) via an instance of COVER if we modify the process template: add an outgoing broadcast transition from state l, and a corresponding receive transition from l into a special state s. Then, the PMC in (iii) becomes equivalent to COVER$_{\mathbf{All}}$ with $C = \{s\}$ and $P = P_{re}$.

---

[1]Recall that in this survey we defined the temporal logics on infinite runs only.

7.4   PARAMETERIZED CONNECTIVITY GRAPHS BP_k, BPC_k, BD_k, C, All

Delzanno et al. [2010, 2011, 2012b] and Abdulla et al. [2013a] studied the PMC problems in ad hoc networks for different classes of parameterized connectivity graphs. The connectivity graphs studied model common topologies met in ad hoc networks. These topologies can be divided into two classes—flat and hierarchical (cf. Karl [2005, Chapter 10]).

In hierarchical topologies, nodes are grouped into clusters, and each cluster has a representative node. All nodes in a cluster communicate directly or via other nodes of the same cluster. Nodes from different clusters do not communicate directly but rather via representative nodes. Below we define bounded path graphs ($\mathbf{BP_k}$) and bounded path clique graphs ($\mathbf{BPC_k}$) that can model hierarchical topologies.

In contrast to hierarchical topologies, in flat topologies there are no representative nodes, and every node is equal with respect to communication. We will define bounded diameter graphs ($\mathbf{BD_k}$) that model flat topologies with a bounded distance between nodes. Cliques ($\mathbf{C}$) are a special case where the distances is always 1, and can be used to model dense ad hoc networks in which every node is in the transmission range of every other node.

The assumption of undirected connection between nodes does not always hold as the discrepancy between a node's transmission and reception range makes the following possible: a node can send messages to some other node, but cannot receive a message from this node. Connectivity graphs with directed edges can model nodes with such discrepancies.

We use the following basic definitions. A *path in a graph* $G = (V, E)$ is a sequence $v_0 e_0 v_1 e_1 \dots v_n \in (VE)^*V$ such that $(v_i, v_{i+1}) \in e_i$ for $i < n$. It is a *simple path* if no node appears twice. A graph is *connected* if there is a path between any two nodes of the graph. The *distance* between two nodes is the number of edges on the shortest simple path between them. The *length* of a simple path is the number of edges on it, thus the length of $v_0 e_0 v_1 e_1 \dots v_n \in (VE)^*V$ is n. A graph $G = (V, E)$ is *undirected* if for any $(v, w) \in E$ it holds that $(w, v) \in E$.

In the following definitions, let $k \in \mathbb{N}_0$.

All, daAll, C.   **All** is the parameterized connectivity graph consisting of all undirected connected graphs, **daAll** the parameterized connectivity graph of all (directed) acyclic graphs, and **C** is the parameterized connectivity graph of all clique graphs.

BD_k.   The *diameter* of a connected undirected graph is the maximal distance between any two nodes of the graph. An undirected connected graph is a *k-bounded diameter graph* if its diameter is less or equal to k. Denote by $\mathbf{BD_k}$ the parameterized connectivity graph of all k-bounded diameter graphs. Intuitively, the graph diameter equals the maximal number of times a message needs to be broadcast in order to reach all nodes.

$\mathbf{BP_k}$, $\mathbf{daBP_k}$.   A graph is a *k-bounded path graph* if all simple paths are of length smaller or equal to k. $\mathbf{BP_k}$ consists of all undirected connected k-bounded path graphs. $\mathbf{daBP_k}$ consists of all directed acyclic k-bounded path graphs. Note that for any $k \in \mathbb{N}_0 : \mathbf{BP_k} \subseteq \mathbf{BD_k}$.

$\mathbf{BPC_k}$.   An undirected connected graph is a *k-bounded path maximal cliques graph* if all simple paths between any of its maximal cliques have lengths smaller or equal to k. $\mathbf{BPC_k}$ consists of all k-bounded path maximal cliques graphs. In terms of expressivity, $\mathbf{BPC_k}$ is between $\mathbf{BP_k}$ and $\mathbf{BD_{2k+1}}$: for any $k \geq 1$, it holds that $\mathbf{BP_k} \subset \mathbf{BPC_k} \subset \mathbf{BD_{2k+1}}$.

Example 7.3   Some examples of graphs as defined above.

- A 1-bounded diameter graph is a clique, and $\mathbf{BD_1}$ consists of all cliques, i.e., is equal to $\mathbf{C}$.

- An undirected star is a 2-bounded path graph, the set of all undirected rings with a central node connected to everyone ("wheel") is in $\mathbf{BD_2}$ but not in $\mathbf{BP_k}$ for any k.

- Undirected trees of depth d are contained in $\mathbf{BP_{2d}}$.

- A directed forest of depth k where all edges are directed away from the roots is containted $\mathbf{daBP_k}$.

- Finally, $\mathbf{BPC_0}$ coincides with the set of all cliques, and stars of cliques are in $\mathbf{BPC_2}$.

7.5   RESULTS FOR (NON-LOSSY) AHNS

The results of Delzanno et al. [2010, 2011, 2012b] for the PMCPs in the classes of graphs defined above are summarized in Figure 7.3.

In the figure the results for the clique column follow from Esparza et al. [1999].

Corollary 7.4   COVER$_\mathbf{C}$ *is decidable,* REPEAT$_\mathbf{C}$ *and* TARGET$_\mathbf{C}$ *are undecidable for* AHNs.

Proof idea. The first item: it is straightforward to reduce COVER$_\mathbf{C}$ for AHNs to PMCP$(\mathcal{P}, \mathbf{C}_\odot, \mathsf{Reg}(A))$ for broadcast systems which is decidable by Theorem 5.7. The proof reduces the PMCP problem to the (decidable) coverability problem for WSTSs. The second and third items follow from a straightforward modification of the construction described in Theorem 5.11 that reduces the (undecidable) non-halting problem for 2CMs to PMCP$(\mathcal{P}, \mathbf{C}_\odot, \omega\mathsf{Reg}(A))$.   □

7.5.1   UNDECIDABILITY RESULTS FOR (NON-LOSSY) AHNS

This section explains all undecidability results for AHNs from Figure 7.3, namely:

- Theorem 7.6 proves that COVER$_\mathbf{All}$ is undecidable;

- Theorems 7.8 and 7.9 cover the case of graphs $\mathbf{BD_k}$;

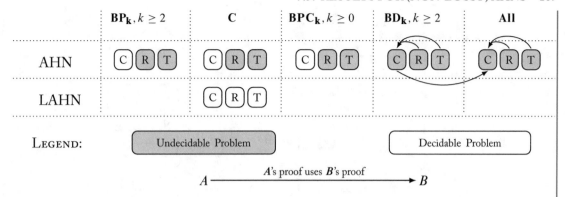

Figure 7.3: Decidability results and reductions for ad hoc networks. The letters c, r, t in the cells stand for Cover, Repeat, Target. The blank cells mean that to the best of our knowledge the problems were not studied in the literature. The results for directed graphs are not shown here—see Theorems 7.12 and 7.19.

- Theorem 7.10 proves that Repeat and Target are undecidable on BP_k for $k \geq 2$;

- Corollary 7.11 proves that Repeat and Target are undecidable on BPC_k for $k \geq 0$; and

- Theorem 7.12 proves that Cover is undecidable on directed graphs (not in the figure).

In the literature, undecidability results for ad hoc networks are usually established via reduction from the halting problem for 2CMs to Cover or, equivalently, from the non-halting problem for 2CMs to the PMC problem.

Most of the undecidability proofs build, for a given 2CM, a protocol that has the following two steps:

1. find a sub-graph of a special form, and

2. simulate the 2CM. The simulation assumes the connectivity graph is of the special form.

Building block: RAO protocol.   All the protocols used in Delzanno et al. [2010, 2011] to prove undecidability results for All, BD_k, BP_k, BPC_k as the first step use a variant of the Req-Ack-OK (RAO) protocol (Figure 7.4) that has the following property.

Lemma 7.5 *[Delzanno et al., 2010, Proposition 1] Let P be the RAO protocol (Figure 7.4(a)), and consider an AHN system instance P^G. If P^G, starting from the initial state, reaches a system state such that some process $v \in V_G$ is in state s_3, then:*

1. *process v is adjacent to exactly one process in state l_3 denoted by w; and*

2. *any other process adjacent to v or w is in state err.*

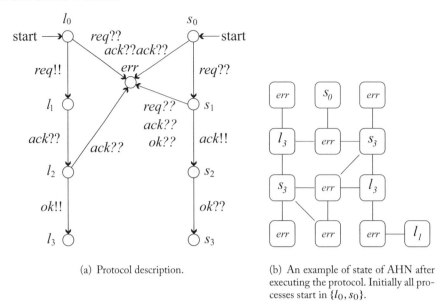

(a) Protocol description.

(b) An example of state of AHN after executing the protocol. Initially all processes start in $\{l_0, s_0\}$.

Figure 7.4: RAO protocol, the building block for protocols to find sub-graphs of a special form [Delzanno et al., 2010].

Proof idea. Note that process v can end in state s_3 only if it receives a broadcast message ok, hence there must be an adjacent process that is in state l_3. By applying the RAO protocol backward, one can show that processes w, v can reach states l_3, s_3 only if they, starting from initial states l_0, s_0, receive messages only from each other. Then, by applying the RAO protocol forwards to processes w, v starting in the initial states, one can show that if w, v reach l_3, s_3 then all their adjacent processes will end in state err. □

Figure 7.4(b) shows an example of a system state after completion of the RAO protocol. Intuitively, the protocol *links* two adjacent processes (that is, a process in state s_3 is linked to a neighbor in state l_3) starting in states l_0, s_0 and sends all other adjacent processes into state err.

Undecidability of Cover$_{All}$.   We are now ready to discuss the first undecidability result in the case of AHNs.

Theorem 7.6   *[Delzanno et al., 2010]* Cover$_{All}$ *for AHNs is undecidable.*

Proof idea. To simulate a 2CM consider process template P that implements a two-phase protocol.

1. Find a sub-graph of the form in Figure 7.5(a), we call it "the controller with two lists."

2. Simulate a 2CM.

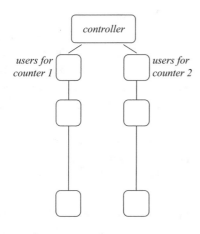 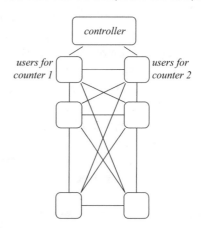

(a) A structure of the sub-graph "the controller with two lists" used in the proof of undecidability of COVER$_{\mathbf{All}}$ for AHNs, Theorem 7.6. There may be connections between left and right users, but they do not affect the simulation phase [Delzanno et al., 2010].

(b) A structure of the sub-graph used in the proof of undecidability of COVER$_{\mathbf{BD_2}}$ for AHNs, Theorem 7.8. This is a special case of the sub-graph on the left. Connection between users from different lists are not used in the simulation phase.

Figure 7.5: Sub-graphs used to simulate a 2CM.

The second phase starts only if the first phase succeeds. Using the protocol we will show that the 2CM halts if and only if there is a graph $G \in \mathbf{All}$ such that system P^G reaches a state with some process in state $halt$.

1st phase: Finding a sub-graph "the controller with two lists."

The first phase can succeed only if the connectivity graph has a sub-graph of a special form: a controller process connected to two lists of user processes. The protocol in Figure 7.6 tries to find such a sub-graph. Initial states are $\{R, C_i', C_i,'' C_i \mid i = 1, 2\}$. Note that it is possible that after the protocol execution the connectivity graph is split into more than a single sub-graph each of the desired form, but these sub-graphs are isolated (nodes that connect them are in the error state and will not participate in the second phase). The transitions leading to the error state are not shown in the figure.

Roughly, the phase guesses a sub-graph of the desired form and then verifies it exists.

The phase can succeed only in executions in which the system starts in an initial state with at least one process in state R (call it the controller) that is connected to two lists of the form $C_i' - C_i'' - C_i - C_i' - C_i'' - C_i - \dots$ (call them list 1 and list 2 for $i = 1, 2$, and call the first nodes of two lists head 1 and 2). Note that non-determinism of the process initial state implies: even if there is a sub-graph "the controller with two lists," it is still possible that the first phase fails because the initial system state is not of the desired form. But it is certain that if there is a desired sub-graph, then there is a desired initial system state.

The phase uses a modified RAO protocol that has the following differences. The original RAO protocol ensures that two adjacent processes that are initially in states l_0 and s_0 can reach states l_3 and s_3 while sending all other adjacent processes into state err. In contrast, the modified RAO protocol in Figure 7.6 describes several-steps protocol that links an R-process with a unique C_1'-process (step 1), that C_1'-process with a C_1''-process (step 2), that C_1''-process with a C_1-process (step 3), and that C_1-process with a C_1'-process (similar to step 1 but the C_1-process plays the role of an R-process).

Step 1 links an R-process with a unique adjacent C_1'-process. All other processes adjacent to the R-process will go either into err state or they belong to another counter and do not change their states. All other processes adjacent to the C_1' process will go either into err except those in C'' state.

Step 2 links a C_1'-process with a unique adjacent C_1''-process, while sending all others adjacent to C_1' into err except the previously linked C_1-process, and sending all others adjacent to C_1'' into err except those in state C_1.

Step 3 links a C_1''-process with a unique adjacent C_1-process, while sending all others adjacent to C_1'' into err except the previously linked C_1'-process, and sending all others adjacent to C_1 into err except those in state C_1'.

In all steps a process that initiates linking with another process (in Step 1 – C_1-process, in Step 2 – C_1'-process, in Step 3 – C_1''-process) non-deterministically chooses between linking with another process or sending $done_1$. Sending $done_1$ completes the initialization of list 1 – the message is transmitted back to the controller (an R-process), and the controller starts initializing list 2 in a similar way. If the initialization of both lists completes (thus the controller is not hanged waiting for a message from head 1 or 2), then the system state is of the form $0_1 - \ldots - 0_1 - L - 0_2 - \ldots - 0_2$, and the controller starts simulating the 2CM.

2nd phase: Simulating a 2CM. If the first phase succeeds, then there is at least one sub-graph of the form in Figure 7.5(a). Consider one such sub-graph. In the simulation phase the controller process simulates transitions of the control state of the 2CM, while user nodes encode values of counters (each user "stores" a bit, and the sum of bits in list i is equal to the value of counter i). To increase the value of counter 1 the controller broadcasts message inc_1 which is received by two head processes. Only head 1 reacts to the message: if it has its bit set, then it passes the message further along list 1, otherwise head 1 sets its bit and sends ack to acknowledge the message. When the controller receives ack, it continues simulation. "Decrease" and "test for zero" work similarly. This completes the description of the simulation phase.

The protocol ensures that the 2CM halts if and only if there is a system where the controller process can reach a halting state, which is an instance of COVER$_{\text{All}}$ problem. □

Example 7.7 Now we can relate the results in Figure 7.3, in particular Corollary 7.4 and Theorem 7.6, with the running example from Section 7.1. Since COVER$_{\text{All}}$ for AHNs is undecidable, there is no single algorithm that can be used to solve all PMCP instances of the form (i)

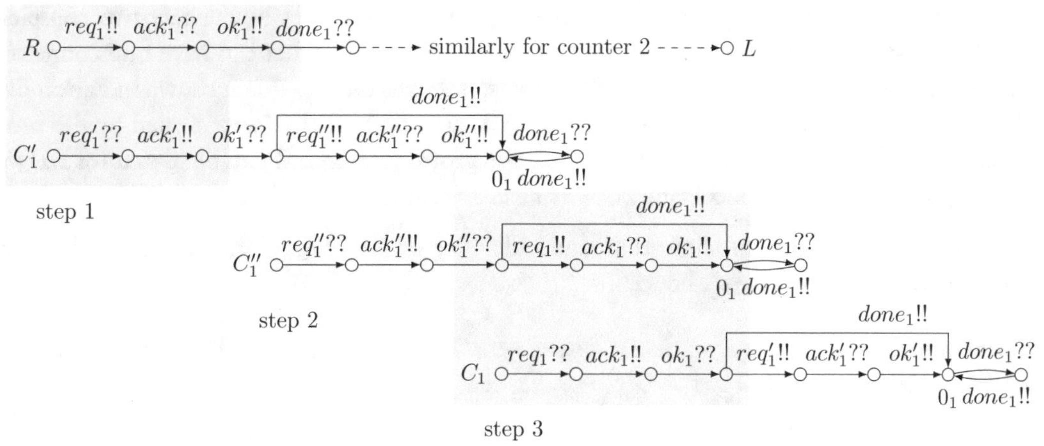

Figure 7.6: A part of the protocol to find a sub-graph "controller with two lists" used in Theorem 7.6. Only the part which looks for a list of processes that store the value of counter 1 is shown. The protocol can be naturally extended for both counters: after receiving $done_1$ the controller runs a similar protocol but with messages $req_2, ack_2 \ldots$ instead of $req_1, ack_1 \ldots$. Transitions to state err are omitted for readability [Delzanno et al., 2010].

from Section 7.1 (recall from Example 7.2 that the PMC in (i) is equivalent to an instance of COVER$_{\textbf{All}}$). In contrast, the corresponding PMCP for AHNs arranged in cliques is decidable by Corollary 7.4—thus, an algorithm that solves COVER$_{\textbf{C}}$ can also be used to answer the PMC question in (ii).

Undecidability for $\textbf{BD}_\textbf{k}$.   Consider the case of a more restricted parameterized connectivity graph $\textbf{BD}_\textbf{k}$. Since $\textbf{BD}_\textbf{1}$ coincides with the set of all cliques, it follows from Corollary 7.4 that COVER$_{\textbf{BD}_\textbf{1}}$ is decidable, and that REPEAT$_{\textbf{BD}_\textbf{1}}$ and TARGET$_{\textbf{BD}_\textbf{1}}$ are undecidable. For $k \geq 2$ COVER$_{\textbf{BD}_\textbf{k}}$ becomes also undecidable.

Theorem 7.8   *[Delzanno et al., 2011, Theorem 1]* COVER$_{\textbf{BD}_\textbf{k}}$, *for AHNs, is undecidable for* $k \geq 2$. Notice that this theorem does not directly follow from the previous one. We prove it differently from Delzanno et al. [2011], where the authors developed a separate protocol for $\textbf{BD}_\textbf{k}$.

Proof idea.   When one tries to prove undecidability of COVER$_{\textbf{BD}_\textbf{2}}$ (other ks follow), the first natural question is "Can we reuse the protocol from **All** case?." It might happen that the sub-graph extracted from **All** (of the form in Figure 7.5(a)) is not present in $\textbf{BD}_\textbf{k}$, which would mean that the protocol that was able to guess and then extract two lists of unbounded length from **All** will not be able to extract such lists from $\textbf{BD}_\textbf{2}$. I.e., when working on graphs in $\textbf{BD}_\textbf{2}$, the protocol from **All** case can guess the presence of a long list but it cannot complete its execution, because $\textbf{BD}_\textbf{2}$ does not contain the list of such length.

This is not the case though, since the protocol for **All** does not extract two completely "isolated" lists (connected to the controller), but rather two lists that can have interconnections between nodes from different lists. In other words, $\mathbf{BD_2}$ has the sub-graph shown in Figure 7.5(b) that i) can be extracted by the protocol from **All** case, ii) is of the form needed by the second phase when simulating a given 2CM. Hence, the protocol from **All** can be reused for $\mathbf{BD_2}$ and $\text{COVER}\mathbf{BD_k}$ for $k \geq 2$ is undecidable. □

It is not difficult to show that undecidability of $\text{COVER}\mathbf{BD_k}$ implies undecidability of $\text{REPEAT}\mathbf{BD_k}$ and $\text{TARGET}\mathbf{BD_k}$, hence:

Corollary 7.9 *[Delzanno et al., 2011, Esparza et al., 1999]* $\text{REPEAT}\mathbf{BD_k}$, $\text{TARGET}\mathbf{BD_k}$, *for AHNs, are undecidable for $k \geq 1$.*

Undecidability of $\text{Target}_{\mathbf{BP_k}}$, $\text{Repeat}_{\mathbf{BP_k}}$, $\text{Target}_{\mathbf{BPC_k}}$, $\text{Repeat}_{\mathbf{BPC_k}}$. Now consider even a more restricted parameterized connectivity graph $\mathbf{BP_k}$. Restricting the graph makes COVER decidable (see Theorem 7.19), but REPEAT and TARGET are still undecidable:

Theorem 7.10 *[Delzanno et al., 2010, Theorem 6]* $\text{TARGET}\mathbf{BP_k}$ *and* $\text{REPEAT}\mathbf{BP_k}$, *for AHNs, are undecidable for $k \geq 2$.*

Proof idea. Here we give an idea how to reduce the halting problem of 2CMs to $\text{TARGET}\mathbf{BP_2}$. The idea can be adapted to $\mathbf{BP_k}$ with $k > 2$. Consider a process template that implements a two-phase protocol:

1. Find a sub-graph of a form "star with a controller in the center."

2. Simulate the 2CM.

The first phase of the protocol is simple in comparison to that of the previous theorems and is shown in Figure 7.7(a). If the first phase succeeds, then nodes that are not in the error state form a graph of the form "star with a controller in the center" with a node in the center called the controller.

In the second phase the controller simulates 2CM, while user nodes store counters values (each user "stores" a bit, the total number of bits being equal to the value of a counter). In the second phase ack_i, ok are different from those used in the first phase. To increase the value of counter i the controller broadcasts $inc_i!!$. If there is a user process in state 0_i, then it responds with $ack_i!!$ and goes to state 1_i. The controller then in its turn acknowledges it with $ok_i!!$ which prevents other processes from sending $ack_i!!$. If the controller though receives several $ack_i!!$ before it manages to send the acknowledgement then it moves into state err and never leaves it. Operation "decrease" works in a similar way. Instead of simulating operation "test for zero" for counter i, the controller non-deterministically guesses the result, and if the guess is zero, then the controller broadcasts $zero_i!!$ and continues simulation. If the guess is wrong and there is a user in state 1_i, then that user moves into state err.

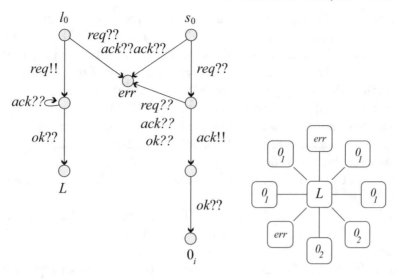

(a) A modified RAO protocol to find the sub-graph "star with a controller in the center" ($i \in 1, 2$).

(b) An example of state of an AHN with the graph from $\mathbf{BP_2}$ after executing the protocol on the left.

Figure 7.7: Finding a star-like sub-graph in graph from $\mathbf{BP_2}$ [Delzanno et al., 2010].

On reaching a halting state the controller sends all users except those in state *err* to a special state *halt* and goes there itself. Therefore, 2CM halts if and only if there is a system where all processes reach *halt*, which is an instance of $\text{TARGET}_{\mathbf{BP_2}}$. □

Recall that if each clique in a graph from $\mathbf{BPC_k}$ is replaced with a single node, then the resulting graph belongs to $\mathbf{BP_k}$. Hence in order to show undecidability of $\text{TARGET}_{\mathbf{BPC_k}}$ and $\text{REPEAT}_{\mathbf{BPC_k}}$ we modify the protocol used in the previous proof and add an initial phase in which in each clique a single representative node is chosen, and the rest of the protocol is unchanged. Hence ($\mathbf{BPC_0}$ coincides with the parameterized clique and was considered in Corollary 7.4):

Corollary 7.11 $\text{TARGET}_{\mathbf{BPC_k}}$ *and* $\text{REPEAT}_{\mathbf{BPC_k}}$, *for AHNs, are undecidable for* $k \geq 0$.

Undecidability of $\text{Cover}_{\mathbf{daAll}}$.   Finally, we state the result of Abdulla et al. [2013a] for the case of directed acyclic graphs:

Theorem 7.12   *[Abdulla et al., 2013a, Theorem 1]* $\text{COVER}_{\mathbf{daAll}}$ *for AHNs is undecidable.*

Proof idea. The previous proofs used the fact that the parameterized graphs are undirected: the basic RAO protocol in Figure 7.13(c) assumes the ability of a process to send and receive broadcast messages to and from all its adjacent nodes. If this is not the case as can be in directed graphs, the RAO protocol's main property ("isolation of pairs of processes," Lemma 7.5) does not hold. Furthermore, the simulation construction described in the proof of Theorem 7.6 breaks in the general case of directed graphs, because the controller is not able to get the feedback about its commands from the user processes. These facts make adaption of the standard proof technique (the reduction from the halting problem for 2CMs to COVER) not easy.

Hence, for the case of parameterized graphs **daAll**, Abdulla et al. [2013a] considered a different undecidable problem called TRANSD. Informally, TRANSD takes as input two automata A and B, and one transducer T, all with the same alphabet (transducer is an automaton that outputs a symbol in each transition). TRANSD outputs "Yes" iff there is $i \in \mathbb{N}_0$ and a word w accepted by A such that i successive applications of the transducer T to the word w results in a word accepted by B.

The authors briefly show in the paper that TRANSD is undecidable. Indeed, a transducer can compute one step of a Turing machine, and thus iterating this transducer simulates arbitrarily many steps of that Turing machine.

To reduce TRANSD to COVER$_{\mathbf{daAll}}$, the authors build a process template that simulates a given automata and a transducer. Initially, every process decide whom it simulates – A, B or T. For the simulation to be correct, it is necessary that the processes will form a graph of the form $A \rightarrow T \rightarrow \ldots \rightarrow T \rightarrow B$, i.e., the first process simulates automaton A followed by a (possibly zero) number of processes simulating transducer T, and then a process that simulates automaton B. Initially every A-process sends a special initiating message intended for a T- or B-process— on receiving it every T-process sends the same message. Every A-, T-, B- process on receiving initiating message twice goes into error state, it also goes into the error if received a message not intended for them or received two messages with no sending in between. After sending the initiating message the A-process starts transmitting a word accepted by A, letter by letter, followed by the end marker. The T-process receives a letter of the word and sends the transduced one further, and so on, to the B-process. The B-process receives a letter and simulates transitions of the automaton B. The B-process goes into state *halt* if it receives the end marker and it is in an accepting state of the automaton.

The control state of COVER consists of a single state *halt*. The construction above ensures: there is an AHN P^G with $G \in \mathbf{daAll}$ where a B-process can go into the control state, if and only if some number of applications of T to a word of automaton A results in a word of automaton B.   □

7.5.2   DECIDABILITY RESULTS FOR (NON-LOSSY) AHNS

In the previous section, in the proofs of undecidability of COVER$_{\mathbf{All}}$ (Theorem 7.6) and COVER$_{\mathbf{BD_k}}$ (Theorem 7.8) we used "lists" of user nodes to store the values of counters of a 2CM. In the general case there is no bound on counter values, so the proofs only work if we can find lists of unbounded length in the parameterized connectivity graph. Thus, the undecidability proofs break for parameterized connectivity graphs in which all graphs have only "lists" of a bounded length, or, in other words, if we restrict the length of simple paths on which a message in the system can travel. In the literature several such parameterized connectivity graphs are considered, namely, $\mathbf{BP_k}$, $\mathbf{BPC_k}$, and $\mathbf{daBP_k}$.

This section proves Theorem 7.19 that states decidability of COVER on $\mathbf{BP_k}$, $\mathbf{BPC_k}$ and on $\mathbf{daBP_k}$, thus covering all decidability results from Figure 7.3 for (non-lossy) AHNs.

The proofs of decidability of COVER of AHNs on these parameterized connectivity graphs use the machinery of well structured transition systems (WSTS) (see Section 3.2.1). The proofs have a similar structure for all the graphs except $\mathbf{daBP_k}$: Abdulla et al. [2013a] first reduced COVER on $\mathbf{daBP_k}$ to COVER on inverted trees—that is, trees that contain a node v such that all other nodes have a directed path to v—of bounded depth.

This section is organized as follows.

1. We define the induced sub-graph relation $\leq_{is}$ on directed graphs.

2. Lemma 7.13 proves that COVER on directed acyclic bounded path graphs ($\mathbf{daBP_k}$) can be reduced to COVER on bounded inverted trees ($\mathbf{BIT_k}$, defined later).

3. Lemma 7.14 and 7.15 prove that $\leq_{is}$ is a well quasi-order on $\mathbf{BPC_k}$, $\mathbf{BP_k}$, $\mathbf{BIT_k}$.

4. We define transition system M, which for given P, $\mathbf{G}$, represents the behavior of all instances of the parameterized AHN $P^{\mathbf{G}}$.

5. Lemma 7.18 proves that the transition system M for AHNs on $\mathbf{BP_k}, \mathbf{BPC_k}, \mathbf{BIT_k}$ is a WSTS with respect to $\leq_{is}$ (the proof uses Lemmas 7.14 and 7.15, and also intermediate Lemmas 7.16 and 7.17).

6. Finally, using Lemmas 7.13 and 7.18, Theorem 7.19 proves decidability of COVER for AHNs on $\mathbf{BP_k}$, $\mathbf{BPC_k}$, and $\mathbf{daBP_k}$.

7. We describe the parameterized model checking algorithm that solves COVER for AHNs on $\mathbf{BP_k}$, $\mathbf{BPC_k}$, and $\mathbf{daBP_k}$, and illustrate how it works.

1. The induced sub-graph relation $\leq_{is}$.   For graphs G_1, G_2 and labeling functions $s_1 : V_1 \to Q$ and $s_2 : V_2 \to Q$ with a set of labels Q define: $(G_1, s_1) \leq_{is} (G_2, s_2)$ iff there is a label preserving injection $h : V_1 \to V_2$ such that $(v, w) \in E_1 \iff (h(v), h(w)) \in E_2$. This is different from the sub-graph relation which preserves labels but allows new edges, i.e., $(h(v), h(w)) \in E_2$ does not necessary imply $(v, w) \in E_1$. Figure 7.8 gives an example.

2. Reducing COVER$_{\mathbf{daBP_k}}$ to COVER$_{\mathbf{BIT_k}}$.   Notice that the induced sub-graph relation $\leq_{is}$ is not a well quasi-order on $\mathbf{daBP_k}$ (an example of infinite decreasing chain is in Abdulla et al. [2013a, Section 8]). This is why we first need to reduce COVER$_{\mathbf{daBP_k}}$ to COVER on inverted trees of bounded depth for which $\leq_{is}$ is a well quasi-order (Lemma 7.15). Let $\mathbf{BIT_k}$ be a parameterized connectivity graph consisting of all inverted trees of depth k. Informally, an inverted tree is a

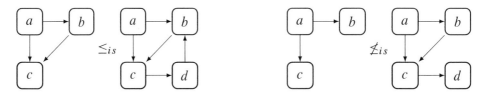

Figure 7.8: Example for the induced sub-graph relation $\leq_{is}$.

tree with all edges pointing toward the root. For the formal definition see, for example, [Abdulla et al., 2013a].

Then the following reduction from $\textsc{Cover}_{\mathbf{daBP_k}}$ to $\textsc{Cover}_{\mathbf{BIT_k}}$ holds.

Lemma 7.13   *[Abdulla et al., 2013a, Theorems 2 and 5] Given a decision procedure for $\textsc{Cover}_{\mathbf{BIT_k}}$, one can construct a decision procedure for $\textsc{Cover}_{\mathbf{daBP_k}}$.*

Proof idea. For a given graph in $\mathbf{daBP_k}$ we build an inverted forest of depth k that preserves all the paths of the the original graph but has new nodes (example in Figure 7.9).

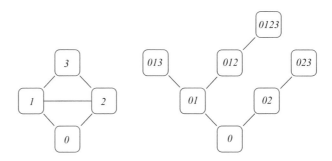

Figure 7.9: [Abdulla et al., 2013a] Directed acyclic graph and a corresponding inverted forest used in Lemma 7.13.

Then: if a process state is reachable in the AHN on a graph from $\mathbf{daBP_k}$, then this state is also reachable in the AHN on the inverted forest of depth k. The idea is to simulate the behavior of the original nodes (e.g., in Figure 7.9 all nodes with names starting with 0 will repeat the behavior of node 0). The other direction—if a process state is reachable in an AHN on an inverted forest of depth k, then it is reachable in the AHN on a graph from $\mathbf{daBP_k}$ – is trivial since any inverted forest of depth k is in $\mathbf{daBP_k}$.

Recall that a forest consists of trees and processes from different trees do not communicate with each other. Hence, a process can reach a control state in the AHN on an inverted forest if and only if a process from one of the trees can reach this state. This means that instead of considering $\textsc{Cover}$ on all inverted forests of depth k we can consider $\textsc{Cover}$ on all trees of those forests, i.e., COVER on all inverted trees of depth k. Finally, this means that $\text{COVER}_{\mathbf{daBP_k}}$ is equivalent to $\text{COVER}_{\mathbf{BIT_k}}$. □

3. $\leq_{is}$ is a well-quasi-order on $\mathbf{BP_k}$, $\mathbf{BPC_k}$, $\mathbf{BIT_k}$.

Lemma 7.14 *[Delzanno et al., 2011, Lemma 2] For fixed $k \in \mathbb{N}$, the induced sub-graph relation $\leq_{is}$ is a well quasi-order on labeled graphs from $\mathbf{BPC_k}$.*

Proof idea. The proof extends that of Ding [1992, Theorem 2.1] for the case of $\mathbf{BP_k}$. The crucial property of $\mathbf{BPC_k}$ (and of $\mathbf{BP_k}$) is that in any graph from $\mathbf{BPC_k}$ there is a vertex such that its removal splits the graph into non-connected graphs from $\mathbf{BPC_{k-1}}$. This property, together with Higman's lemma [Higman, 1952] (informally: if $\leq$ is a well quasi-order on Q, then the component-wise variation $\leq^*$ is a well quasi-order on Q^*), leads to an inductive proof. □

$\mathbf{BP_k} \subset \mathbf{BPC_k}$ for any $k \geq 1$, hence by the lemma $\leq_{is}$ is a well quasi-order on $\mathbf{BP_k}$ too (the case of $k = 0$ is trivial).

Abdulla et al. [2013a] introduced a special class of multi-sets that can encode inverted trees of depth k, and then prove that these sets are well quasi ordered and so are inverted trees of depth k. Here, instead, we show that inverted trees of depth k are well quasi-ordered with the induced sub-graph relation $\leq_{is}$.

Lemma 7.15 *For a fixed $k \in \mathbb{N}$, the induced sub-graph relation $\leq_{is}$ is a well quasi-order on labeled graphs from $\mathbf{BIT_k}$.*

Proof idea. We use the fact that $\leq_{is}$ is a well quasi-order on labeled $\mathbf{BP_k}$ [Ding, 1992, Theorem 2.1].

First, any inverted tree of depth k can be uniquely up to isomorphism mapped to a $3k$-bounded path graph. For example, the inverted tree $a \to b$ maps to $a - v - w - b$, where v, w are two auxiliary nodes to help encode edge directions[2].

Take any infinite sequence $G_1, G_2, \ldots$ of inverted trees of depth k. We will show that there is $i < j$ with $G_i \leq_{is} G_j$.

Consider the sequence $G'_1, G'_2, \ldots$ of encoding graphs. They are from $3k$-bounded path graphs which are well quasi ordered with $\leq_{is}$ [Ding, 1992, Theorem 2.1], and therefore the sequence has $i < j$ with $G'_i \leq_{is} G'_j$.

Thus, for original graphs, $G_i \leq_{is} G_j$ also holds: by induction we can show that the induced sub-graph relation preserves exact paths, hence for any path $a - v - w - b$ in G'_i there is a path $h(a) - h(v) - h(w) - h(b)$ in G'_j, hence for edge $a \to b$ in G_i there is edge $h(a) \to h(b)$ in G_j. The other direction (for any edge $h(a) \to h(b)$ there is edge $a \to b$) can be proven similarly.[3] □

---

[2]This encoding was suggested to us by authors of [Abdulla et al., 2013a], in particular by Othmane Rezine.

[3]Here, h is a label preserving injection $V(G'_i) \to V(G'_j)$ as required by the definition of $\leq_{is}$, we also assume that for any i: $V(G'_i) = V(G_i) \cup$ *auxiliary nodes*, and we reused h to show that $G_i \leq_{is} G_j$.

4 & 5. Parameterized AHNs on $\mathbf{BP_k}$, $\mathbf{BPC_k}$, $\mathbf{BIT_k}$ are WSTSs wrt. $\leq_{is}$.   For given parameterized AHN $\overline{P}^{\mathbf{G}}$ define the *transition system M* (in Lemma 7.18 we prove it is a WSTS).

- The set of states consists of all pairs (G, s) with $G \in \mathbf{G}$, $s \in S$ where S is the set of states of P^G, and the set I of initial states $I = \{(G, s_0) \mid G \in \mathbf{G}, s_0 \in S_0\}$. Notice that I is downward closed with respect to $\leq_{is}$.

- The transition relation contains $(G, s) \to (G, s')$ iff there is a transition $s \to s'$ in P^G.

Intuitively, the transition system M is an infinite state system that represents all instances of a given parameterized AHN $P^{\mathbf{G}}$.

Now we can state the following.

Lemma 7.16   *[Delzanno et al., 2010, Lemma 2]* [4] *Fix $\overline{P}^{\mathbf{G}}$, and let M be defined as above. Then the induced sub-graph relation $\leq_{is}$ is monotonic with respect to the transition system M.*

Proof idea. Let $(G, s) \leq (G', s')$ for some states s, s' in S and G, G' in $\mathbf{G}$ (where S is the set of states of $\overline{P}^{\mathbf{G}}$). Consider the case when $(G, s) \to (G, t)$ happens via a broadcast by process v in system $\overline{P}^{G}$. Then there is a process v' of $\overline{P}^{G'}$ which is in the same state as process v, and v' is connected to processes in the same states as neighbors of v. Then if the process v' in $\overline{P}^{G'}$ makes the same broadcast action as v in $\overline{P}^{G}$ then all the neighbors of v' in G' behave the same way as neighbors of v in G, and possibly neighbors of v' in $G' \setminus G$ also change state.   □

Recall from Section 3.2: for a given set C of states of transition system M, $Pred(C)$ is defined as the union of C and all one-step predecessors of C; a basis of an upward closed set D is set B s.t. $D = \uparrow B$. Now we are ready to state:

Lemma 7.17   *[Abdulla et al., 2013a, Delzanno et al., 2010, 2011]*
  Fix $k \in \mathbb{N}_0$, $\overline{P}^{\mathbf{G}}$ where $\mathbf{G}$ is one of $\mathbf{BP_k}$, $\mathbf{BPC_k}$, $\mathbf{BIT_k}$, and let M be the transition system defined as before. Then given a basis of an upward closed set C, one can compute a basis of $Pred(C)$ for the transition system M.

Proof idea. A variation of the algorithm is in Algorithm 1. The authors do not provide the proof of the algorithm correctness, but the insight is: to compute $Pred(\uparrow B)$ for some finite $B = ((G_1, s), .., (G_i, s_i), .., (G_k, s_k))$, it is enough to compute all predecessors of all (G_i, s_i) in B, and compute all predecessors of all (G_i^+, s_i^+) resulting from (G_i, s_i) by adding a single node making a broadcast transition. The termination follows from the finiteness of iterated objects.   □

---

[4] The original lemma is for graphs from $\mathbf{BP_k}$, but the proof applies to general graphs as well.

Algorithm 1: BPred: Computing a finite basis of a predecessor (Lemma 7.17).

Input: $P, G \in \{\mathbf{BP_k}, \mathbf{BPC_k}, \mathbf{BIT_k}\}$, a finite set T of states of the transition system M

Output: *a basis of $Pred(\uparrow T)$*

def BPred($P, \mathbf{G}, T$):

    $B = T$

    for $(G, s) \in T$:

        for $q' \xrightarrow{act} q$ of P :

            $A = \mathtt{pred1}(G, s, q' \xrightarrow{act} q)$

            add to B all $(G, s) \in A$ that are not in $\uparrow B$

            if $q' \xrightarrow{act} q$ *is a broadcast send transition* :

                $T^+ = \{(G^+, s^+) \mid$ *it is* (G, s) *with one new node in state* q *and* $G^+ \in \mathbf{G}\}$[5] **for**

                $(G^+, s^+) \in T^+$:

                    $A = \mathtt{pred1}(G^+, s^+, q' \xrightarrow{act} q)$

                    add to B all $(G, s) \in A$ that are not in $\uparrow B$

    return B

def pred1($G, s, q' \xrightarrow{act} q$):

    $A = \emptyset$

    for $v \in G$ *with* $s(v) = q$:

        if $q' \xrightarrow{act} q$ *is internal* :

            add (G, s') to A where s' is the predecessor of s corresponding to $q' \xrightarrow{act} q$

        elif $q' \xrightarrow{act} q$ *is broadcast send* $q' \xrightarrow{a!!} q$:

            if *process* v *has a neighbor*[6] *in state* r *and* $r' \xrightarrow{a??} r$ *for some* r :

                continue

            $\{v_1, .., v_k\}$ = the neighbors of v that received a (for every v_i $\exists r_i' \xrightarrow{a??} s(v_i)$[7])

            for *subset* $\in 2^{\{v_1, ..., v_k\}}$:

                $S' = \{s' \mid s'$ *is a predecessor of* s *where* v *synchronizes only with subset*[8]$\}$

                add (G, s') to A for every $s' \in S'$

    return A

---

[5]To optimize, consider only G^+s where the new node is connected to at least one node that will be able to receive the broadcast.

[6]"v has a neighbour v'" means there is an edge from v to v'.

[7]For each v_i there might be more than one r_i' with $r_i' \xrightarrow{a??} s(v_i)$.

[8]I.e., $\forall v_i \in subset : s'(v_i) \xrightarrow{a??} s(v_i)$ is a transition of P, $\forall v' \in G \setminus \{v, v_i\} : s'(v') = s(v'), s'(v) = q'$.

Lemma 7.18   *Fix* $k \in \mathbb{N}_0$, $\overline{P}^{\mathbf{G}}$ *where* $\mathbf{G}$ *is one of* $\mathbf{BP_k}$, $\mathbf{BPC_k}$, $\mathbf{BIT_k}$, *and let* M *be the transition system defined as before. Then* M *is a well structured transition system with respect to* $\leq_{is}$.

Proof. M and $\leq_{is}$ satisfy all items of the definition of a WSTS wrt. $\leq_{is}$ (Section 3.2.1):

- $\leq_{is}$ is a well quasi-order on states of M (Lemmas 7.14 and 7.15),

- $\leq_{is}$ is monotonic with respect to M (Lemma 7.16), and

- a basis of $Pred(\uparrow B)$ for a given finite set B of states of M is computable (Lemma 7.17)

□

6. Cover is decidable.   Finally, we are ready to prove the main result of this section.

Theorem 7.19   *[Abdulla et al., 2013a, Delzanno et al., 2010, 2011]* COVER *is decidable for* AHNs *on i)* $\mathbf{BPC_k}$, *ii)* $\mathbf{BP_k}$, *iii)* $\mathbf{daBP_k}$.

Proof idea.   Consider the case of $\mathbf{BPC_k}$, the cases of $\mathbf{BP_k}$ and $\mathbf{BIT_k}$ (which implies the result for $\mathbf{daBP_k}$ by Lemma 7.13) is similar. For simplicity assume that the set of control states given to COVER consists of a single state.

We reduce COVER$_{\mathbf{BPC_k}}$ to the coverability problem for WSTSs and then apply Theorem 3.3.

Fix process template P, $k \in \mathbb{N}_0$, and a single control state c in COVER$_{\mathbf{BPC_k}}$. For given P, k build the transition system M defined as before. Consider the instance of coverability problem for WSTS M with control states set $\{(G_1, s) \mid s(1) = c\}$ where G_1 is the graph with a single vertex. M is a WSTS (by Lemma 7.18) with downward closed initial states, hence by Theorem 3.3 we can compute the answer to the coverability problem for M which is equal to the answer to COVER$_{\mathbf{BPC_k}}$ for $P^{\mathbf{BPC_k}}$. Hence, COVER$_{\mathbf{BPC_k}}$ for AHNs is decidable.   □

7. Putting it all together: the parameterized model checking algorithm.   Let us develop the parameterized model checking algorithm that solves COVER$_{\mathbf{G}}$ for AHNs for $\mathbf{G} \in \{\mathbf{BPC_k}, \mathbf{BP_k}, \mathbf{BIT_k}\}$. The soundness and completeness of the algorithm will follow from Theorem 7.19 and Theorem 3.3. The algorithm computes predecessors of C using procedure BPred from Algorithm 1 until the fixpoint is reached, and checks if predecessors has a non-empty intersection with the initial states. Algorithms of such form are called set saturation algorithms in Finkel and Schnoebelen [2001].

For simplicity assume that the set of control states given to COVER consists of a single state called c, thus $C = \{c\}$. Also, let G_c denote the graph with a single node in state c.

Algorithm 2: Solving COVER.

Input: $P, c, \mathbf{G} \in \{\mathbf{BP_k}, \mathbf{BPC_k}, \mathbf{BIT_k}\}$
Output: the answer to COVER$_\mathbf{G}$ for $P, c, \mathbf{G}$
$b\_reach = \emptyset$
$b\_reach' = \{G_c\}$
while $b\_reach \neq b\_reach'$:
    $b\_reach = b\_reach'$
    $b\_reach' = \text{BPred}(P, \mathbf{G}, b\_reach)$
    if b_reach' *contains an initial system state* :
        return YES
return NO

Example 7.20 Let us apply Algorithm 2 to the process template P_{re} from the running example in Figure 7.1, the parameterized graph $\mathbf{BP_2}$ ("stars"), and for different control states C.

First, consider $C = \{err\}$. Thus, we answer PMC question (i) from Section 7.1 specialized to $\mathbf{BP_2}$: "In AHNs composed of processes of P_{re}, is there a graph from $\mathbf{BP_2}$ and a process that reaches err?"

- The first iteration gives: $\text{BPred}(P, \mathbf{BP_2}, \{G_{err}\}) = \{err, init - l'\}$[9].

- The second iteration gives: $\text{BPred}(P, \mathbf{BP_2}, \{err, init - l'\}) = \{err, init - l'\}$. Fixpoint!

- $\{err, init - l'\}$ does not contain an initial system state, hence return NO.

Now consider $C = \{hub\}$ and thus the question is "In AHNs composed of processes of P_{re}, is there a graph from $\mathbf{BP_2}$ and a process that reaches hub?"

- The first iteration gives: $\text{BPred}(P, \mathbf{BP_2}, \{G_{hub}\}) = \{hub, init - u, init - u', u - u'\}$.

- For simplicity, consider only labeled graph $init - u'$ calculated in the previous item: $\text{BPred}(P, \mathbf{BP_2}, \{init - u'\}) = \{init - u', init - init - init\}$. The set contains initial system state $init - init - init$, hence return YES.

7.6 DECIDABILITY RESULTS FOR LOSSY AD HOC NETWORKS

Recall from Section 7.2 that in LAHNs a broadcast message can be non-deterministically lost by some of the receivers.

---

[9]Here, a denotes the graph consisting of a single node labeled a. Also, $a - b$ denotes the graph consisting of two connected vertices labeled a and b. Finally, $a - b - c$ denotes the graph which is a pipeline of three nodes labeled a, b, and c, respectively.

The following two theorems were proved for *mobile* ad hoc networks, but as shown in Delzanno et al. [2012b, Proposition 1], mobile ad hoc networks are equivalent to lossy ad hoc networks on cliques.

Theorem 7.21   *[Delzanno et al., 2010, Corollary 2]* COVER$_C$, REPEAT$_C$, TARGET$_C$ *are decidable for LAHNs.*

Proof idea. The problems can be reduced to decidable problems for Petri nets (or equivalently to vector addition systems) described in Chapter 3. The reduction works only for systems arranged in cliques, so does not apply to **BP$_k$**, **BD$_k$**, **BPC$_k$**, etc.

To reduce the problems for LAHN to decidable problems for Petri nets the authors suggest the construction of the Petri net shown in Figures 7.10 and 7.11 (the construction depends on the process template of a LAHN under consideration). The construction ensures that the answer to a given LAHN problem is YES if and only if the answer to a corresponding problem for the Petri net is YES.

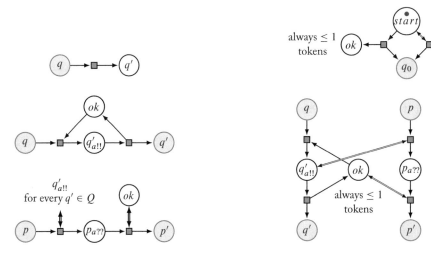

Figure 7.10: Top to bottom, Petri net constructions for transitions: internal, broadcast-send $q \xrightarrow{a!!} q'$, and receive $p \xrightarrow{a??} p'$.

Figure 7.11: On the top—the initilization, on the bottom—illustration of broadcast synchronization $q \xrightarrow{a!!} q'$ and $p \xrightarrow{a??} p'$.

Assuming that COVER, REPEAT, TARGET has control sets with a single state, the reductions are the following.

- COVER$_C$ is reduced to the coverability for Petri nets: the control configuration has "1" in a place that corresponds to a control state, and "0" in all other places.

- REPEAT$_C$ is reduced to the repeated coverability for Petri nets: the control configuration is defined similarly to the previous case.

- TARGET$_C$ is reduced to the reachability for Petri nets, but the Petri net constructed according to Figures 7.10 and 7.11 additionally has:

  - place *end*,

  - transition from *ok* to *end*, and

  - transition from *end, q* to *end* for every state *q* of the process template.

  Then the control configuration is: "1" in place *end*, and "0" in all other places.

Now let us look how the reduction works.

Direction "Run in the LAHN → *computation in the Petri net"*: take a run in the LAHN that satisfies a given problem property, let us build a run in the Petri net that also satisfies the corresponding property. First, the Petri net builds an initial state of the LAHN (Figure 7.11, top): the Petri net "pumps" an arbitrary number of tokens from *start* into place q_0, then the token from *start* moves into *ok*. At this moment the configuration of the Petri net (with *n* tokens in q_0) corresponds to the initial state of the LAHN with *n* processes.

After the initial configuration is built, the Petri net starts simulating transitions of the LAHN. Consider the case of a broadcast transition: send $q \xrightarrow{a!!} q'$ and receive $p \xrightarrow{a??} p'$ (Figure 7.11, bottom). Suppose there is a process in state *q* in the LAHN and some number of processes in state *p* – in the Petri net this corresponds to a token in place *q*, and a number of tokens in *p* (the number of tokens in *p* is equal to the number of processes in state *p*). Let the *q*-process and *m* processes in state *p* take the broadcast synchronized transition—in the Petri net this corresponds to a sequence of transitions that moves a single token from *q* to *q'* and *m* tokens from *p* to *p'* (and no tokens are left in $p_{a??}$). This completes the description of the simulation of the broadcast transition. The simulation ensures that the computation of the Petri net satisfies the corresponding property (over Petri net configurations).

Direction "Faithful computation in the Petri net → *run in the* LAHN." We call *faithful computation* a computation in the Petri net that does not leave tokens in place $p_{a??}$ between broadcast simulations. Then the proof of this direction follows from two claims.

(i) If there is a computation that (repeatedly) covers the corresponding control configuration mentioned in the reductions before, then there is a faithful computation in the Petri net that does this,

(ii) Any faithful computation of the Petri net has a corresponding run in the LAHN.

The intuition behind item (i) is as follows. If in a non-faithful computation there are tokens left in state $p_{a??}$, then in a faithful corresponding computation we move all the tokens from $p_{a??}$ to state *p'* and do not move them until the tokens in $p_{a??}$ get moved in the original non-faithful computation. The second item (ii) follows from the observation that any faithful transition of the Petri corresponds to some transition in the LAHN.

Finally, the decidability of $\text{COVER}_\mathbf{C}$, $\text{TARGET}_\mathbf{C}$, $\text{REPEAT}_\mathbf{C}$ for LAHNs follows from the decidability of corresponding problems for Petri nets. □

Example 7.22   Consider process template in Figure 7.12(a) which is a part of the running example process template P_{re} in Figure 7.1 from Section 7.1. Constructing the Petri net according to Figures 7.10 and 7.11 gives the net in Figure 7.12(b).

Consider PMC question (i) from Section 7.1 adapted to LANHs: "Is there a LAHN build from process template in Figure 7.12(a) that reaches state err?." It is easy to see that two tokens in the initial state ι are enough to cover state err in the Petri net: consider computation where, first, one token moves from ι to l', and then both tokens move: the token in l' moves to err while the token from ι moves to l'. Hence, the answer to our PMC question is YES.

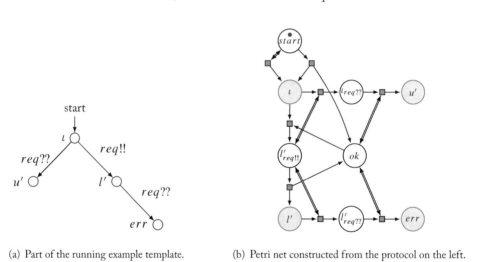

(a) Part of the running example template. (b) Petri net constructed from the protocol on the left.

Figure 7.12: Example of the conversion of a protocol into a Petri net simulating LAHNs.

Note on complexities.   The proof of Theorem 7.21 reduces $\text{COVER}_\mathbf{C}$ and $\text{TARGET}_\mathbf{C}$ for LAHNs to ExpSpace-complete and -hard problems on Petri nets, and does not provide the lower bound. In the follow-up paper Delzanno et al. [2012a] explore the complexities. We state their results without providing the proofs.

Theorem 7.23   *[Delzanno et al., 2012a, Theorem 1 and 2] For* LAHNs $\text{COVER}_\mathbf{C}$ *is* P-*complete and* $\text{TARGET}_\mathbf{C}$ *is* NP-*complete (with respect to the size of the process template).*

7.7   DISCUSSION

In ad hoc networks, the nature of the parameterized connectivity graph separates the decidable cases from undecidable. Delzanno et al. [2010, 2011] gave the first characterization of those graphs on which COVER is decidable ($\mathbf{BPC_k}$) and on which it is undecidable ($\mathbf{BD_k}$). Figure 7.13 illustrates the decidability boundary for this problem. If we consider the more expressive problems

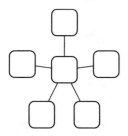
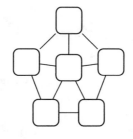
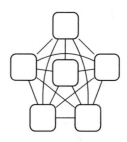

(a) COVER is decidable on star-like graphs for AHNs (bounded-path graphs).

(b) COVER is undecidable on wheel-shaped graphs for AHNs (unbounded-path bounded-diameter graphs).

(c) COVER is decidable on cliques for AHNs (unbounded-path graphs with diameter equal to 1).

Figure 7.13: The decidability boundary for Cover for AHNs.

REPEAT or TARGET in ad hoc networks without losses, then we get undecidability for all the graphs considered in this chapter.[10] Finally, in ad hoc networks with lossy broadcast transitions, all these problems are decidable. Table 7.1 summarizes the decidability results for ad hoc networks.

Decidability proof techniques in both non-lossy and lossy cases are based on well-structuredness of the systems, and do not exhibit cutoffs that are independent of the process template as in Chapter 4.

Undecidability proofs, similarly to other chapters, reduce from the halting problem for 2CMs. Thus, for a given 2CM, the proofs build a protocol that simulates its execution. In contrast to other chapters, the exact connectivity graph is unknown a priori (what is known is a class to which the graph belongs to), so the protocols for simulating a given 2CM have two steps. In the first step they ensure the right form of the connectivity graph, and the second step does the simulation relying on the particular form of the graph. Another difference is the case of directed acyclic graphs (Theorem 7.12) where the information from process to process flows in one direction only. Thus the controller that simulates the control of a given 2CM cannot receive the feedback from processes it broadcasts messages to. In this case the undecidability proof uses the fact that TMs can be simulated by iterating finite-state transducers.

---

[10]Possibly except for directed parameterized connectivity graph $\mathbf{daBP_k}$.

Table 7.1: Decidability results for Ad Hoc Networks and their sources

Result	Network type	Graphs	Specification	References
undecidability	AHN	**All**	Cover	[Delzanno et al. 2010]
undecidability	AHN	**BD$_k$**	Cover	[Delzanno et al. 2011]
undecidability for $k \geq 2$	AHN	**BP$_k$**	Target, Repeat	[Delzanno et al. 2010]
undecidability	AHN	**daAll**	Cover	[Abdulla et al. 2013a]
decidability	AHN	**BPC$_k$,** **BP$_k$,** **daBP$_k$**	Cover	[Delzanno et al. 2010] [Delzanno et al. 2011] [Abdulla et al. 2013a]
decidability	LAHN	**C**	Cover, Repeat, Target	[Delzanno et al. 2010]

7.7.1   VARIATIONS OF THE MODEL

Delzanno et al. [2012b] study AHNs with many other failure types (we considered only message losses). They distinguish between failures in nodes and in communication.

Node failures include non-deterministic restarts and crashes. They show by reduction from the undecidable Cover in AHNs (without failures) that the PMCPs for such models are undecidable.

Communication failures include non-deterministic message losses (covered here as LAHNs), message conflicts, and message conflicts with conflict detection. A message conflict happens when a node senses broadcasts from two or more nodes simultaneously. The model with message conflicts makes Cover decidable (and the proof uses the ideas from the LAHN section), while the model with conflict detection makes the PMCPs undecidable (via reduction from undecidable Cover for AHNs).

Abdulla et al. [2011] studied PMC problems for AHNs composed of processes being timed automata, and Delzanno et al. [2013] studied the case of LAHNs of processes being register automata.

Delzanno and Traverso [2013] studied PMC problems for AHNs where broadcasts are asynchronous. In this model each process has an unbounded (local) buffer for incoming messages. When a process broadcasts a message, it is enqueued into buffers of all receiving processes, and later the processes asynchronously handle the messages (in our model broadcasts are synchronous, i.e., a broadcast message is immediately and simultaneously handled by all receiving processes).

CHAPTER 8

Related Work

In this book we focused on established decidability results in parameterized model checking. As this topic is a lively field, we cannot make any claim about completeness of our survey. In particular, we left out the large body of research that includes invariant-based techniques, regular model checking, symbolic methods, techniques for counter automata, and abstraction-based methods. In this chapter we give a brief overview of these methods and give further references to the interested reader. Our classification of the techniques is unavoidably subjective, as except for several cornerstone papers, many techniques adopted multiple different ideas.

For the reader interested in practical applications of parameterized model checking techniques, we give an overview of PMC tools in Chapter 9.

8.1 ABSTRACTION TECHNIQUES

The general idea of abstraction-based techniques is as follows. One identifies a class of process templates that have a common structure.[1] To construct a new abstraction, one defines an abstraction mapping α that builds a finite-state system $\alpha(P)$ of a given process template P. Further, one proves that α preserves the specifications from a predefined class S: for every specification $\varphi \in S$ and every process template P, if $\alpha(P) \models \varphi$, then for every number of processes $n \geq 1$, it holds that $P^n \models \varphi$. This proof is the most complicated part of the technique. Typically, the proof is done by showing that $\alpha(P)$ simulates each system P^n, for $n \geq 1$, which implies that $\alpha(P)$ satisfies all ACTL*-formulas that are satisfied by every system instance from P^n for $n \geq 1$ (see Clarke et al. [1999, Theorem 16]). Hence, for a given process template P, the parameterized model checking problem amounts to constructing the abstraction $\alpha(P)$ and checking whether the property holds for $\alpha(P)$.

Abstraction introduces new behavior and thus, when $\alpha(P)$ does not satisfy the property φ to be verified, one cannot immediately conclude whether the property is satisfied in the parameterized family $\{P^n \mid n \geq 1\}$. If $\alpha(P) \not\models \varphi$, the model checking tool will provide a counterexample, and the user has to analyze the counterexample with the goal of refining the abstraction $\alpha(P)$. Sometimes, $\alpha(P)$ can be refined automatically, see e.g., Abdulla et al. [2010] and John et al. [2013]. However, refinement techniques for parameterized model checking are, by design, incomplete. Therefore, abstraction-based techniques do not characterize decidable classes of the parameterized model checking problem, in contrast to the techniques described in this book.

---

[1]For instance, $\{0, 1, \infty\}$-counter abstraction by Pnueli et al. [2002] is applicable to process templates that can be represented with the SLP language.

Notwithstanding, this incompleteness property, abstraction methods have been successfully applied to many practical examples.

Pnueli et al. [2002] highlighted $\{0, 1, \infty\}$-*counter abstraction*. There, a state of the abstraction $\alpha(P)$ consists of global variables over some finite domain and abstract counters $\kappa_1, \ldots, \kappa_m$ over the domain $\{0, 1, 2\}$. Counter κ_i represents the abstract number of processes in the i-th local state as follows: value 0 corresponds to zero processes; value 1 corresponds to exactly one process; value 2 corresponds to "many" processes (i.e., more than one). By using the finite abstract domain to count processes, one constructs the finite abstraction $\alpha(P)$ for a process template P. The atomic propositions allow one to check how many processes there are in a certain local state, e.g., $\kappa_{\ell_1} = 1$ asserts that there is exactly one process in the local state ℓ_1, while $\kappa_{\ell_2} > 1$ asserts that that several processes are in the state ℓ_2. Pnueli et al. [2002] showed that for every 1-LTL\X-formula φ, if $\alpha(P) \models \varphi$ holds, then $\forall n \geq 1.\ P^n \models \varphi$ holds as well. It is easy to see that this abstraction works especially well for mutual exclusion properties: the formula $\mathsf{G}(\kappa_{\ell_C} < 2)$ expresses that never two processes are in the critical section at the same time. Pnueli et al. [2002] applied their abstraction to reason about safety and liveness of Szymanski's mutual exclusion algorithm and of simplified Bakery. The abstractions were checked with the NuSMV model checker [Cimatti et al., 2002].

Ip and Dill [1999] discussed an abstraction similar to $\{0, 1, \infty\}$-counter abstraction, but they focused only on safety properties. They implemented their abstraction in Murφ [Dill, 1996, 2008] and verified safety of Peterson's mutual exclusion algorithm and of the cache coherence protocols MESI, ICCP, and DCCP.

John et al. [2013] generalized $\{0, 1, \infty\}$-counter abstraction to counter abstraction over *parametric intervals* (PIA-counter abstraction). In their abstraction, each counter is assigned an abstract value that corresponds to an interval, e.g., if $\kappa_i = [(n+1)/2, n+1)$, then a majority out of n processes is in state ℓ_i. Hence, $\{0, 1, \infty\}$-counter abstraction is a special case of PIA-counter abstraction over the intervals $[0, 1)$, $[1, 2)$, and $[2, n+1)$. John et al. [2013] implemented their abstraction in the tool ByMC and verified safety and liveness of reliable broadcast algorithms in the presence of a parameterized number of faults (e.g., crash and Byzantine). The abstract systems were checked with the Spin model checker [Holzmann, 2003].

Clarke et al. [2008] introduced environment abstraction, which can also be seen as a generalization of $\{0, 1, \infty\}$-counter abstraction. In their framework, an abstraction of a global state is a formula that describes the state of a special process (called the *reference* process) and a summary of the states of the other processes (called the *environment*). A system transition is abstracted as a step of the reference process as follows: the reference process checks whether the environment satisfies the precondition; if so, the reference process changes its local state and the state of the environment. After the transition has been made, another process in the environment can become the reference process. The abstract semantics of the transitions is defined individually for each protocol class. Clarke et al. [2008] applied their technique to verify the following protocols: readers/writers, Szymanski's mutual exclusion, simplified Bakery, German's cache coherence protocol, and the Flash cache coherence protocol. Their work was extended by Talupur and Tuttle [2008].

Basler et al. [2009] applied $\{0, 1, \infty\}$-counter abstraction on boolean programs to verify concurrent programs with the parameterized number of threads. They proposed a symbolic exploration algorithm that has been implemented in the tool BOOM and scales well for boolean programs in practice.

Jensen and Lynch [1998] introduced a parameterized simulation relation and used it to prove soundness of their specific abstraction of Burns' mutual exclusion algorithm. In their abstraction, they mapped a system of n processes to a system of two processes AP_0 and AP_1: intuitively, AP_0 and AP_1, respectively, represent the processes with indices i and j for $1 \leq i < j \leq n$. Jensen and Lynch [1998] proved soundness of the abstraction in the Larch Proof Assistant and verified safety of the abstraction with Spin.

Calder and Miller [2003] verified the Firewire protocol with Spin and introduced a specific abstraction for the parameterized case.

8.2   REGULAR MODEL CHECKING

Regular model checking (RMC) is a symbolic technique built upon automata representation of transition relations; see Abdulla [2012] for a detailed survey. RMC assumes a linear order $\prec$ on a set of processes. Such an order comes naturally when the processes of a parameterized system are organized in a ring or a line. Let P be a process template with a *finite* set Q of local states. Then, a global state of a system P^n is represented as a word $w \in Q^n$ of length n, where the letter $w[i]$ corresponds to the local state of the i-th process (in the order $\prec$) for $1 \leq i \leq n$.

In RMC, the set of global states S is required to be a language of a finite-state automaton A_S over the alphabet Q. Similarly, a finite-state automaton A_R over the alphabet $Q \times Q$ represents the union of transition relations in the parameterized family $\{P^n \mid n \geq 1\}$. As the automaton A_R models systems that do not dynamically create or destroy processes, the language of A_R is size-preserving, that is, the language $\mathcal{L}(A_R)$ of the automaton A_R is a subset of $\{(w, w') \mid w, w' \in Q, |w| = |w'|\}$.

Given a process template P, one has to construct the following automata that represent the union of the transition systems in the parameterized family $\{P^n \mid n \geq 1\}$:

- an automaton A_I to represent the set of the initial states,

- an automaton A_B to represent the set of bad states (violating the reachability specification), and

- an automaton A_R to represent the transition relation.

These automata are given as the input to the RMC technique. Their construction is not part of the RMC technique.

The main goal of the RMC technique is to compute the reflexive and transitive closure A_R^* of the automaton A_R: an automaton that only accepts pairs of words $w, w' \in Q^*$ that are connected by a path $w_1, \ldots, w_k \in Q^*$, that is, $w = w_1$, $w_k = w'$ and $(w_i, w_{i+1}) \in \mathcal{L}(A_R)$ for $1 \leq i < k$. Once A_R^* is built, one applies automata-theoretic operations to check whether one of the systems in the family $\{P^n \mid n \geq 1\}$ violates the specification: let us denote by $\mathcal{L}(A_R^*(A_I))$ the set of words $\{w' \in Q^* \mid w \in \mathcal{L}(A_I), (w, w') \in \mathcal{L}(A_R^*)\}$, which symbolically represents all reachable states. Then, no system P^n reaches a bad global state (i.e., a state in the language of the automaton A_B), if and only if $\mathcal{L}(A_R^*(A_I)) \cap \mathcal{L}(A_B) = \emptyset$.

Computing A_R^* is the main bottleneck of the RMC technique. Indeed, in general, the closure is neither regular, nor computable. Several less general solutions were introduced, e.g., *acceleration* of process transitions [Abdulla et al., 1999], *quotienting* of automata by state merging [Abdulla et al., 2002, Bouajjani et al., 2000], and *abstraction* [Bouajjani et al., 2004].

We make two observations about the representation. First, alphabet Q is finite and for each $n \geq 1$, automaton A_S accepts finitely many words of length n. However, as the language of A_S can be infinite, the automaton is able to capture global states of all systems P^n, for $n \geq 1$. This brings us to the second observation: not every set of global states S is regular, i.e., there may not be an ordering $\prec$ under which S can be encoded with a finite-state automaton, and thus RMC techniques may not apply. The same applies to the automaton A_R.

Finally, To and Libkin [2010] introduced algorithmic metatheorems that generalize reasoning found in regular model checking research. A tool that implements regular model model checking is T(O)RMC [Legay, 2008].

8.3 SYMBOLIC TECHNIQUES

Similar to regular model checking (Section 8.2), symbolic techniques do not represent state sets and transition relations explicitly, but use symbolic representations. While RMC is based on one form of symbolic representation, namely, finite automata, the symbolic techniques presented in this section apply various logical theories to represent states and transitions.

Henriksen et al. [1995] proposed to use *monadic second order logic* as a "highly succinct alternative to regular expressions." Elgaard et al. [1998] implemented their framework in the tool MONA.

General principles for parameterized symbolic model checking were laid out by Kesten et al. [1997]. There, the authors used a *finitary second-order theory of one successor* (FS1S) and FS*S, which have the same expressive power as finite automata and tree automata respectively. Further, Pnueli and Shahar [2000] investigated liveness and acceleration in this framework. These techniques were implemented in the tool called TLV [Pnueli and Shahar, 1996], and have been re-implemented in JTLV [Pnueli et al., 2010].

Maidl [2001] introduced a framework, in which parameterized systems are represented as formulas over Presburger arithmetic. Apart from local and global variables, the formulas contain special variables that represent process indices. The framework encompasses token passing and broadcast systems. The authors give a semi-algorithm based on proof tree construction and give sufficient conditions of its termination for safety properties.

Reachability checking for array-based systems.   There are a number of techniques that are similar to RMC in that they model the state of a parameterized system as a finite word, or equivalently an array of values from some logical background theory, but are different from RMC in that they represent sets of states and the transition relation of the system as constraints in this theory.

A first representative of this approach developed directly out of RMC and was initially called *regular model checking without transducers* [Abdulla et al., 2007]. The system model assumes an order on the processes, and allows them to communicate via shared variables, rendezvous, or broadcast. In addition, transitions can be guarded with global conditions that take into account the order of processes. Systems are verified by an approximate backward reachability check, where potentially infinite sets of system configurations are represented as (finite) constraints on system variables. To ensure termination, the approach considers a *monotonic abstraction* of the transition relation, which guarantees that transitions are monotonic with respect to the subword relation on configurations. As a result, the algorithm can always work on *upwards closed sets* of configurations, and thus one considers an abstraction of the original system which is a *well-structured transition system*. The approach has later been extended by Abdulla et al. [2009] to systems with infinite-state components by also supporting numerical variables. To ensure decidability of the reachability computation, sets of valuations of numerical variables can only be expressed as *gap-order constraints*. The tool Undip implements both the finite- and infinite-state case. As an alternative to monotonic abstraction, the approach for finite-state processes has recently been combined with counter abstraction, which in contrast to monotonic abstraction allows to refine the abstraction if verification is not successful [Ganty and Rezine, 2014]. An implementation of this extension is available in the tool PWC.

Ghilardi et al. [2008] introduced an approach that generalizes the basic idea of representing states and transitions as constraints on arrays over a suitable background theory. They define the notion of *array-based systems*, where a state of the system is represented as an unbounded array of values from a (parametric) first-order theory of elements. As another generalization, the approach also supports a parametric index theory for the array, allowing to model non-linear topologies. Then, sets of states can be represented as formulas over the theories of indices and elements, and transition relations as formulas that relate the possible pre- and post-states. In both cases, formulas can be quantified, making the problem potentially undecidable due to the undecidability of first-order logic. Instead of an abstraction to a well-structured system, this approach uses SMT solvers and quantifier elimination methods to directly reason on these constraints. For combinations of systems and theories such that all quantifiers can be effectively eliminated and the ground satisfiability problem is decidable, one obtains the fully automated technique of *Model Checking Modulo Theories (MCMT)* [Ghilardi and Ranise, 2010]. In addition to an implementation (called MCMT) by its inventors, the approach has been implemented by Conchon et al. [2012] in the tool Cubicle.

Completeness of MCMT relies on the one hand on existing decidability results for first-order theories, and on the other hand on proving new results for decidability or the possibility of quantifier elimination in the theories that are necessary for describing systems and properties. For some expressive classes of array-based systems, full model checking may not be possible. In such cases, one may resort to invariant checking or bounded model checking, which can both be expressed as a single first-order constraint over a suitable theory. The framework of *local theory extensions* allows to define configurations and transitions of array-based systems as extensions of a given first-order theory, providing a decision procedure for such constraints [Faber et al., 2010, Jacobs and Sofronie-Stokkermans, 2007].

8.4   DYNAMIC CUTOFF DETECTION

Many of the results presented in this survey solve the PMCP by providing a *cutoff*, i.e., a maximal number of processes that need to be considered for a given class of systems and specifications. While such cutoff results let us decide the PMCP, they are restricted to the classes of systems and specifications for which the proof methods have been designed. A related approach is *dynamic cutoff detection*, which does not depend on *a priori* proven cutoff theorems, but instead tries to automatically detect a suitable cutoff for a given system template, and possibly also a given specification.

Kaiser et al. [2010] considered the problem of finding cutoffs that are specific to a given parameterized system and a safety property. To this end, their algorithm first computes the set of reachable *thread-states*, i.e., combinations of shared and local state, in a system of fixed size k. For the class of shared-memory systems under consideration, a sufficient and necessary condition for the existence of new reachable thread-states in systems of size $n > k$ is identified. In a nutshell, if any new thread-states are reachable for $n > k$, then among those there is one thread-state (s, l) with minimal distance from the initial state. Furthermore, by the characteriztics of their model, this thread-state (s, l) must be reachable from those that are reached in a system of size k by a transition that does not change the shared memory part s. This gives rise to an analysis for *thread-state candidates* that could be reached in a system of size $k + 1$. Whether this actually is the case can be decided for each candidate by a backward coverability analysis, which is decidable for fixed k. Since there can only be a finite number of candidates, this procedure will terminate for the given k. If none of the candidates can be reached, then k is a cutoff, otherwise the procedure is iterated for $k + 1$.

Abdulla et al. [2013b] also detected property- and system-specific cutoffs for safety properties. Their system model is close to the one presented in Chapter 6, with connectivity graphs that can be different from cliques and guarded updates that can take into account this topology. To find a cutoff, the procedure computes in parallel the exact set of reachable states for a system of size k, and an over-approximation of the reachable states with respect to a *view abstraction*, also parameterized by k. Roughly, for this overapproximation we view a global state as a word over local states of the system, and not only consider words that are reachable, but also words that can be constructed from subwords of reachable words. By a separate argument, the authors show that for their class of systems it is sufficient to consider words of size $k + 1$ in this procedure in order to obtain completeness. If the concrete computation finds an error trace, then the given safety property does not hold. If the abstract computation does not find an error trace, then k is a cutoff and the safety property holds for all instances of the system. If neither is the case, then the procedure is iterated for $k + 1$.

The dynamic cutoff techniques are applicable to very expressive classes of systems, such that the PMCP is in general undecidable even for safety properties. Thus, the search for a suitable cutoff can in general not be guaranteed to terminate, but only in restricted cases that are decidable. For instance, the approach by Abdulla et al. [2013b] is guaranteed to terminate for well-quasi ordered transition systems. Cutoffs that are specific to a property and a process template can be much smaller than pre-determined cutoffs that hold for *all* elements of a class of systems and properties.

8.5 NETWORK INVARIANTS

Invariant-based techniques use inductive arguments to reason about parameterized systems. Intuitively, these arguments state that if a certain property is satisfied in a system of n process it also holds in a system of $n + 1$ processes. There is a number of such techniques in the literature that apply induction to reason about parameterized systems. The techniques discussed here thus exploit invariants over a sequence of systems, rather then invariants of computations, that is, over a sequence of steps. The techniques discussed differ in the following ingredients.

(invariant specification) This defines the object that is invariant for a sequence of system instances, e.g., an invariant can be a labeled transitions system that simulates every system instance in the sequence.

(invariant preservation) A formal definition of what it means for a system instance P^n to preserve an invariant, e.g., simulation.

(inductive step) An inductive step to prove that a system instance P^{n+1} preserves an invariant, if a system instance P^n does.

The first results on using induction for parameterized model checking were obtained independently by Kurshan and McMillan [1989] and Wolper and Lovinfosse [1989]. Wolper and Lovinfosse [1989] introduced the framework of *network invariants*. Kurshan and McMillan [1989] introduced *the structural induction theorem*.

In the framework of network invariants, an invariant I is specified in the same language as a process template P, namely, as a process in the framework of Hoare's Communicating Sequential Processes (CSP). Invariant preservation is defined with the means of an implementation relation $\preceq$ on labeled transition systems, e.g., trace inclusion, bisimulation, or observational equivalence. The technique consists of proving two properties for some $k \geq 1$:

- the base system P^k implements I, i.e., $P^k \preceq I$, and

- the parallel composition of I and P implements I, i.e., $I \parallel P \preceq I$.

Wolper and Lovinfosse [1989] showed by induction that whenever P and I satisfy these two properties, it holds that $P^n \preceq I$ for $n \geq k$. Hence to prove a property for all n, it just remains to check the specification against I, and against instances $P^1, \ldots, P^{k-1}$. The crucial point of this method is how to generate invariants. One may try $I = P$ or $I = P^2$, which works for simple examples. If this guess fails, an invariant candidate must be provided by the user.

Kurshan and McMillan [1989] obtained similar results in the form of the structural induction theorem in the framework of Milner's Calculus of Communicating Systems (CCS). They also note that one can use various implementation relations, e.g., "may" preorder on CCS processes, language containment, strong and weak bisimulation, or the "implements" relation of I/O automata.

Network invariants and network grammars. Shtadler and Grumberg [1990] extended the framework of network invariants to parameterized systems whose connectivity graph is derived by a network grammar. In their work, they used a special form of computation equivalence.

Clarke et al. [1995] also used network grammars to capture the connectivity graph. Instead of equivalence relations, e.g., bisimulation, they use a preorder on labeled transition systems, namely, simulation. The key feature of their work is to specify expected behavior with automata over regular expressions,[2] as opposite to indexed temporal logics. For invariant generation, Clarke et al. [1995] gave a method to generate invariant candidates. The method takes the specification as input and has better chances of generating useful invariants than a more general technique that does not consider the specification. Still, if the generated invariant candidate is not an invariant, the user must help the verification tool. The original framework was formulated for synchronous systems. Later, Clarke et al. [1997] extended the framework to asynchronous systems.

Lesens et al. [1997] followed up the work by Clarke et al. [1995] and introduced several invariant synthesis heuristics based on *widening techniques*. If the technique fails to find an invariant, the user can manually refine the widening operator and thus give a hint to the technique. This is the key improvement over other techniques, which cannot be tuned by the user. Kesten and Pnueli [2000] transferred the framework of network invariants to fair-discrete systems, in which processes communicate via shared variables, as opposed to rendezvous communication used in the other work discussed in this section. Konnov and Zakharov [2010] also applied network grammars to generate connectivity graphs. As simulation is typically too restrictive for asynchronous systems, they introduced several weak forms of simulation: block simulation, quasi-block simulation, and semi-block simulation. They have implemented the technique in the tool CHEAPS.

---

[2]Similar to regular model checking, the alphabet is the set of local states Q.

8.6   INVISIBLE INVARIANTS

The notion of invariants used in the techniques based on invisible invariants is closer to the one used in the analysis of programs (loop invariants) or algorithms. Pnueli et al. [2001] introduced an approach to invariant detection in concurrent programs parameterized by the number of processes. The method targets verification of k-indexed formulas, e.g., the 2-indexed formula $\forall i, j \neq i.\, \mathsf{G}(at_i \neq critical \vee at_j \neq critical)$. In the technique of invisible invariants, a model checker is run on a fixed-size system instance to collect the reachable *global* states R. Given k, the technique projects the reachable global states R on all combinations of k process indices and thus computes the reachable combinations of the *local* states of k processes. The result of this projection — that is, the set of combinations of local states — is called an *invisible invariant*. For parametrized model checking, Pnueli et al. [2001] proved a small model property for concurrent programs with (bounded) shared variables, from which follows that an invisible invariant of a fixed-size system instance is also an invariant of the parameterized system.

Fang et al. [2006] combined invisible invariants with ranking functions, in order to verify liveness properties. McMillan and Zuck [2011] investigated connections between invisible invariants and abstract interpretation. Johnson and Mitra [2012] extended the small model theorem by Pnueli et al. [2001] to the networks of rectangular hybrid automata. They implemented their technique in the tool PASSEL [Johnson, 2013].

8.7   OTHER ASPIRING APPROACHES

Fully symmetric parameterized systems, e.g., cache coherence protocols, can be naturally encoded as *counter automata* [Delzanno, 2003, Leroux and Sutre, 2005]. A counter automaton is a graph, whose edges are labeled with counter updates and guards over counters and parameters (such as the number of processes). Typically, the guards and updates are expressed in linear integer arithmetic. Delzanno [2003] applied backward reachability on the systems with linear arithmetic constraints to analyze cache coherence protocols. Leroux and Sutre [2005] introduced flat (and flatable) counter automata, whose reachability can be checked with terminating acceleration techniques. This technique is implemented in the tool FAST [Bardin et al., 2008].

Esparza et al. [2013] introduced *non-atomic networks* to model parameterized asynchronous shared memory systems. A non-atomic network consists of a single leader and many contributors that write to and read from a shared register store. The authors showed that safety verification of non-atomic networks of processes modeled with state machines is decidable and at least PSPACE-hard. Further, they showed that safety verification of non-atomic networks of processes modeled with pushdown machines is undecidable.

Bouajjani et al. [2008] studied parameterized model checking of *resource allocation systems* (RASs). Such systems have a bounded number of resources, each owned by at most one process at any time. Processes are pushdown automata, and can request resources with high or normal priority. RASs are similar to conjunctive guarded protocols in that certain transitions are disabled unless a process has a certain resource. RASs without priorities and with processes being finite state automata can be converted to conjunctive guarded protocols (at the price of blow up), but not vice versa. The authors study parameterized model checking wrt. LTL\X properties on strong-fair or all runs, and wrt. (local or global) deadlocks on all runs. The proof structure resembles that of Emerson and Kahlon [2000].

Farzan et al. [2014] introduced *counting proofs* to reason about parameterized shared memory programs. Their technique automatically generates auxilliary counters and synthesizes a small proof of partial correctness of a concurrent program. Farzan et al. [2015b] also introduced *proof spaces*, where they construct a finite set of correctness proofs that capture all traces of a parameterized program. The proofs are constructed from predicate automata [Farzan et al., 2015a], an infinite-state generalization of alternating finite automata.

CHAPTER 9

Parameterized Model Checking Tools

The results covered in this book show that the parameterized model checking problem is only decidable for rather restricted classes of system models and specifications. In addition to that, parameterized model checking is computationally hard even in cases where it is decidable. As a result, there are only few software tools that implement decision procedures for the PMCP, and most of the available tools are implementations of the semi-decision procedures covered in Chapter 8. For researchers who want to get some hands-on experience with parameterized model checking, we give an overview of parameterized model checking tools that are available at the time of this writing. Table 9.1 summarizes the approaches of the available tools, and Table 9.2 shows where they can be obtained.

The only tool that uses decidability results from this book is PARTY [Khalimov et al., 2013b]. PARTY supports synthesis of concurrent systems in a token ring topology, with specifications in indexed LTL\X. It uses the cutoff results from Chapter 4, together with an SMT-based approach to solve the synthesis problem for a process template that satisfies the specification in the cutoff topology. By constraining the implementation of the process template such that it only allows one implementation, the approach can also be used to solve the PMCP in token rings.

Several of the approaches from the previous chapter have been implemented in tools such as BOOM [Basler et al., 2009], T(O)RMC [Legay, 2008], MONA [Elgaard et al., 1998], TLV [Pnueli and Shahar, 1996] and JTLV [Pnueli et al., 2010], Undip [Abdulla et al., 2009], MCMT [Ghilardi and Ranise, 2010], CHeAPS [Konnov and Zakharov, 2010], Cubicle [Conchon et al., 2012], ByMC [John et al., 2013], and PCW [Ganty and Rezine, 2014]. We refer to the previous chapter for an explanation of their respective approaches to parameterized model checking.

Furthermore, there is a number of tools that implement more general forms of infinite-state model checking, in particular with support for integer-valued variables. With a suitable encoding of parameterized systems into systems with integer variables, these tools can be used for parameterized model checking. Examples of such tools are ALV [Yavuz-Kahveci and Bultan, 2009], BRAIN [Rybina and Voronkov, 2002], FAST [Bardin et al., 2008], and NUXMV [Cavada et al., 2014].

Finally, there is a number of tools for the verification of hybrid systems, like KeYmaera [Platzer, 2012, Platzer and Quesel, 2008] and Passel [Johnson, 2013]. Both systems allow

Table 9.1: Parameterized model checking tools: approaches

Tool	Authors	Implements
ALV	Yavuz-Kahveci and Bultan [2009]	approximate infinite-state reachability
BRAIN	Rybina and Voronkov [2002]	symbolic infinite-state reachability
BOOM	Basler et al. [2009]	counter abstraction
ByMC	John et al. [2013]	counter abstraction
CHEAPS	Konnov and Zakharov [2010]	network invariants
Cubicle	Conchon et al. [2012]	symbolic backward reachability
FAST	Bardin et al. [2008]	acceleration-based inf.-state reachability
IIV	Balaban et al. [2005]	invisible invariants
JTLV	Pnueli et al. [2010]	semi-automatic verification platform
KeYmaera	Platzer and Quesel [2008]	semi-automatic verification platform
Murϕ	Dill [1996]	counter abstraction
MCMT	Ghilardi and Ranise [2010]	symbolic backward reachability
MONA	Henriksen et al. [1995]	monadic second-order logic
NUXMV	Cavada et al. [2014]	infinite-state model checking
PARTY	Khalimov et al. [2013b]	(static) cutoff detection
Passel	Johnson [2013]	invisible invariants
PCW	Ganty and Rezine [2014]	symbolic reachability, counter abstraction
TLV	Pnueli and Shahar [1996]	semi-automatic verification platform
T(O)RMC	Legay [2008]	regular model checking
Undip	Abdulla et al. [2009]	approximate backward reachability

for the verification of distributed hybrid systems with a parametric number of components. While Passel is based on a completely automatic combination of reachability checking and detection of invisible invariants, KeYmaera is a very powerful semi-automatic theorem prover.

Table 9.2: Parameterized model checking tools: availability

Tool	URL
ALV	http://www.cs.ucsb.edu/~bultan/composite/
BOOM	http://www.cprover.org/boom/
BRAIN	http://www.cs.man.ac.uk/~voronkov/BRAIN/
BYMC	http://forsyte.tuwien.ac.at/software/bymc/
CHEAPS	http://lvk.cs.msu.ru/~konnov/cheaps/index_en.html
Cubicle	http://cubicle.lri.fr
FAST	http://tapas.labri.fr/trac/wiki/FASTer
JTLV	http://jtlv.ysaar.net/
KeYmaera	http://symbolaris.com/info/KeYmaera.html
MCMT	http://users.mat.unimi.it/users/ghilardi/mcmt/
MONA	http://www.brics.dk/mona/
Murϕ	http://formalverification.cs.utah.edu/
NUXMV	Murphi/https://nuxmv.fbk.eu
PARTY	https://github.com/5nizza/Party
Passel	https://publish.illinois.edu/passel-tool/
PWC	http://www.ahmedrezine.com/tools/
TLV	http://www.cs.nyu.edu/acsys/tlv/
T(O)RMC	http://www.montefiore.ulg.ac.be/~legay/TORMC/index-tormc.html
Undip	http://www.ahmedrezine.com/tools/

CHAPTER 10

Conclusions

In this book, we provided a general model for uniform concurrent systems that captures a large class of systems from the literature. Our model includes different forms of communication, like token-passing, rendezvous, or broadcast, as well as different communication graphs, like cliques, rings, stars, or even dynamic topologies that change at runtime.

For this class of systems, we surveyed the existing decidability results, drawing a map that focuses on the border between decidability and undecidability, and highlighting some of the uncharted territory in this research area.

Regarding undecidability results, we noticed that unrestricted forms of communication make it possible even for uniform parameterized systems to simulate Turing machines. Such communication is thus a source of undecidability. This even holds for quite simple systems, e.g., with a simple token in a bidirectional ring architecture, or a two-valued token in a unidirectional ring architecture. The reason is essentially that arbitrary amounts of information can be exchanged over an infinite run of a system, even if a single synchronization can only transmit one bit of information. Typically, this allows to represent Turing machines with tapes of arbitrary length, which leads to undecidability.

Many (but not all) decidability results give a constructive way to solve the PMCP for interesting subclasses, e.g., by a decomposition into several finite-state model checking problems. However, in many cases there either is no constructive result, or the decomposition is too big to be model checked in practice. Thus, additional research is needed to obtain effective ways to solve the PMCP.

Regarding specifications, it is worth noting that the token passing systems of Chapter 4 are the only ones known to us for which branching-time logics, like certain fragments of indexed-CTL*\X, are known to have decidable PMCP. This is in contrast to pairwise rendezvous and disjunctively guarded systems that are known to have undecidable PMCP for CTL*, while for ad hoc networks and conjunctively guarded systems the problem does not seem to have been studied.

Another set of open problems concerns lower bounds and computational complexity of the PMCP. A few exact bounds for PMCP are known: rendezvous systems and 1-index LTL\X specifications are ExpSpace-complete (and PSpace-complete if there is no controller) [Esparza, 2014, German and Sistla, 1992]; disjunctively guarded systems and 1-index LTL\X specifications are PSpace-complete [Aminof et al., 2014b]; and broadcast systems and safety specifications have "Ackermanian complexity" [Schmitz and Schnoebelen, 2013].

While the theoretical results presented give some insight in the problems of verifying large concurrent systems, it should be noted that the systems considered here are still quite limited compared to practical concurrent programs. In this book, we considered parallel compositions $P \parallel \cdots \parallel P$ of n copies of a fixed finite-state process P — that is, P is independent of n. As systems consist of copies of the same process, processes cannot use unique identifiers (IDs). IDs are, however, quite natural in many applications, and from a theoretical viewpoint they are quite powerful as they can be used to break symmetries. Similarly, the processes have a fixed state space independent of the system size. Consequently, processes cannot use counting arguments (e.g., a majority of processes are in certain states) that are useful to decide on coordinated actions.

Of course, we can think of more complicated systems. Consider parallel compositions $P(1, n) \parallel \cdots \parallel P(n, n)$ where $P(i, n)$ is a finite-state process that has a unique ID i as well as "knowledge" of the number of processes n in the system; consequently, the local state space of the processes is parameterized. Such systems seem quite natural, and actually there is a sizeable amount of literature on such systems, e.g., in the area of distributed algorithms [Attiya and Welch, 2004, Lynch, 1996]. This model is rarely addressed in the parameterized model checking literature, and as discussed above, in most cases the PMCP is undecidable. However, we believe that in this area theoretical work must also be done in order to design procedures that allow one to reason about such systems.

Bibliography

Parosh Aziz Abdulla. Regular model checking. *STTT*, 14(2):109–118, 2012. DOI: 10.1007/s10009-011-0216-8. 131

Parosh Aziz Abdulla, Kārlis Čerāns, Bengt Jonsson, and Yih-Kuen Tsay. General decidability theorems for infinite-state systems. In *LICS*, pages 313 –321, 1996. DOI: 10.1109/LICS.1996.561359. 25, 26, 99

Parosh Aziz Abdulla, Ahmed Bouajjani, Bengt Jonsson, and Marcus Nilsson. Handling global conditions in parametrized system verification. In *CAV*, pages 134–145. Springer, 1999. DOI: 10.1007/3-540-48683-6_14. 132

Parosh Aziz Abdulla, Bengt Jonsson, Marcus Nilsson, and Julien d'Orso. Regular model checking made simple and efficient. In *CONCUR*, pages 116–130, 2002. DOI: 10.1007/3-540-45694-5_94. 132

Parosh Aziz Abdulla, Giorgio Delzanno, Noomene Ben Henda, and Ahmed Rezine. Regular model checking without transducers (on efficient verification of parameterized systems). In *TACAS*, volume 4424 of *LNCS*, pages 721–736. Springer, 2007. DOI: 10.1007/978-3-540-71209-1_56. 133

Parosh Aziz Abdulla, Giorgio Delzanno, and Ahmed Rezine. Approximated parameterized verification of infinite-state processes with global conditions. *Formal Methods in System Design*, 34(2):126–156, 2009. DOI: 10.1007/s10703-008-0062-9. 133, 139

Parosh Aziz Abdulla, Yu-Fang Chen, Giorgio Delzanno, Frédéric Haziza, Chih-Duo Hong, and Ahmed Rezine. Constrained monotonic abstraction: A CEGAR for parameterized verification. In *CONCUR*, pages 86–101, 2010. DOI: 10.1007/978-3-642-15375-4_7. 129

Parosh Aziz Abdulla, Giorgio Delzanno, Othmane Rezine, Arnaud Sangnier, and Riccardo Traverso. On the verification of timed ad hoc networks. In *FORMATS*, volume 6919 of *LNCS*, pages 256–270. Springer, 2011. DOI: 10.1007/978-3-642-24310-3_18. 128

Parosh Aziz Abdulla, Mohamed Faouzi Atig, and Othmane Rezine. Verification of directed acyclic ad hoc networks. In *FORTE*, volume 7892 of *LNCS*, pages 193–208. Springer, 2013a. DOI: 10.1007/978-3-642-38592-6_14. 19, 103, 107, 115, 116, 117, 118, 119, 120, 122

Parosh Aziz Abdulla, Frédéric Haziza, and Lukáš Holík. All for the price of few. In *VMCAI*, volume 7737 of *LNCS*, pages 476–495. Springer, 2013b. DOI: 10.1007/978-3-642-35873-9_28. 134, 135

Benjamin Aminof, Swen Jacobs, Ayrat Khalimov, and Sasha Rubin. Parameterized model checking of token-passing systems. In *VMCAI*, volume 8318 of *LNCS*, pages 262–281, January 2014a. DOI: 10.1007/978-3-642-54013-4_15. 31, 35, 39, 40, 41, 42, 45, 46, 47

Benjamin Aminof, Tomer Kotek, Sasha Rubin, Francesco Spegni, and Helmut Veith. Parameterized model checking of rendezvous systems. In *CONCUR*, volume 8704, pages 109–124. Springer, 2014b. DOI: 10.1007/978-3-662-44584-6_9. 46, 63, 101, 143

Benjamin Aminof, Sasha Rubin, Florian Zuleger, and Francesco Spegni. Liveness of parameterized timed networks. In *ICALP (Part II)*, volume 9135 of *LNCS*, pages 375–387, 2015. DOI: 10.1007/978-3-662-47666-6_30. 64

Krysztof R. Apt and Dexter C. Kozen. Limits for automatic verification of finite-state concurrent systems. *Information Processing Letters*, 15:307–309, 1986. DOI: 10.1016/0020-0190(86)90071-2. 2, 3

Hagit Attiya and Jennifer Welch. *Distributed Computing*, 2nd ed. John Wiley & Sons, 2004. DOI: 10.1002/0471478210. 144

Christel Baier and Joost-Pieter Katoen. *Principles of model checking*. MIT Press, 2008. 1, 2, 12, 14, 83, 97

Ittai Balaban, Yi Fang, Amir Pnueli, and Lenore D. Zuck. IIV: an invisible invariant verifier. In *CAV*, pages 408–412, 2005.

Valmir C. Barbosa and Eli Gafni. Concurrency in heavily loaded neighborhood-constrained systems. *ACM Trans. Program. Lang. Syst.*, 11(4):562–584, 1989. DOI: 10.1145/69558.69560. 48

Sébastien Bardin, Alain Finkel, Jérôme Leroux, and Laure Petrucci. FAST: acceleration from theory to practice. *STTT*, 10(5):401–424, 2008. DOI: 10.1007/s10009-008-0064-3. 137, 139

Gerard Basler, Michele Mazzucchi, Thomas Wahl, and Daniel Kroening. Symbolic counter abstraction for concurrent software. In *CAV*, volume 5643 of *LNCS*, pages 64–78. Springer, 2009. DOI: 10.1007/978-3-642-02658-4_9. 131, 139

Ahmed Bouajjani, Bengt Jonsson, Marcus Nilsson, and Tayssir Touili. Regular model checking. In *CAV*, pages 403–418, 2000. DOI: 10.1007/10722167_31. 132

Ahmed Bouajjani, Peter Habermehl, and Tomás Vojnar. Abstract regular model checking. In *CAV*, pages 372–386, 2004. DOI: 10.1007/978-3-540-27813-9_29. 132

Ahmed Bouajjani, Peter Habermehl, and Tomás Vojnar. Verification of parametric concurrent systems with prioritised FIFO resource management. *Formal Methods in System Design*, 32(2): 129–172, 2008. DOI: 10.1007/s10703-008-0048-7. 48, 137

Michael C. Browne, Edmund M. Clarke, and Orna Grumberg. Characterizing finite kripke structures in propositional temporal logic. *Theor. Comput. Sci.*, 59:115–131, 1988. DOI: 10.1016/0304-3975(88)90098-9. 29

Michael C. Browne, Edmund M. Clarke, and Orna Grumberg. Reasoning about networks with many identical finite state processes. *Information and Computation*, 81(1):13–31, 1989. DOI: 10.1016/0890-5401(89)90026-6. 14

Muffy Calder and Alice Miller. Using spin to analyse the tree identification phase of the ieee 1394 high-performance serial bus (firewire) protocol. *Formal Aspects of Computing*, 14(3):247–266, 2003. DOI: 10.1007/s001650300004. 131

Roberto Cavada, Alessandro Cimatti, Michele Dorigatti, Alberto Griggio, Alessandro Mariotti, Andrea Micheli, Sergio Mover, Marco Roveri, and Stefano Tonetta. The nuXmv symbolic model checker. In *CAV*, volume 8559 of *LNCS*, pages 334–342, 2014. DOI: 10.1007/978-3-319-08867-9_22. 139

K. M. Chandy and J. Misra. The drinking philosophers problem. *ACM Transactions on Programming Languages and Systems (TOPLAS)*, 6(4):632–646, 1984. DOI: 10.1145/1780.1804. 48

Allan Cheng, Javier Esparza, and Jens Palsberg. Complexity results for 1-safe nets. In *FSTTCS*, volume 761 of *LNCS*, pages 326–337. Springer, 1993. DOI: 10.1007/3-540-57529-4_66. 105

Alessandro Cimatti, Edmund M. Clarke, Enrico Giunchiglia, Fausto Giunchiglia, Marco Pistore, Marco Roveri, Roberto Sebastiani, and Armando Tacchella. NuSMV 2: An opensource tool for symbolic model checking. In *CAV*, volume 2404 of *LNCS*, pages 359–364, 2002. DOI: 10.1007/3-540-45657-0_29. 130

Edmund Clarke, Orna Grumberg, Hiromi Hiraishi, Somesh Jha, David Long, Kenneth McMillan, and Linda Ness. Verification of the futurebus+ cache coherence protocol. Technical report, DTIC Document, 1992. DOI: 10.1007/BF01383968. 1

Edmund Clarke, Orna Grumberg, and Doron Peled. *Model Checking*. MIT Press, 1999. 1, 2, 13, 14, 129

Edmund Clarke, Muralidhar Talupur, Tayssir Touili, and Helmut Veith. Verification by network decomposition. In *CONCUR 2004*, volume 3170, pages 276–291, 2004. DOI: 10.1007/978-3-540-28644-8_18. 2, 19, 25, 31, 40, 41, 42

Edmund Clarke, Murali Talupur, and Helmut Veith. Proving ptolemy right: The environment abstraction framework for model checking concurrent systems. In *TACAS*, pages 33–47. Springer, 2008. DOI: 10.1007/978-3-540-78800-3_4. 130

Edmund M Clarke, Orna Grumberg, and Somesh Jha. Verifying parameterized networks using abstraction and regular languages. In *CONCUR*, pages 395–407. Springer, 1995. DOI: 10.1007/3-540-60218-6_30. 136

Edmund M. Clarke, Orna Grumberg, and Somesh Jha. Verifying parameterized networks. *ACM Transactions on Programming Languages and Systems (TOPLAS)*, 19(5):726–750, 1997. DOI: 10.1145/265943.265960. 136

Sylvain Conchon, Amit Goel, Sava Krstic, Alain Mebsout, and Fatiha Zaïdi. Cubicle: A parallel smt-based model checker for parameterized systems - tool paper. In *CAV*, volume 7358 of *LNCS*, pages 718–724. Springer, 2012. DOI: 10.1007/978-3-642-31424-7_55. 133, 139

Giorgio Delzanno. Constraint-based verification of parameterized cache coherence protocols. *Formal Methods in System Design*, 23(3):257–301, 2003. DOI: 10.1023/A:1026276129010. 137

Giorgio Delzanno and Riccardo Traverso. Decidability and complexity results for verification of asynchronous broadcast networks. In *LATA*, volume 7810 of *LNCS*, pages 238–249. Springer, 2013. DOI: 10.1007/978-3-642-37064-9_22. 128

Giorgio Delzanno, Jean-François Raskin, and Laurent Van Begin. Towards the automated verification of multithreaded Java programs. In *TACAS*, volume 2280 of *LNCS*, pages 173–187, 2002. DOI: 10.1007/3-540-46002-0_13. 51

Giorgio Delzanno, Arnaud Sangnier, and Gianluigi Zavattaro. Parameterized verification of ad hoc networks. In *CONCUR*, volume 6269 of *LNCS*, pages 313–327, 2010. DOI: 10.1007/978-3-642-15375-4_22. 12, 19, 103, 107, 108, 109, 110, 111, 113, 114, 115, 120, 122, 124, 127

Giorgio Delzanno, Arnaud Sangnier, and Gianluigi Zavattaro. On the power of cliques in the parameterized verification of ad hoc networks. In *FOSSACS*, volume 6604 of *LNCS*, pages 441–455. Springer, 2011. DOI: 10.1007/978-3-642-19805-2_30. 19, 103, 107, 108, 109, 113, 114, 119, 120, 122, 127

Giorgio Delzanno, Arnaud Sangnier, Riccardo Traverso, and Gianluigi Zavattaro. The cost of parameterized reachability in mobile ad hoc networks. *CoRR*, abs/1202.5850, 2012a. DOI: 10.1007/978-3-642-30793-5_15. 126

Giorgio Delzanno, Arnaud Sangnier, and Gianluigi Zavattaro. Verification of ad hoc networks with node and communication failures. In *FORTE*, volume 7273 of *LNCS*, pages 235–250. Springer, 2012b. DOI: 10.1007/978-3-642-41036-9_11. 19, 103, 105, 106, 107, 108, 124, 128

Giorgio Delzanno, Arnaud Sangnier, and Riccardo Traverso. Parameterized verification of broadcast networks of register automata. In *RP*, volume 8169 of *LNCS*, pages 109–121. Springer, 2013. DOI: 10.1007/3-540-61474-5_86. 128

David L Dill. The mur ϕ verification system. In *CAV*, pages 390–393. Springer, 1996. DOI: 10.1007/978-3-540-69850-0_5. 130

David L. Dill. A retrospective on mur*phi*. In *25 Years of Model Checking - History, Achievements, Perspectives*, volume 5000 of *LNCS*, pages 77–88. Springer, 2008. DOI: 10.1002/jgt.3190140406. 130

Guoli Ding. Subgraphs and well-quasi-ordering. *Journal of Graph Theory*, 16(5):489–502, 1992. DOI: 10.1002/jgt.3190160509. 119

Jacob Elgaard, Nils Klarlund, and Anders Møller. MONA 1.x: new techniques for WS1S and WS2S. In *CAV*, volume 1427 of *LNCS*, pages 516–520. Springer, 1998. DOI: 10.1007/BFb0028773. 132, 139

E. Allen Emerson and Edmund M. Clarke. Characterizing correctness properties of parallel programs using fixpoints. In *ICALP*, volume 85 of *LNCS*, pages 169–181. Springer, 1980. DOI: 10.1007/3-540-10003-2_69. 1

E. Allen Emerson and Vineet Kahlon. Reducing model checking of the many to the few. In *CADE*, volume 1831 of *LNCS*, pages 236–254. Springer Berlin Heidelberg, 2000. DOI: 10.1007/10721959_19. 19, 29, 65, 73, 74, 81, 82, 84, 86, 89, 95, 100, 101, 138

E. Allen Emerson and Vineet Kahlon. Model checking large-scale and parameterized resource allocation systems. In *TACAS*, volume 2280 of *LNCS*, pages 251–265, 2002. DOI: 10.1007/3-540-46002-0_18. 48

E. Allen Emerson and Vineet Kahlon. Exact and efficient verification of parameterized cache coherence protocols. In *CHARME*, volume 2860 of *LNCS*, pages 247–262. Springer, 2003a. DOI: 10.1007/978-3-540-39724-3_22. 19, 65, 74, 99, 101

E. Allen Emerson and Vineet Kahlon. Model checking guarded protocols. In *LICS*, pages 361–370. IEEE, 2003b. DOI: 10.1109/LICS.2003.1210076. 18, 19, 23, 51, 58, 59, 62, 73, 74, 76, 79, 81, 95, 96, 97, 98, 99, 100

E. Allen Emerson and Vineet Kahlon. Rapid parameterized model checking of snoopy cache coherence protocols. In *TACAS*, volume 2619 of *LNCS*, pages 144–159. Springer, 2003c. DOI: 10.1007/3-540-36577-X_11. 19, 65, 74, 99, 101

E. Allen Emerson and Vineet Kahlon. Parameterized model checking of ring-based message passing systems. In *CSL*, volume 3210 of *LNCS*, pages 325–339. Springer, 2004. DOI: 10.1007/978-3-540-30124-0_26. 19, 44, 45, 48

E. Allen Emerson and Kedar S. Namjoshi. Reasoning about rings. In *POPL*, pages 85–94, 1995. DOI: 10.1145/199448.199468. 2, 12, 14, 16, 19, 23, 24, 25, 29, 31, 35, 36, 38, 39, 40, 42, 84

E. Allen Emerson and Kedar S. Namjoshi. Automatic verification of parameterized synchronous systems. In *CAV*, volume 1102 of *LNCS*, pages 87–98. Springer, 1996. DOI: 10.1007/3-540-61474-5_60. 18, 73, 74, 77

E. Allen Emerson and Kedar S. Namjoshi. On model checking for non-deterministic infinite-state systems. In *LICS*, pages 70–80. IEEE Computer Society, 1998. DOI: 10.1109/LICS.1998.705644. 18, 19, 100

E. Allen Emerson and Kedar S. Namjoshi. On reasoning about rings. *Int. J. Found. Comput. Sci.*, 14(4):527–550, 2003. DOI: 10.1142/S0129054103001881. 12, 14, 16, 19, 24, 25, 29, 31, 35, 36, 38, 39, 40, 42, 43

E. Allen Emerson and A. Prasad Sistla. Symmetry and model checking. *Formal Methods in System Design*, 9:105–131, 1996. DOI: 10.1007/BF00625970. 25

Javier Esparza. Decidability and complexity of petri net problems - an introduction. In *In Lectures on Petri Nets I: Basic Models*, pages 374–428. Springer-Verlag, 1998. DOI: 10.1007/3-540-65306-6_20. 25, 27

Javier Esparza. Keeping a crowd safe: On the complexity of parameterized verification. In *STACS*, 2014. DOI: 10.4230/LIPIcs.STACS.2014.1. 63, 64, 143

Javier Esparza and Mogens Nielsen. Decidability issues for petri nets - a survey. *Bulletin of the EATCS*, 52:244–262, 1994. 95

Javier Esparza, Alain Finkel, and Richard Mayr. On the verification of broadcast protocols. *LICS*, page 352, 1999. ISSN 1043-6871. DOI: 10.1109/LICS.1999.782630. 10, 19, 51, 58, 59, 99, 100, 108, 114

Javier Esparza, Pierre Ganty, and Rupak Majumdar. Parameterized verification of asynchronous shared-memory systems. In *CAV*, pages 124–140, 2013. DOI: 10.1007/978-3-642-39799-8_8. 137

Johannes Faber, Carsten Ihlemann, Swen Jacobs, and Viorica Sofronie-Stokkermans. Automatic verification of parametric specifications with complex topologies. In *IFM*, volume 6396 of *LNCS*, pages 152–167. Springer, 2010. DOI: 10.1007/978-3-642-16265-7_12. 134

Yi Fang, Kenneth L. McMillan, Amir Pnueli, and Lenore D. Zuck. Liveness by invisible invariants. In *FORTE*, pages 356–371, 2006. DOI: 10.1007/11888116_26. 137

Azadeh Farzan, Zachary Kincaid, and Andreas Podelski. Proofs that count. In *POPL*, pages 151–164, 2014. DOI: 10.1145/2535838.2535885. 138

Azadeh Farzan, Matthias Heizmann, Jochen Hoenicke, Zachary Kincaid, and Andreas Podelski. Automated program verification. In *LATA*, pages 25–46, 2015a. DOI: 10.1007/978-3-319-15579-1_2. 138

Azadeh Farzan, Zachary Kincaid, and Andreas Podelski. Proof spaces for unbounded parallelism. In *POPL*, pages 407–420. ACM, 2015b. DOI: 10.1145/2676726.2677012. 138

Alain Finkel and Philippe Schnoebelen. Well-structured transition systems everywhere! *Theoretical Computer Science*, 256(1–2):63–92, 2001. DOI: 10.1016/S0304-3975(00)00102-X. 25, 26, 122

Matthias Függer and Josef Widder. Efficient checking of link-reversal-based concurrent systems. In *CONCUR*, volume 7454 of *LNCS*, pages 486–499, 2012. DOI: 10.1007/978-3-642-32940-1_34. 48

Pierre Ganty and Ahmed Rezine. Ordered counter-abstraction — refinable subword relations for parameterized verification. In *LATA*, volume 8370 of *LNCS*, pages 396–408. Springer, 2014. DOI: 10.1007/978-3-319-04921-2_32. 133, 139

Steven M. German and A. Prasad Sistla. Reasoning about systems with many processes. *J. ACM*, 39(3):675–735, 1992. ISSN 0004-5411. DOI: 10.1145/146637.146681. 12, 18, 19, 29, 51, 52, 54, 55, 58, 59, 64, 99, 143

Silvio Ghilardi and Silvio Ranise. Backward reachability of array-based systems by SMT solving: Termination and invariant synthesis. *Logical Methods in Computer Science*, 6(4), 2010. DOI: 10.2168/LMCS-6(4:10)2010. 133, 139

Silvio Ghilardi, Enrica Nicolini, Silvio Ranise, and Daniele Zucchelli. Towards SMT model checking of array-based systems. In *Automated Reasoning*, volume 5195 of *LNCS*, pages 67–82. Springer, 2008. DOI: 10.1007/978-3-540-71070-7_6. 133

Jim Gray. Notes on data base operating systems. In *Operating Systems, An Advanced Course*, volume 60 of *LNCS*, pages 393–481. Springer, 1978. DOI: 10.1007/3-540-08755-9_9. 103

Orna Grumberg and Helmut Veith, editors. *25 Years of Model Checking - History, Achievements, Perspectives*, volume 5000 of *LNCS*, 2008. 1

Jesper G. Henriksen, Jakob L. Jensen, Michael E. Jørgensen, Nils Klarlund, Robert Paige, Theis Rauhe, and Anders Sandholm. Mona: Monadic second-order logic in practice. In *TACAS*, volume 1019 of *LNCS*, pages 89–110. Springer, 1995. DOI: 10.1007/3-540-60630-0_5. 132

Graham Higman. Ordering by divisibility in abstract algebras. *Proceedings of the London Mathematical Society*, s3-2(1):326–336, 1952. DOI: 10.1112/plms/s3-2.1.326. 119

Gerard Holzmann. *The SPIN Model Checker: Primer and Reference Manual*. Addison-Wesley Professional, 2003. 130

C. Norris Ip and David L. Dill. Verifying systems with replicated components in Murφ. *Formal Methods in System Design*, 14(3):273–310, 1999. DOI: 10.1023/A:1008723125149. 130

Swen Jacobs and Viorica Sofronie-Stokkermans. Applications of hierarchical reasoning in the verification of complex systems. *Electr. Notes Theor. Comput. Sci.*, 174(8):39–54, 2007. DOI: 10.1016/j.entcs.2006.11.038. 134

Henrik Jensen and Nancy Lynch. A proof of Burns n-process mutual exclusion algorithm using abstraction. In *TACAS*, volume 1384 of *LNCS*, pages 409–423. Springer, 1998. DOI: 10.1007/BFb0054186. 131

Annu John, Igor Konnov, Ulrich Schmid, Helmut Veith, and Josef Widder. Parameterized model checking of fault-tolerant distributed algorithms by abstraction. In *FMCAD*, pages 201–209, 2013. DOI: 10.1145/2484239.2484285. 3, 129, 130, 139

Taylor T. Johnson. *Uniform Verification of Safety for Parameterized Networks of Hybrid Automata*. PhD thesis, University of Illinois at Urbana-Champaign, Urbana, IL 61801, 2013. 137, 139

Taylor T. Johnson and Sayan Mitra. A small model theorem for rectangular hybrid automata networks. In *FORTE*, pages 18–34, 2012. DOI: 10.1007/978-3-642-30793-5_2. 137

Alexander Kaiser, Daniel Kroening, and Thomas Wahl. Dynamic cutoff detection in parameterized concurrent programs. In *CAV*, volume 6174 of *LNCS*, pages 654–659. Springer, 2010. DOI: 10.1007/978-3-642-14295-6_55. 134

Holger Karl. *Protocols and architectures for wireless sensor networks*. Wiley, Hoboken, NJ, 2005. ISBN 978-0-470-09510-2. DOI: 10.1002/0470095121. 103, 107

Yonit Kesten and Amir Pnueli. Control and data abstraction: The cornerstones of practical formal verification. *International Journal on Software Tools for Technology Transfer*, 2(4):328–342, 2000. DOI: 10.1007/s100090050040. 136

Yonit Kesten, Oded Maler, Monica Marcus, Amir Pnueli, and Elad Shahar. Symbolic model checking with rich assertional languages. In *CAV*, pages 424–435. Springer, 1997. DOI: 10.1007/3-540-63166-6_41. 1, 132

Ayrat Khalimov, Swen Jacobs, and Roderick Bloem. Towards efficient parameterized synthesis. In *VMCAI*, volume 7737 of *LNCS*, pages 108–127. Springer, 2013a. DOI: 10.1007/978-3-642-35873-9_9. 38, 40

Ayrat Khalimov, Swen Jacobs, and Roderick Bloem. PARTY parameterized synthesis of token rings. In *CAV*, volume 8044 of *LNCS*, pages 928–933. Springer, 2013b. DOI: 10.1007/978-3-642-39799-8_66. 139

Igor V. Konnov and Vladimir A. Zakharov. An invariant-based approach to the verification of asynchronous parameterized networks. *J. Symb. Comput.*, 45(11):1144–1162, 2010. DOI: 10.1016/j.jsc.2008.11.006. 136, 139

Panagiotis Kouvaros and Alessio Lomuscio. Automatic verification of parameterised multi-agent systems. In *AAMAS*, pages 861–868, 2013a. 64

Panagiotis Kouvaros and Alessio Lomuscio. A cutoff technique for the verification of parameterised interpreted systems with parameterised environments. In *IJCAI*, 2013b. 64

Panagiotis Kouvaros and Alessio Lomuscio. A counter abstraction technique for the verification of robot swarms. In *AAAI Conference on Artificial Intelligence*, pages 2081–2088, 2015. 64

Robert P Kurshan and Ken McMillan. A structural induction theorem for processes. In *Proceedings of the eighth annual ACM Symposium on Principles of distributed computing*, pages 239–247. ACM, 1989. DOI: 10.1145/72981.72998. 135, 136

Leslie Lamport. Checking a multithreaded algorithm with +CAL. In *Distributed Computing*, pages 151–163. Springer, 2006. DOI: 10.1007/11864219_11. 2

Axel Legay. T(O)RMC: A tool for (omega)-regular model checking. In *CAV*, volume 5123 of *LNCS*, pages 548–551. Springer, 2008. DOI: 10.1007/978-3-540-70545-1_52. 132, 139

Jérôme Leroux and Grégoire Sutre. Flat counter automata almost everywhere! In *ATVA*, volume 3707 of *LNCS*, pages 489–503, 2005. DOI: 10.1007/11562948_36. 137

David Lesens, Nicolas Halbwachs, and Pascal Raymond. Automatic verification of parameterized linear networks of processes. In *POPL*, pages 346–357. ACM, 1997. DOI: 10.1145/263699.263747. 136

Nancy Lynch. *Distributed Algorithms*. Morgan Kaufman Publishers, Inc., San Francisco, USA, 1996. 14, 144

Monika Maidl. A unifying model checking approach for safety properties of parameterized systems. In *CAV*, pages 311–323. Springer, 2001. DOI: 10.1007/3-540-44585-4_29. 132

Kenneth L. McMillan and Lenore D. Zuck. Invisible invariants and abstract interpretation. In *SAS*, pages 249–262, 2011. DOI: 10.1007/978-3-642-23702-7_20. 137

Robin Milner. *Communication and concurrency*. PHI Series in computer science. Prentice Hall, 1989. ISBN 978-0-13-115007-2. 3, 31

Marvin L. Minsky. *Computation: finite and infinite machines*. Prentice-Hall, Inc., Upper Saddle River, NJ, USA, 1967. ISBN 0-13-165563-9. 23, 24

André Platzer. A complete axiomatization of quantified differential dynamic logic for distributed hybrid systems. *Logical Methods in Computer Science*, 8(4), 2012. DOI: 10.2168/LMCS-8(4:17)2012. 139

André Platzer and Jan-David Quesel. Keymaera: A hybrid theorem prover for hybrid systems (system description). In *IJCAR*, volume 5195 of *LNCS*, pages 171–178. Springer, 2008. DOI: 10.1007/978-3-540-71070-7_15. 139

Amir Pnueli and Elad Shahar. A platform for combining deductive with algorithmic verification. In *CAV*, volume 1102 of *LNCS*, pages 184–195. Springer, 1996. DOI: 10.1007/3-540-61474-5_68. 132, 139

Amir Pnueli and Elad Shahar. Liveness and acceleration in parameterized verification. In *CAV*, pages 328–343, 2000. DOI: 10.1007/10722167_26. 132

Amir Pnueli, Sitvanit Ruah, and Lenore Zuck. Automatic deductive verification with invisible invariants. In *TACAS*, volume 2031 of *LNCS*, pages 82–97. Springer, 2001. DOI: 10.1007/3-540-45319-9_7. 137

Amir Pnueli, Jessie Xu, and Lenore Zuck. Liveness with $(0,1,\infty)$- counter abstraction. In *CAV*, volume 2404 of *LNCS*, pages 93–111. Springer, 2002. DOI: 10.1007/3-540-45657-0_9. 3, 129, 130

Amir Pnueli, Yaniv Sa'ar, and Lenore D. Zuck. JTLV: A framework for developing verification algorithms. In *CAV*, volume 6174 of *LNCS*, pages 171–174. Springer, 2010. 132, 139

Jean-Pierre Queille and Joseph Sifakis. Specification and verification of concurrent systems in cesar. In *International Symposium on Programming*, volume 137 of *LNCS*, pages 337–351. Springer, 1982. DOI: 10.1007/3-540-11494-7_22. 1

Tatiana Rybina and Andrei Voronkov. BRAIN : Backward reachability analysis with integers. In *AMAST*, volume 2422 of *LNCS*, pages 489–494. Springer, 2002. DOI: 10.1007/978-3-642-14295-6_18. 139

Sylvain Schmitz and Philippe Schnoebelen. The power of well-structured systems. In *CONCUR*, volume 8052 of *LNCS*, pages 5–24. Springer, 2013. Invited paper. DOI: 10.1007/978-3-642-40184-8_2. 63, 143

Ze'ev Shtadler and Orna Grumberg. Network grammars, communication behaviors and automatic verification. In *Automatic Verification Methods for Finite State Systems*, pages 151–165. Springer, 1990. DOI: 10.1007/3-540-52148-8_13. 136

T.K. Srikanth and Sam Toueg. Simulating authenticated broadcasts to derive simple fault-tolerant algorithms. *Distributed Computing*, 2:80–94, 1987. DOI: 10.1007/BF01667080. 3, 14

Ichiro Suzuki. Proving properties of a ring of finite-state machines. *Inf. Process. Lett.*, 28(4): 213–214, July 1988. DOI: 10.1016/0020-0190(88)90211-6. 3, 23, 31, 42

Murali Talupur and Mark R. Tuttle. Going with the flow: Parameterized verification using message flows. In *FMCAD*, pages 1–8. IEEE, 2008. DOI: 10.1109/FMCAD.2008.ECP.14. 131

Anthony Widjaja To and Leonid Libkin. Algorithmic metatheorems for decidable LTL model checking over infinite systems. In *Foundations of Software Science and Computational Structures*, pages 221–236. Springer, 2010. DOI: 10.1007/978-3-642-12032-9_16. 132

Moshe Y. Vardi. An automata-theoretic approach to linear temporal logic. In *Banff Higher Order Workshop*, pages 238–266, 1995. DOI: 10.1007/3-540-60915-6_6. 55

Pierre Wolper and Vinciane Lovinfosse. Verifying properties of large sets of processes with network invariants. In *Automatic Verification Methods for Finite State Systems*, volume 407 of *LNCS*, pages 68–80, 1989. DOI: 10.1007/3-540-52148-8_6. 3, 135, 136

Tuba Yavuz-Kahveci and Tevfik Bultan. Action language verifier: an infinite-state model checker for reactive software specifications. *Formal Methods in System Design*, 35(3):325–367, 2009. DOI: 10.1007/s10703-009-0081-1. 139

Hsu-Chun Yen. A unified approach for deciding the existence of certain petri net paths. *Information and Computation*, 96(1):119 – 137, 1992. DOI: 10.1016/0890-5401(92)90059-O. 25

Authors' Biographies

RODERICK BLOEM

Roderick Bloem is a professor at Graz University of Technology. He received an M.Sc. in computer science from Leiden University in the Netherlands (1996) and a Ph.D. from the University of Colorado at Boulder (2001). His thesis work, under the supervision of Fabio Somenzi, was on formal verification using Linear Temporal Logic.

Since 2002, he has been an assistant professor at Graz University of Technology and a full profesor since 2008. His research interests are in formal methods for the design and verification of digital systems, including hardware, software, and combinations such as embedded systems. He studies applications of game theory to the automatic synthesis of systems from their specifications, connections between temporal logics and omega-automata, model checking, and automatic fault localization and repair.

SWEN JACOBS

Swen Jacobs is a postdoc at Saarland University. He received his Ph.D. (Dr. Ing.) from Saarland University for his work on decision procedures for the verification of complex systems at the Max-Planck-Institute for Informatics.

He worked at École Polytechnique Fédérale de Lausanne (EPFL), at Technical University Graz, and has been a visiting professor at the University of Ljubljana. His current work focuses on the automated verification and synthesis of distributed systems, based on a combination of logical and game-theoretic methods.

AYRAT KHALIMOV

Ayrat Khalimov is a Ph.D. student at Technical University of Graz, Austria. He received his master's degree in applied physics and Mathematics at Moscow Insitute of Physics and Technology (MIPT), with the thesis focusing on a method of calculation of current leakages in hardware circuits. Later, he joined Dependable Systems Lab at École Polytechnique Fédérale de Lausanne (EPFL) for an internship where he researched symbolic execution techniques for software verification. His current area of research is parameterized synthesis and verification.

IGOR KONNOV

Igor Konnov is a postdoc (Universitätsassistent) at the Formal Methods in Systems Engineering Group, Institute of Information Systems of TU Wien (Vienna University of Technology). His research interests include model checking, parameterized model checking, and verification of distributed algorithms.

He received his Specialist (comparable to M.Sc.) and Ph.D. degrees in applied mathematics and computer science from Lomonosov Moscow State University. In his Ph.D. thesis, he introduced new techniques for parameterized model checking.

SASHA RUBIN

Sasha Rubin is a postdoc at the Università degli Studi di Napoli "Federico II" (University of Naples). He is broadly interested in the connections between automata theory and logic, and in particular, in formal verification, game theory, and finite model theory. He received his Ph.D. from the University of Auckland and was awarded the Vice-chancellor's prize for the best doctoral thesis in the Faculty of Science. He previously held a New Zealand Science and Technology Postdoctoral Fellowship. He is currently a Marie Curie fellow of the Istituto Nazionale di Alta Matematica.

HELMUT VEITH

Helmut Veith is a professor at the Faculty of Informatics of TU Wien (Vienna University of Technology), and an adjunct professor at Carnegie Mellon University. He has a diploma in Computational Logic and a Ph.D. sub auspiciis praesidentis in Computer Science, both from TU Wien. Prior to his appointment to Vienna, he held professor positions at TU Darmstadt and TU Munich.

In his research, Helmut Veith applies formal and logical methods to problems in software technology and engineering. His current work focuses on model checking, software verification and testing, embedded software, and computer security.

JOSEF WIDDER

Josef Widder is an assistant professor (Privatdozent) at the Faculty of Informatics of TU Wien. His primary area of interest is the theoretical approach to distributed algorithms, currently focusing on automated verification of fault-tolerant distributed algorithms.

He received his Ph.D. (Doctor technicae), and his habilitation in computer science from TU Wien. He worked at the Embedded Computing Systems group and the Formal Methods in Systems Engineering group of TU Wien (Austria), the Laboratoire d'Informatique de l'Ecole polytechnique (France), and the Parasol Lab at Texas A&M University (USA).

Printed in the United States
by Baker & Taylor Publisher Services